Curtis Hammond

10 February 2010

A
FIGHTER'S
HEART

A FIGHTER'S HEART

ONE MAN'S JOURNEY THROUGH
THE WORLD OF FIGHTING

SAM SHERIDAN

Atlantic Monthly Press
New York

Excerpts from *Cut Time: An Education at the Fights* by Carlo Rotella. Copyright © 2003 by Carlo Rotella. Reprinted by permission of Houghton Mifflin Company. All rights reserved.
Rope Burns: Stories from the Corner by F. X. Toole. Copyright © 2000 by F. X. Toole. Reprinted by permission of HarperCollins Publishers.
The Professional by W. C. Heinz. Copyright © by W. C. Heinz. Reprinted by permission of William Morris Agency, Inc. on behalf of author.
Excerpt from *Chinese Boxing: Masters and Methods* by Robert W. Smith. Published by North Atlantic Books, copyright © 1990 by Robert W. Smith. Reprinted by permission of publisher.
"These are forces . . . redefines the possible" by Ronald Levao and ". . . when we did not . . . we were high and dry . . ." by Ted Hoagland from *Reading the Flights: The Best Writing About the Most Controversial of Sports*, edited by Joyce Carol Oates and Daniel Halpern, copyright © 1998 by Joyce Carol Oates and Daniel Halpern. Reprinted by permission of Henry Holt and Company, LLC.
"No doubt much . . . hunters than ourselves" and "thus the ritual . . . is a carnivore" by Barbara Ehrenreich from *Blood Rites: Origins and History of the Passions of Wars* copyright © 1997 by Barbara Ehrenreich. Reprinted by permission of Henry Holt and Company, LLC.
Excerpt from *The Fight* by Norman Mailer, copyright © 1997 by Norman Mailer, Vintage Books, a division of Random House, Inc.
Excerpt from *Shawdowbox* by George Plimpton. Copyright © 1977 by George Plimpton. Reprinted by the permission of Russell and Volkening as agents for the author's estate.
Excerpts from *Without Apology* by Leah Hager Cohen, copyright © 2005 by Leah Hager Cohen, Random House, a division of Random House, Inc.
Excerpts from *On Bullfighting* by A. L. Kennedy, copyright © 1999 by A. L. Kennedy, Anchor Books, a division of Random House, Inc.
Excerpts from *On Agression* by Konrad Lorenz, copyright © by Deutscher Taschenbuch Verlag GmbH & Co. English translation copyright © 1966 by Konrad Lorenz. Harvest Books, a division of Harcourt Brace & Company.
Excerpt from *A Neutral Corner: Boxing Essays* by A. J. Liebling, edited by Fred Warner and James Barbour. Compilation copyright © 1990 by Norma Liebling Stonehill. Reprinted by permission of North Point Press, a division of Farrar, Straus and Giroux, LLC.
Excerpts from *Manhood in America: A Cultural History*, copyright © 1996 by Michael Kimmel. Oxford University Press.
Excerpts from *On Boxing* copyright © 1987, 1995 by Joyce Carol Oates, used by permission of Harper Perennial.

Published simultaneously in Canada
Printed in the United States of America

Library of Congress Cataloging-in-Publication Data
Sheridan, Sam.
    A fighter's heart : one man's journey through the world of fighting / Sam Sheridan.
        p. cm.
    ISBN-10: 0-87113-950-2
    ISBN-13: 978-0-87113-950-4
    1. Sheridan, Sam.   2. Martial artists—United States—Biography.
I. Title.
    GV1113.S243S45 2007
    796.8092—dc22
    [B]   2006043084

Atlantic Monthly Press
an imprint of Grove/Atlantic, Inc.
841 Broadway
New York, NY 10003

Distributed by Publishers Group West

www.groveatlantic.com

07 08 09 10 11   10 9 8 7 6 5 4 3

To my parents, Susan and Michael, for the unwavering support

To Claudia, thanks, regrets, love

To Panio, my brother

1

THE RESPONSIBILITY
TO FIGHT

Apidej sit-Hirun at Fairtex Gym, Bangkok, Thailand, May 2000.

Elephant behind Fairtex Gym.

Ibn Khaldun, the immortal Tunisian historian, says that events often contradict the universal idea to which one would like them to conform, that analogies are inexact, and that experience is deceptive.

—A. J. Liebling, *A Neutral Corner*

Every talent must unfold itself in fighting.
—F. Nietzsche, "Homer on Competition," 1872

Samrong Stadium, in Bang Pli, an hour from Bangkok, is dirty, dingy, and high ceilinged, with concrete floors, rows of folding chairs, and crowds milling around drinking Singha beer and smoking Krum Thip cigarettes. A fight has just ended and the canvas ring is brightly lit and empty. Now it's my turn to fight, and I look at Johann, a short, muscular, bald Belgian, and say, "Win or lose, I want a beer in my hand as soon as I climb out of the ring." He smiles tightly and nods. I roll my neck like a real fighter and step through the vermilion ropes. I'm wearing a robe designed for Thais who fight at 130 pounds and it barely covers my oily thighs.

My heavily tattooed opponent ignores the screaming crowd and I ignore him, even though I can feel his eyes on me across the ring, his attempt to engage me in a samurai stare-down. I am absurdly, frenetically excited, and yet calm in the knowledge that I'm as ready as possible for my first fight. I can ignore my opponent's mind games because, hey—we'll find out who's tougher soon enough. I suppress an urge to smile at him. I have no ill will toward the guy.

My body is aglow with the power of recuperation and heating oils, and my face is greased with a layer of Vaseline. The harsh blatting horn, the lilting pipes, and the stomping drum begin their song. There is nothing left to fear.

When I was in junior high, at the Eaglebrook School in the green hills of Massachusetts, I read a book about John F. Kennedy that said he used to carry an anonymous poem with him in his wallet:

> Bullfight critics, ranked in rows,
> Crowd the enormous plaza full.
> But only one is there who knows,
> And he's the man that fights the bull.

I loved that quote. I carried it in my own wallet for years, well through college, until that wallet was lost when I flipped the dinghy during a hurricane in Bermuda. I wanted to be the one who knows. To me, the quote wasn't just about critics and performers and artists. The man in the ring knows, and not just about that particular bullfight and whether or not he did a good job. He *knows*.

I grew up romanticizing fighting and fighters: matadors, soldiers, knights, samurai. There was nothing more noble. That boys should worship fighters was as unquestioned as patriotism, bred into the fabric of masculinity. Little boys pick up sticks and turn them into swords and guns no matter what their mothers might do.

I went to high school at Deerfield Academy, a fancy prep school where my father was the business manager. I had a circle of friends who were locals and sons of teachers, and we had our own sort of world between the rich kids who lived in the dormitories and the surrounding rural public school kids.

We watched a lot of kung fu movies, but we didn't fight. Deerfield wasn't that kind of place; nobody fought, although they did wrestle, and in hindsight I wish I had wrestled, too. Our favorite part of any kung fu movie wasn't necessarily the climactic fights; it was the training sequence, when the hero becomes an invincible warrior.

I played sports, football and lacrosse, and was a mediocre varsity athlete. I was a not-so-secret nerd, really. I played Advanced Dungeons

& Dragons, sometimes by myself as I got older and it became less socially acceptable. I read voraciously and insatiably. I had one girl-friend for a few weeks, and she pretty much hated me.

After high school I joined the merchant marines out of a burn-ing need to escape before college and an attempt to see the world in a supremely clichéd fashion. I took the three a.m. train from an un-manned station in Amherst down to Maryland, to the Seafarers Harry Lundenburg School of Seamanship, in Piney Point. When my mom dropped me off, in a pool of light from a street lamp at the deserted train station, with my dad's old navy duffel bag, I was a living Norman Rockwell painting.

The school was run like a boot camp—shave your head, shine your boots, do push-ups till you puke—and my "class," number 518, started out with about twenty-eight guys and finished, four months later, with thirteen. Classes usually lost five or ten guys, but we were gutted. Some of this was due to racial tension; the class was half white and half black, and there were some fights. The black guys, it seemed to me at the tender age of eighteen, had a better handle on how to deal with the pressure, and the endless work: They did just enough to coast through, while the white guys were killing themselves trying to complete the Sisyphean tasks put to us by an unusually cruel bosun. I found a way to live in both worlds, and I learned one of the most important lessons in life: Keep your mouth shut. It was my introduction to the world of tough guys.

Half of the class had been in jail for one reason or another, and I told no one about my prep school background or Ivy League future. One of my best friends there had a spiderweb tattooed on his face, right under his eye. I dared him to cut my hand off one night on the meat slicer, laid my hand on it, stared him in the eye, and said, "Fuck you, do it" (everybody had to talk that way). He gave me a small, tight-eyed look and then looked away. On the first ship he got on, he stabbed the chief mate three times.

We would fight in the weight room with some old boxing gloves, and looking back with the benefit of some experience, I realize we had no idea what we were doing. There was a tall black kid named Sypes, from Mississippi, who spoke like birds chirping and claimed to have been a pro boxer, but when he was sparring with Walzer, a five-foot blond redneck who would just windmill, Sypes didn't look that good. Walzer in his fury caught Sypes and blasted his eyebrow open, and blood sprayed everywhere. Sypes dashed to the bathroom clutching his eye, leaving long spatters of blood on the filthy linoleum. We mopped up the blood, rusty stains trailing like a big orange-brown paintbrush. I got in there and tried to box with a few people, and I was hesitant and awkward. A tough kid from Florida, Davey Dubois, racked me with an uppercut, and for days my jaw clicked in a funny way. Still, I got in there; my curiosity edged out my fear. I had to know. I wanted to *know*.

A few years later, an art critic named Peter Schjeldahl, who was teaching at Harvard (I was an art major), said to me, "You're wondering what all young men wonder: Am I a coward or not?" That was part of it, though I knew I probably wasn't a coward. Bravery is something different. Bravery has to be proved.

My dad had been a Navy SEAL, Explosive Ordnance Disposal, and the military was an obvious choice after college, maybe a little too obvious. It didn't really grab me, partially because of my merchant marine experiment but mostly because I learned too much history, too much about politicians and great-power politics. I don't want to kill people, and I didn't want to be a tool, a tooth in the cog of a great machine. My idea of a war hero is Hawkeye on *M*∗*A*∗*S*∗*H*: If you have to go to war, then you go; but if you don't, then you don't.

Bar brawling didn't interest me, either; when I'm in a bar, I'm interested in having fun. What appealed was the dynamic of a duel: What is it like to meet a man on open ground, a man who is ready for you, a man who is your equal in most measurable ways?

At Harvard I tried tai chi and tiger kung fu, and one day I happened upon the boxing gym, where Tommy Rawson was the coach. He was about four foot five and maybe eighty years old. He'd been a professional fighter in the thirties and New England lightweight champ in 1935 with a record of 89–6, and he was magical. Finally, here was real fighting and sparring, with headgear and a mouth guard and big sixteen-ounce gloves. Tommy couldn't remember anyone's name, but he understood boxing in his bones. "Hey slugger, don't start weaving until he gives you trouble," he'd call in a harsh voice that had yelled out things like that for fifty years. He always had a gleeful smile on his handsome, crumpled face.

Once I started boxing, I prized hammering away on a big bag, working the speed bag, running stairs, jumping rope. Of course, I still smoked two packs a day and drank five nights a week—this was college. Sparring with headgear comes as a revelation, because you get hit and it doesn't really hurt. It becomes like a chess match: You think, *Hey, he jumped back when I did this, so next time I'll fake this and actually do that*—and then you have the satisfaction of burying a hook to the side of his head. There is the battle rage that is so enthralling, the berserker emotion that doesn't discern friend from foe but simply rejoices in blood. This was the feeling I was after. My adrenal glands were triggered and I was fully engaged in the moment: Someone was trying to kill me. The door opened on a new world.

By senior year, I was boxing less and less. College was winding down, and I was wondering what the hell comes next. I was signed up with the Marine Corps, but also to go to Honduras with the Peace Corps, both to begin right after graduation. I vacillated daily, hourly. I used to say, "Peace Corps or Marine Corps, just so long as it's hard core." Hilarious. Then, about two weeks after graduation in 1998, my godmother told me that a friend of hers had just bought a yacht and was looking for crew. I sent him my scrawny résumé and we talked and I kept my mouth shut (that essential survival skill learned in the merchant marine) and didn't reveal my cluelessness, and he hired me. He was going to pay me good money to help fix up his yacht and sail it around the world with him. It was a once-in-a-lifetime opportunity, impossible to refuse, and so I spent a year and a half on the boat, seeing her through three captains, five stewardesses, two engineers, and a variety of guests. I made it all the way to Australia, where I finally had had enough of being part of a rich man's toy and stepped off onto dry land.

I was twenty-four, in Darwin, Australia, loaded with cash, and I planned not to work again until I'd spent it all. I got a room in a hostel and started working out in a local gym; I stopped smoking and began thinking again about fighting. It occurred to me, slowly, that I could return to fighting now, without distractions. I started taking classes in muay Thai, the Thai variation of kickboxing that utilizes elbows and knees, with the local Aussies. The instructor, a thin, bald, narrow-faced former professional fighter named Mike, had trained in Thailand.

Muay Thai is considered by the sport-fighting world to be the premier "stand-up" ring sport, for the simple reason that it allows the most dangerous moves. Western-style boxing is all hands, and punches must be above the waist. Kickboxing, full-contact tae kwon do, and karate all allow kicks, but they're restricted to above the waist. Muay Thai, on the other hand, allows kicks anywhere, which dramatically changes the style of fighting, as leg kicks are quicker, nastier, faster, and easier to execute. Perhaps more telling is that muay Thai also allows fighting in the clinch. In Western boxing, the clinch—when fighters come together and lock up arms—is a safe haven. The clinch in muay Thai is very different: The fighters wrestle for control, looking to throw knees and elbows; the clinch is where most of the damage is done.

After a few weeks training with Mike, when he could see I was getting more serious, he told me that months spent training in Thailand were worth years of training anywhere else, including his gym. He also said, "You can either be tough or you can be quick." When I asked him which he was, he smiled ruefully and said, "Quick." I thought that maybe I could fake tough.

I left Darwin with Craig, the engineer on the yacht I had crewed on, traveling in a Kombi-van with flowers painted all over it. We spent a few months driving across Australia, telling girls we were professional long-board surfers but the waves were too small for us today. Along the way, I kept thinking about muay Thai, and at campsites I would throw three hundred kicks with each leg at trees, amusing and occasionally alarming the other backpackers.

We ended the road trip in Sydney, and I found my way into a gym where I met a short, mean-looking Maori who had spent a year training in Thailand. His legs were a lattice of scars and veins: In muay Thai, the leg kick uses the shin as a striking point, and the only way to counter a shin kick is to block it with your own shin. Shin-on-shin contact is very painful—at least until all the nerve endings there have died. The Maori told me that if I was going to get serious about muay Thai, I should cover an empty bottle with a little oil and vigorously roll the bottle up and down my shins while pressing hard, a procedure that if repeated enough times would eventually kill the nerve endings.

I started doing the bottle rub back in the hostel while watching *The Simpsons* and figuring out how I could become a real muay Thai fighter. I had the money, I had the time, I had the inclination—so I decided to train in Thailand. I'd always wondered what would happen if I could train all the time, like the Shaolin monks who were raised in the temple, the samurai, the Spartans. No drinking, or smoking, or coffee, or girls—just fighting all the time.

I wanted to find a contact before I went over to Thailand and on a whim bought a copy of *International Kickboxer* magazine, which featured a full-page ad for a muay Thai camp called Fairtex. I began a tentative e-mail correspondence with its manager, and he was matter of fact: Come on over and stay as long as you can, no experience necessary.

I arrived in Bangkok around midnight on Valentine's Day of '00. A gentle, round-faced Thai named Han picked me up at the airport and drove me the hour to Fairtex, where he unceremoniously deposited me at my room. There were two men inside asleep when I stumbled in and flicked on the lights; they half-woke to curse me out in French before I hurriedly shut off the light and lay down on a mattress on the floor.

I was too jet-lagged to sleep, and tossed and turned in the dark with the snoring of strangers in my ears, the unfamiliar heat thick in the air. I stared at the ceiling for long minutes or hours, ears pricking at strange noises. Finally, I crept from my room, trying not to wake my unseen roommates, and padded down the stairs into the green wash of morning. The camp was silent, still and deserted. I glanced briefly at the boxing rings; the heavy bags hung like a neat row of lynched corpses. I could hear dogs barking and a nearby cock marking the morning.

I found my way out of the camp through leafy bowers over cracking concrete and scurrying geckos. At the end of the driveway, at a loss for which way to go, I turned right and walked up onto a curving concrete bridge. It was warm and light already, although nobody else seemed to be up yet. The sun was low in the eastern sky, nearly obscured by the muggy clouds of gray and pearl. The river was still and black and silver, and a low mist hung on it, getting thicker farther upstream. Rickety wooden houses and piers stood in the white shrouds of fog; a lone Thai woman with a broad straw hat poled her boat through the murk. I finally felt the full strangeness of where I was, this movie set of the Far East, the mystic Orient.

That first day I didn't train, on the say-so of the camp manager, an American-born Chinese named Anthony, the guy I'd been e-mailing. He told me to let my body adjust after the long journey, so I sat and watched.

One of the first things one notices about muay Thai is the youth of the fighters: The boys are often six or seven when they climb into the ring for their first fights, and they're generally considered to peak at about seventeen. Muay Thai, like many of the ring fighting arts, is a way out for the very poor. The prize money can support families who can't afford to send their children to school. It is an extremely grueling sport, not only the fights themselves, but the training. Most Thais are surprised that anyone would pay to come to train in muay Thai, because it is such a horrible, painful way to live.

I sat next to the far ring, which was reserved for the Lumpini fighters—Lumpini is the premier fighting stadium in Thailand, where the best muay Thai fighters in the world compete—and watched them train. They were working the pad rounds, which I learned are the heart of training. A trainer with shin guards, a thick belly pad, and pads on his forearms takes the fighter through rounds of kicking, punching, elbows, and knees. The noise was tremendous: The fighters yelled with every kick and every punch. In other martial arts, you execute moves at 70 percent of full speed and power; in muay Thai, everything is 100 percent all the time. The din of twenty men and boys all yelling and hitting is a strange, desperate noise. That noise was my introduction to the urgency of a real fight.

The trainers were older, heavier Thais with battered faces and scarred brows. They would drill their fighters relentlessly, switching through positions smoothly, and the fighters would follow, kicking and punching and kneeing, screaming something like "*Aish*," while the noise of their legs hitting the pads crackled like gunshots. The fighters resembled oiled, tireless machines, functioning beautifully. Competence displayed is always fun to watch, but this kind of speed and power and skill was mesmerizing.

The next morning, I had my first training session, with a trainer named Kum. He asked me to put on my wraps, the binding fighters "wrap" around their fists and wrists for padding and protection. I rushed through it, doing it the old Harvard boxing way, with short wraps not going between the fingers, instead of asking him to show me the way they do it. He let me go on because, I sensed, he couldn't care less. There was such frequent turnover of foreigners who couldn't speak Thai and who stayed for only a few days that I could understand why trainers didn't take new people seriously, at least until they showed something. Kum was arguably the best trainer for the foreigners, or *farang,* as they are called in Thai. The larger, and therefore slower, *farang* were unsuited to the Lumpini fighters' style of kicking, which is very quick and precise. Kum's style, with its emphasis on power and heavier, more deliberate kicks—every blow devastating—was much more effective for the bigger *farang.*

That first day, I managed only a few super-slow, barely moving rounds with a tall, thin trainer named Pepsi (a junior man), who cared even less about me than Kum did. My punches had no snap, my kicks landed poorly and hurt my own shins, and I was sweating like a horse—I was chubby compared to anyone else at the camp, even the other *farang*. I stumbled around, huffing and grimacing, trying to maintain an air of seriousness, as if I were a real fighter, too. I soon met the other *farang,* who were mostly hard-muscled, flinty-eyed Aussies who had done muay Thai back home and were here to gear up for fights. Everyone was tattooed, including me.

The camp operated as a big family, with Philip, the owner, and Anthony, the manager, the father figures. There were between thirty and forty Thais living there: fighters, trainers, and their wives and families; older fighters and their wives and children; and the workers who made training gear. They all lived in a row of dormitories at the camp, along with their fighting cocks and dogs. At Fairtex, everything fights—the roosters, the dogs, the men.

After a few days, I was in shape enough to train every day, twice a day; it became all consuming, the backdrop to all thought and action. It began in the early morning, with the youngest fighters waking us up, calling, "Jogging, jogging" in soft voices. I'd clamber out of bed and down the stairs in my shorts and running shirt. The fighters would congregate; we'd sit in the dawn glow on the edge of the ring and put our socks and running shoes on. We'd all walk in a line, usually a dozen or so, sometimes two abreast, with the Lumpini fighters in front, then the second-tier fighters, followed by the up-and-comers, and the *farang* would bring up the rear. After maybe a quarter-mile walk, we'd break into a jog. We'd run on paved empty roads through the rice fields, past temples and apartment complexes with birdcages raised high on poles for decoration; down red-dirt roads, past rice farmers and squatters' huts; past shrines gilded and glittering with glass and stones, and shrines where garlands of flowers hung from tree branches and candles moldered in the damp. It was always hot and still, and as the sun rose, it got hotter. Depending on your level of fitness, you'd run anywhere from three to nine miles; the last quarter mile we would walk back into camp, where the trainers would be getting ready for us. The other fighters would silently put on their wraps. The human hand is a terrible club, full of moving parts and delicate bones and tendons that have to be protected. It's far safer to hit someone with an elbow. The glove provides the bulk of the padding, while the wrapping pads keep the bones and tendons from spreading apart—especially after you've been punching for years and have learned to punch hard.

Apidej (AP-ee-day) Sit-Hirun, one of the trainers, would be eager to get going and we'd be out shadowboxing before anyone else. Apidej is a living legend, the greatest muay Thai fighter of the century, so proclaimed by the king of Thailand. He won a record seven titles, kicking harder than anyone ever had. None of his students—including his son—has ever been able to replicate his power. He wore a golden "dollar-sign" ring on his right hand, his "money" hand. There are statues of him ready to be erected in Bangkok once he dies. He was sixty when I trained with him, and his style of muay Thai was out of favor, much like the style of Western boxing from the thirties and forties is out of favor today. Apidej still trained fighters for Philip at Fairtex, although at that point he primarily taught *farang*. Somehow he picked me as a student during that first month, mostly because I'd been persistent.

In muay Thai, the better the fighter, the more humble and good the person; and you could feel goodness, humbleness, and happiness radiating off Apidej. He had an infectious laugh, a deep sense of glee, and the gentle manner of a lifelong Buddhist. He had a trick that gave him great pleasure: He would beckon me over with something hidden in his hands, motion for me to put out my hands, and then he would gently, quietly deposit a tiny frog into my palm and chuckle.

And yet there was the other side, the fighting side. Apidej would show me how to move, sliding around the ring like a leopard, his eyes dark and serious, his motion effortless, his aura menacing. His eyes would go flat and cold, the naked enmity toward another man in the ring just under the surface.

The fighters warmed up by shadowboxing. The other fighters generally took it easy at first, shadowboxing lightly, going through the motions without focus, but Apidej wanted me to actually work, to move crisply, to throw fakes. He was always serious in the ring.

In muay Thai, whoever is in better shape wins. The primary tool to get you there is the pad rounds, which work like actual fighting rounds: You kick and punch and knee continuously for five or six minutes with thirty-second breaks between rounds. I would, at my best, do five or six rounds of straight pads with Apidej, followed by two or three rounds of just punching the smaller "focus pads" that were used to improve my accuracy. The strenuousness of the workout, the "maxing out" of your system, is why so many fighters get sick, why little cuts take weeks to heal and often get infected. The training is so hard that the immune system can bottom out, the fighter's body pushed past the edge of its abilities.

After the pad rounds, you went straight to the heavy bags and did about five or six rounds on them. This was still pretty hard, but you could relax, as often your trainer would be distracted doing the pads with someone else. If you had a fight coming up, the trainer would come and stand behind you and say, "*Lao lao*," which means hurry up, and generally make your life miserable. Then you would take your wraps off and either spar or clinch. Because the Thais fight every month, they essentially learn to fight in the ring, in real fights, from a young age. This makes their sparring very laid back, the priority being not to get hurt while refining their timing and trying things out. This lack of intensity was bad for us, the *farang* with no fights under our belts, but it was the way they did things.

The clinch was different. The clinch is an essential part of muay Thai, and it is often neglected by *farang*. It's where most of the points in a bout are scored, and where many of the knockouts happen. To practice the clinch, two fighters without gloves or wraps, of more or less equal size and strength, come together and work for position, trying to get their arms around the other man's neck and inside his arms, taking control of his head and body. It's a little like wrestling, but with both feet on the ground. When a fighter achieves position in the clinch, he then throws a knee into his opponent's stomach or side. A fighter also tries to pull his opponent's head down, which can lead to a knee in the face, and then it's lights out.

After the sparring or clinching, the session was over. On my own I would do three sets of pull-ups and sit-ups, as would the other fighters. Toward the end of my training, I would do five hundred sit-ups of various types a session—more than a thousand a day—but I never got a six-pack. Then we'd head to the big shower room, where, out of either respect for one another or modesty, the Thai fighters all wore their underwear, so we *farang* did too. Then Apidej would fill a large, square concrete bath with the hottest water you could stand. It was better than a massage, he'd say, and cheaper, too. The tub room was cavernous, like a grotto, despite the thick beams overhead and the dirty, slatted windows that let chinks of light in. Sometimes I would get the tub to myself, and I could submerge my whole body in it, as if returning to the womb. I would hear my pulse, a feathery thudding in my ears.

Afterward, shaky from the heat and exhaustion, I'd shower again and eat breakfast. The food was good, but never enough: soup and rice and chicken and noodles and some sliced pineapple or lychees. And always a lot of water, twelve pints a day. I'd rest a little, wander over to the office to check e-mail and chat with Anthony, who would be dealing with business. After e-mailing, it was time for the one-hour afternoon nap through the hottest part of the day. Exhausted and feverishly hot, I would burrow into bed, my body aching. I dreamt strange dreams and punched in my sleep. I would sweat into my mattress, and when I got up, it looked like an invisible man was still sleeping in my bed.

Sometimes I would take the afternoon nap in the hammocks that hung by the fence right next to the rings, cooler with a breath of air off the swamp. The swamp out back was full of high grass, stretching out to infinity, and there were often elephants and handlers hanging out there, sometimes right against our chain-link fence, the elephants methodically tearing the grass and eating it, and the handlers sleeping beneath them or nearby. I would lie diagonally in the small Thai hammock and maybe three feet away an elephant would be grazing peacefully, and his handler resting, and all of us dozing in the steady thrush of the elephant's trunk curling and ripping long bunches of grass.

At three-thirty we'd start again—jogging (a far shorter distance, just a couple of miles), then another full training session, during which the pad rounds and sparring and clinching might go on longer and the sparring would be a bit more aggressive. We'd finish with a few rounds of shadowboxing—the Lumpini fighters would do it while holding five-pound dumbbells—and then sit-ups and push-ups and all the rest: shower–hot tub–shower, and the grueling cycle was finally done for the day by five-thirty. At night, the goal was to do as little as possible, just to get some rest and stay hydrated for the next morning's run.

The days crawled by. At first, each day felt endless, and then they began to flow together. After three weeks, I could stumble through four rounds of pad work with Apidej, and my kicks were finally acquiring some snap. I now had massive, horny calluses instead of bloody blisters on the balls of my feet. The tender feet of the *farang* were often a problem; because of the two training sessions and rough canvas and stone floors, the foreigners often tore their feet up, got them infected, and had to go to the hospital. Actually, I was the only *farang* I knew who stayed for long at Fairtex and never went to the hospital once.

When I first started with the pad rounds, I was too embarrassed and self-conscious to scream like the Thais did. Finally, one day, maybe a month in, I just started doing it, yelling "Aish!" with every kick, my voice a few notes lower than those around me. I remember a Lumpini fighter named Neungsiam (the best fighter in the camp), who looked at me as I got out of the ring, and nodded. I was beginning to get it. Neungsiam and I would eventually become friends. He was my age, had been a Lumpini superstar at eighteen, had quit for a few years, and was now making his comeback. He was a tranquil guy, with pinpoint punching. He would come hang out in my room and we would bullshit in English, Thai, and sign language. I showed him pictures of the girls I hung out with in L.A., and I think that cemented the friendship. He loved those blond girls and thought maybe I could hook him up.

During my stay at Fairtex, I lived in the cheapest room. It was at the top of the stairs, above the rings, and hot and airless and foul with stale sweat, even with both windows open and the fan going. The room was small and high-ceilinged, maybe fifteen feet wide and twenty-five long. It was noisy, with traffic across the swamp and the boys calling and adults hollering and sandals flapping in the hall outside. There was the murmur of talk and breeze, the dogs occasionally barking like mad. There was barely space for the three people in there, the broke-ass lifers; the other *farang* who came through stayed for weeks or even days, and they all stayed in a nicer set of rooms with—God forbid—air-conditioning.

In our room, we slept on three single mattresses on the floor, evenly spaced, with green-and-white-checked bedspreads and sheets; girls would wash them about once a month. It was a little dirty, but we had wooden straw brooms if we wanted to sweep up (we didn't). In addition to standing portable closets that were fairly useless, we had a little table and two chairs. Our stuff was strewn everywhere, or piled high in the corners. The mice would sometimes hide in it, and we couldn't be bothered to chase them out. Despite the roughness, it was a haven for us, a refuge, where I spent a lot of time reading. By the end of my six months, I had something like two hundred English paperbacks stacked around the room.

There were two guys in the room when I got there, Michael and Johnny. Michael was Italian Swiss, a short, stocky man, slightly balding with thick, curly black hair and a hairy chest. He had been at Fairtex for three or four months already and had fought twice, winning both times against Thais. He spoke English, and, although he and Johnny at first resented my intrusion into their little domain, he was friendly to me.

There were ants everywhere, and when Michael spilled food, he would look at me in false shock and then sing, in his heavily accented English, "Don't worry, the ants will get it." And the ants *would* get it, just like they got everything; if you were drinking some juice and put the cup down, the next time you glanced at it there would be ants swarming thick along the rim. On the floor, on the table, it didn't matter. Sometimes the big ants would wake you up at night when they ran over you. You got used to it.

Michael would also frequently go to Pattaya, a capital for the tourist sex trade, and when he got back, he would spend hours detailing his exploits in lascivious detail for Johnny. He tried to tell me about them until I made it clear I didn't really want to hear what he had been up to. When the lights went out, he would talk with Johnny in his silky, low accent and chuckle to himself in an evil, delighted little burble.

Michael spoke a fair bit of Thai, and he fought at Samrong, the same place I would, and I went to see his last fight, against a Frenchman who trained out on the islands. It was agonizing to watch Michael chase this guy around, without the energy or the snap to connect with anything. The other guy wasn't much better but was in slightly better shape, and that's all it took. After that fight, Michael hung around, half-training, and then left Fairtex to go look at other, cheaper camps. He became convinced that his victories had been fixed, that he couldn't have beat a Thai. I only spent maybe a month with Michael.

Johnny Deroy, on the other hand, I spent four and half months with. He was nineteen and this was the first time he had ever been out of Montreal. After finishing high school, he flew to Thailand to pursue his dream of being a muay Thai fighter. Before he left Canada, he dreamt that he had been stung by a scorpion on his leg but survived it, and he had a scorpion tattooed on his leg. He had gone north at first to a camp at Chiang Mai and been ignored and robbed. Instead of giving up, he found his way to Fairtex.

I was deeply impressed by his courage. When I was his age, I had gone backpacking around Europe, which is a far cry from Southeast Asia. Like Michael, Johnny didn't like me at first, but we warmed up talking about movies and *The Simpsons* and then got along famously. He taught me to swear in gutter Canadian French, and I helped him with his English.

He was small, thin, and leanly muscled with a narrow, angular face. He would stand in front of the full-length mirror with his arms raised and yell, "I'm nature's greatest miracle!" completely tongue-in-cheek.

I had been at Fairtex for about two months when Johnny got his first fight. Kum set it up back at his village, Chayaphum, where there was going to be a festival, and so naturally there would be fights. Johnny asked me to come (Michael had just left), and although it would break my training, I knew he would like to have a friend around. I was also curious to see some of the countryside.

On the second weekend in May, we packed up and took a cab from Fairtex to the bus station, Kum slick in his Fairtex jacket and movie-star hair. The bus station was the size of a major airport, a massive, chaotic edifice of concrete. I didn't see any *farang* among the maze of levels and stairs crowded with people, and it wasn't surprising, because you would have to be able to speak Thai. There weren't many signs or numbers that I could see—I would have been completely lost on my own. The *farang* buses all left from Khao San, where tourists were herded together and charged five times the normal price. In Thailand, there is a 300 percent tax on foreigners, and it's still an inexpensive place. I had flown there on an airplane; compared to most Thais, I was a millionaire.

We rode the bus, air-conditioned and smelling sweet, for about four hours, and then disembarked in a little town. Kum wandered around until he found a guy with a pickup truck who agreed to take us in the bed out to Kum's house, about a forty-minute ride, with a few other Thais, who stared openly at us. The villages were havens for chickens and dogs, and the jungle walled us in.

Kum's house was a big place for the village, with a tiled ground floor lined with glass cabinets. There was running water; a single spigot in the house filled a large concrete cistern in the only bathroom, on the first floor. This cistern or pool was ubiquitous; you'd find it in restaurants and hostels in Bangkok. There was a plastic bowl floating in it for dumping water, usually freezing cold, over your head. There was no toilet paper, but we'd brought some.

The second floor was bare, uneven, and unpainted wood. We slept in a big room there, in a line on little pads, a mosquito coil burning at our feet. Michael had convinced Johnny that the mosquito coils were deadly poison, and I agreed with him. That smoke has *got* to be toxic. Still, at times it was necessary. I woke up much earlier than the other two and crept from the creaking room.

Kum had a wife, Dee, and two sons, the younger of whom was called Suphumvit and was beautiful in his hammock crib that rose in steep walls around his dense little body. Dee was also beautiful, with a warm matronly body and a smile that lit up her face and squeezed her eyes shut. She was always laughing, and the three of us got along great, Dee and Suphumvit and I. We sat on the front porch that morning while everyone else was still asleep, and I held Suphumvit and we ate mango. After I finished the mango, I put the plate down on the tile floor and washed the copius juice off my face and hands and arms. By the time I got back, the plate was crawling with several types of ants. I could hear Michael in my head singing, "Don't worry, the ants will get it."

After everyone else woke up, we went out to get Johnny weighed in and find an opponent for him. The event was being organized at a *wat,* or temple; it was jammed with men and boys, and the drinking had already started. As Johnny weighed in, the Thais crowded around to see him. An older Thai wanted to fight him, a tall, thin, mustachioed man with tattoos on his shoulders, but Kum wouldn't hear of it. I'm not sure whether Johnny would have killed this guy or this guy would have killed Johnny. They started with the music, traditional Thai stuff, and began a sort of mini-parade around the wat, dancing and twisting their arms. They gestured for Johnny to join in, and like a good sport, he did, stepping delicately in his imitation Tevas.

We rode in the back of a different pickup that night out to the festival, and got there as the sun was setting. It was a small-town fairground, with Porta-Potties and garish lights strung up and little vendors selling everything. The area where the fights were going to be was cordoned off, and we went in there and found a corner of the grass to set up on.

The ring was homemade and small and lit by a string of four bright, bare bulbs that hung diagonally over it. The fights began with really little kids, maybe eight or nine, but the crowd followed closely and shouted and cheered. The kids were deadly serious, although they couldn't hit hard enough to hurt each other too much (although one little boy was cut by an elbow), and the crowd rejoiced ecstatically.

Johnny was getting nervous, jumpy. He had been putting on a relaxed face all day, but now the nerves were setting in. He started to get his prefight massage from Kum, lying on a couple of towels on the pavement in the parking lot. Kum and I were going to be his cornermen.

It was a wild scene, with a cheerful, carnival atmosphere. The thick outdoor crowd milled tightly around the ring, hundreds of people drunk and shouting. There wasn't another foreign face for a hundred miles. Because his fight was delayed through three or four matches, Johnny was getting more anxious. He had warmed up and then cooled off, which wastes energy. Kum was also angry, and insulted. I think Johnny was something of a draw, and Kum was a man of some standing around town.

Before the fight, Johnny danced the full *wai khru* and *ram muay* that the Lumpini fighters do, and the crowd roared its approval, cheering him on; the Thai fight enthusiasts always love it when the *farang* respect their traditions. The *wai khru* and *ram muay* are traditional dances that all Thai fighters perform before they fight, dances to honor their families and teachers. The dance appeases superstitious spirits but also centers the fighter, brings him back to himself. The musicians played throughout the fight, blowing and thumping with cigarettes in their hands.

After he finished, Johnny looked at me and the heaving sea of brown faces and said, "I've never been so scared in my life."

Johnny had a right to be scared. He was fighting a Thai who had been born into the sport. The Thai looked young, but just the fact that he was Thai was scary enough: He might be sixteen, but have five years and fifty fights.

In the beginning of the fight, Johnny dominated. He was bigger and stronger, and every time they clinched, Johnny would throw his man to the ground. But there was a cost. He was too tense, too worked up, and tiring quickly. After every clinch, his hands were lower; he was obviously struggling for air. Kum was trying to get through to him, calling, "*Sabai sabai,*" and I was translating, yelling, "Relax!" at him. Kum picked it up, and trying to be heard over the din, began yelling with me, "Re-lax!"

Johnny counted himself out in the third—just lay back on the ropes and gestured "No more" to the referee. The other fighter couldn't believe it and threw his hands in the air like he'd just won a title. I was angry with John at first, although I understood the line of fear and exhaustion he was walking. He wasn't hurt at all, just completely out of breath, and I knew within twenty seconds he was going to be wondering why he had quit like that. He was quiet on the way home. We sat in the pickup bed and watched the stars.

Eventually, we talked a little about the fight, just Johnny and me. We came through to a rationale. The problem was breathing. Whenever Johnny was in the clinch, straining to throw his opponent down, for a split second he would hold his breath. This was a deadly mistake because with muay Thai you are operating at your anaerobic threshhold for almost the entire fight. Those split-second breath holds were killing Johnny. Kum and the other trainers can't talk about this with us (here the language gap makes itself felt), but breathing is critical. In the clinch, what the Thais do is stay loose, stay on their toes, and breathe. There isn't any straining or wrestling, or if there is, it is quick, smooth moves in rhythm with the breathing.

Johnny was unhurt, but his voice was shaky. I could tell he was angry and a little ashamed to have lost the fight, but as we talked and figured out what had happened, he cheered up, and by the time the sun rose the next day, he was back to his old form, cracking jokes about everything he saw.

The next morning, Kum commandeered a truck, and we rode through the countryside in the hot sun, past rice paddies and thick forest, and stopped and wandered up to a waterfall. We all stripped down to our underwear for a dip and annoyed the hell out of a Thai teenager and his girlfriend who were up there for a make-out session.

After the swim, Kum took us to a Buddhist monastery, a huge complex up in the mountains that stood on a cliff and overlooked the valley. There were monkeys in dismal cages and a strange sculpture garden depicting the afterlife of a bad person. It was deeply disturbing, a wide area filled with hundreds of human-size wooden carvings. There were demons with animal heads and human bodies attacking the humans: cutting into a pregnant woman's stomach, piercing eyeballs—real serious gore. The carvings were all painted to look lifelike. Over all this presided two huge statues, twenty feet tall, thin and wooden in the same style: a man and a woman with their skin flayed off and their eyes melted out and their tongues hanging past their waists.

We went back to Kum's house and then wandered down through the one-road village to the square and grabbed some folding chairs. We sat there for a parade of elephants, all dressed out in finery and ridden by monks and children. Some of the elephants were walking billboards for Red Bull and Coca-Cola. There were a few hundred people in the square, mostly children running and shrieking and carrying on. Several columns of dancers in traditional costume came through. Although we were all exhausted from the unfamiliar sun—living at the camp, we never got any sun, as we were training under cover and resting through the days—we sat stoically through it.

After the parade was finished, we wandered back down to Kum's house. On the way there I saw an elephant handler, a big, heavily muscled, tattooed guy punch his wife, hard, in the stomach, and Johnny saw it, too. I thought we should do something, but Johnny, from inner-city Montreal, said to just stay out of it. I looked around for Kum, but he was far behind us. The moment passed, and I did nothing. So much for the tough fighters.

Then there was the participatory parade around the village that we joined in—strangely crowded for such a small village—an endless line of trucks and vans and people. There was music, and we danced as we walked, and people sprayed us with water, which was welcome in the stifling heat. The Thais seemed happy to have us there, and we were happy to be there, willing to enjoy ourselves.

That night we caught the rickety old run-down bus that passed through town. It was full of people and children and chickens, so we clambered up onto the luggage rack and prostrated ourselves on the bags and baskets. The night air was thick with fat white locusts. We stayed as flat as possible, with our mouths clamped shut, watching the stars roll by. It was a mad, dreamlike ride, and I kept eyeballing the cheap, shitty welds that held the rack to the bus and thinking that we might go around a corner and the rack would shear off, that this is how tourists die in Southeast Asia, but the night was shimmering and the magic of travel and silence took away my free will.

Back in camp, time stretched on and on, but things were changing. The trainers began to notice me. Yaquit, a big, handsome Thai who looked a little like Elvis, would sometimes train me, and he would kick the crap out of me and chuckle with delight. Kum would watch me kick the bag and frown and shake his head, then demonstrate a fuller extension or a thrust of the hips. Slowly, Apidej took more and more of an interest in me, and when I started doing whatever he told me without question—like eating a raw egg in the morning with a Sprite—he decided that I was his property.

Anthony would at times come and lean on the ropes and watch us train. We'd chat and he'd ask me if I was ready to fight. At Fairtex, the *farang* could fight when they felt they were ready, but I'd put him off for two months while I was still getting my bearings. Then one day, as I was unwrapping my hands and covered in a cool film of sweat, Anthony, dressed in his usual black, sidled up to the ring. We bullshitted about training for a few minutes, and then he raised his eyebrows and asked again if I wanted a fight. "Sure, why not?" I said. He nodded, satisfied, and walked away. I hung up my wraps to dry in the afternoon breeze and realized that I had just committed to stepping into the ring for a professional muay Thai fight. Just like that.

Once a month the Lumpini fighters from Fairtex would go to Lumpini stadium, and two or more would have fights. These were big-money fights—career fights—with purses of eighty thousand *baht* (around two thousand dollars U.S.), which is serious money in Thailand. A large part of the camp would go with them, a retinue of trainers and observers and fighters dressed in their Sunday best. We would leave in a parade of vehicles, from tricked-out, low-slung pickups (Yaquit used to drag-race his) to a decrepit old van.

Lumpini stadium was what I came to Thailand for. It epitomizes the romantic lure of Southeast Asia: the heat, the noise, the adrenaline, the betting, and the wildness. On a big night, Lumpini feels full of possibilities, with a dark and bloodstained edge. The concrete amphitheater probably holds anywhere from four to ten thousand people. There are three main sections of seats: The uppermost section consists of benches; it's where seats are the cheapest and also where the gambling is the heaviest. The middle section has folding chairs that waitresses navigate to bring beer and food. Ringside seats are the most expensive, about twenty dollars U.S. There can be anywhere from nine to twelve fights in a night, with the main-draw fights scheduled about three-quarters of the way through the evening.

Although my fight was not likely to happen for at least another several months—and when it did, it was not going to be in front of four to six thousand people in the Lumpini stadium—Philip wanted me to be a cornerman for Neungsiam's comeback fight. He wanted me to get used to being in the ring in front of people, to confront that stage fright. The cornermen in muay Thai are directly involved with the fighters during the fight, much more than they are in Western boxing. When a round ends, both cornermen dart from outside the ropes and set up a stool and begin vigorously massaging and rubbing the fighter's arms and legs. The previous week, Neungsiam had shown me what he wanted.

In the back room there was an assembly line processing the fighters: A fighter stripped down for a vigorous massage with hot liniment, which had the effect of warming him, fully, without him having to waste a drop of energy. He then had Vaseline smeared on his face and chest so that the gloves would slide off his skin and not cut him. When his massage was finished, the fighter got off the table and the next one took his place, with his trainer as his masseur. After the oil massage, the fighter got his cup tied on and put on his fight shorts, emblazoned with his name and the name of his trainer or gym. He warmed up a bit, but not too hard, with a few minutes of shadowboxing. His trainer tied his armbands on, recited short Buddhist or Catholic prayers, and then the *mongkol*—a headdress that used to be made from rolled-up Buddhist scrolls but is now made of decorative plastic—was placed on his head. The mongkol, usually blessed by a priest, helped protect the fighter from harm. Fighters sported different styles of mongkols, some with tassels, some without, many with a Las Vegas garishness. While all this was happening, you could hear the pipes and drums tinking and plinking in their dissonant way, and the crowd outside shouting "*Oh-way!*" in response to a fighter's good technique or solid hit.

I watched Neungsiam get lubed and then start his warm-up, marching up and down the alleys in the backstage room, throwing a few punches. He seemed extremely confident and calm, even eager. He received his blessings and had his robe threaded onto him, and then Kum and I went out in our traditional red vests and took up position behind Neungsiam's corner. Although I knew what to do, and it wasn't that complicated, I was still a little nervous.

Neungsiam's bout was one of the main events of the evening, and a key step in his comeback. The Thais called him "Mr. Smart," and if you watched him fight, you knew exactly what they were talking about: He was cold and calculating and explosive. Above all, he was patient, his dark eyes missing nothing, blocking everything, and he loved to punch. A fight was just finishing and Neungsiam was up next.

A typical muay Thai fight starts out slowly. The trainers or promoters are good at matching fighters, and there are few knockouts. The fighters begin by feeling each other out, probing for an obvious weakness. The first round or two might see just a few kicks and blocks per round; the fighters are aware that they must carefully conserve energy for the ordeal of the rounds deeper into the fight. The later rounds, the third and fourth, are where the fights are usually decided. The fighters often go straight into the clinch as they tire, looking to land knees for the most points. The pace quickens, and there is no way to communicate how strenuous this is. Going twelve rounds in Western boxing is a breeze compared to going five in muay Thai—at least, that's according to Apidej, who had boxed professionally as well.

Neungsiam's opponent was a current top fighter, higher ranked, and the betting favorite. He was younger and leaner, but he seemed quickly intimidated by Neungsiam's calm hostility and heavy touch. Neungsiam had power as well as speed, and his careful thinking and reasoning were apparent from ringside. I was too focused on the match to feel any stage fright when Kum and I leapt into the ring to massage Neungsiam between rounds; I just didn't want to screw up my tiny part of the whole effort. In the corner between rounds, I filled my mouth with water and sprayed it onto Neungsiam's legs and then roughly and vigorously massaged him, while Kum did the same to his upper body. The crowd breathed like the sea around us.

The fight turned into a muay Thai clinic: Neungsiam took his opponent apart. He checked the kicks and counter-kicked with devastating power, and he punished his man whenever he tried something. Muay Thai matches are very much about composure: breathing through the nose, appearing unwinded and unhurt. Neungsiam's calm, utterly hostile gaze cut through his man and everyone could see it. He hit too hard and his defense was too complete for his opponent; the man couldn't find a rhythm and looked more and more ill at ease while trying to appear calm and collected. In the middle of the third round, Neungsiam chased him down in a flurry of pinpoint hard punches—you almost never jab in muay Thai—and knocked him out. He strode coolly away, shaking his right fist in triumph. It was awesome. His opponent left in a wheelchair.

One day when I was in the office, e-mailing my mom, Anthony strode in and said he'd found an opponent for me. I finished the e-mail without mentioning it. The fight was set for July 14, nearly two months away, and I would be facing a heavyweight Japanese fighter who was also new to muay Thai. Anthony was relieved to have found an opponent for me; there were maybe only two Thais fighting near my weight (around 185 pounds) in the whole country, and they both would have obliterated me.

Once my fight was scheduled, it loomed like a long, dark cloud on the horizon. I trained as hard as I could each day, full out. I joined the long morning runs with the Lumpini fighters who were about to fight, out in the dark before anyone else would go. I was discovering the key to building endurance: Push on when you feel you can't, and next time that moment will come later. I had to push hard, because the fight was a "professional" fight, meaning five rounds.

I had some doubts that would eat into my heart late at night, or when waking from an afternoon nap, but strangely enough my confidence seemed boundless; I couldn't really imagine a bad outcome. But the fight drew closer and closer, and I began to feel that maybe I was overtraining, or getting sick, and the fears would plague me like a swarm of gnats.

I stayed at it, training hard, and the days crept by until suddenly I was a week away. When gearing up for a fight, the fighter takes two or three days off from training immediately before the event, to allow his now rapacious stamina to rebuild and his body to heal. There were always little things: blisters, cuts, bruises. For my last morning run, I went out with Johann, a bald Belgian fighter with a scorpion tattooed on his ribs (clearly scorpions were a popular motif with the muay Thai crowd), and we went farther than usual. We turned around after five miles and noticed that a dark and dirty monsoon had been sneaking up on us the whole time. Big drops began to sizzle and splatter on the pavement like bleeding flies. In Thailand, for a fighter, the rain is death. The added stress of cold water on a fighter's already maxed-out immune system almost guarantees sickness, and a sick fighter in a fight has about a third of his normal stamina, sometimes less.

The rain was coming down so hard it misted off the ground up past my knees—a real tropical deluge—and it stripped the humidity out of the air, leaving a chill. About halfway back, Johann stopped to relieve himself; I decided to push on through the red mud and deepening puddles. My socks turned crimson and my calves were coated. When I finally got back to the camp, Apidej was worried, warming up the van to come find me. He hustled me into the hot tub and we skipped training that morning. Luckily, I didn't get sick.

The next day, Anthony and I received a startling fax from the Japanese promoter of my fight. The other fighter was going to try to make 203 pounds but would probably be over; he was thirty-eight years old; and here was the kicker: He was the 1994 Western Osaka heavyweight karate champion. It was my first fight ever and I weighed 187 pounds. Sometimes a professional fighter gives up two or three pounds. Sixteen pounds would be considered suicide. A larger man hits harder with more weight behind his blows. He also just takes up more space; he can do so much more, he can control the ring. When I sparred with Johnny, who weighs about 140 pounds, we were both surprised; he had better technique and moved well, but I was so much bigger, I could dominate him. I stumbled back to my room, thinking, *How many fights did my opponent have to fight to become a champion?*

Fifteen? Twenty? Full-contact karate wasn't muay Thai, but it was definitely full contact.

A German guy named Bippo, who at twenty-eight had spent a lot of time in Thailand studying muay Thai, had helped me during my training. When I told him about the fax, he looked worried and made no effort to hide it. "You should cancel the fight," he said. "This is a setup." He talked about ax-kicks and other bone-breaking karate techniques that I would be completely unprepared for and might walk into blindly. Mostly, though, he talked about experience. "In my first fight, I was so nervous I couldn't punch," he told me.

I left Bippo and went upstairs to my room. I thought about his advice. I could quit. I could get out of this! I felt the lure of escape, of dodging responsibility. When I was in junior high school, I loathed the pressure of football games and had a few times faked illness to get out of practice, though I always went to the games. Here was an excuse, an escape hatch. I sat on my dingy bed and stared at the fax. I realized that the guy was trying to psych me out. It enraged me, the idea that this guy thought he could play mind games with me.

I turned it over in my mind. I was a long way from junior high. I was a lot stronger, and I was a better fighter than I'd been an offensive tackle. I was never going to be here again, and I had invested so much. To not fight would be to miss an unrepeatable opportunity. And somehow I couldn't see losing; I just couldn't imagine it.

When I went downstairs for the afternoon session, I told Bippo, "I don't care who he is, I'm going to kick his ass," and Bippo smiled— he understood that braggadocio is part of gearing up for a fight. He understood, but he still thought I was in trouble.

On the last day before the fight, resting in my room, I took a picture of my stuff hanging on the wall: my mongkol, my warm-up gear, my towel. Kum had made the mongkol out of thick red plastic string. I had reassured my mom via e-mail that it was blessed by Buddhist monks and would protect me. In a funny way, I was growing calmer.

We drove down to Samrong, which was about twenty minutes away, and I could tell Anthony was nervous. Traffic was bad, and if it continued like this, we might not have enough time to prep. I stared out the window, watched the cars, and waited. Everything I could do was done. I was surprised at how relaxed I felt. I even found myself smiling.

We got to Samrong with time to spare, and I met Bippo on the way in. I nodded hello but kept my head down. I didn't really want to look at anybody I knew.

I saw my opponent when I walked in the door of the stadium. I was taller than he was, and although he was as wide as a tree, height made a difference. He had a broad, pleasant face, and glasses, and his hair was cropped short. He was wearing karate *gi* pants and a T-shirt and his heavy forearms were covered in tattoos. We shook hands, smiling, and talked through our promoters. We nodded at each other, agreeing that this was a friendly match and we were not there to kill each other. Yeah, right, I thought. I may have been uninitiated, but I wasn't stupid. This was a fight, not a sparring session, and he was going to try to hurt me. I knew I was supposed to be intimidated by him, but I was also aware that he wasn't as cool as he pretended to be. Showing up in my Fairtex warm-up suit and being big and tall, I looked a lot more professional than I was.

National Geographic was there to film a Westerner having his first muay Thai fight, part of a documentary they were doing on the sport, but it was easy to ignore them. I sat down in the stands, paranoid about wasting energy; I knew that I would need absolutely everything. Yaquit taped up my hands. Finally, it was me getting my hands taped—tape was different than the wraps, tighter, stronger, permanent. My opponent was walking around, a towel around his neck and both hands on it. He was big and burly, but, I reminded myself, thirty-eight years old. He should really sit down.

Yaquit and I moved to the tables, and I lay down and got the hot-oil massage. It tingled and then stung. We didn't talk much. Johann and Bippo and a few other *farang* stood around, nervous. I had a new roommate at Fairtex, a giant Swede named Blue, who was one of my cornermen and probably more nervous than I was. Blue was about as unsuitable for muay Thai as one could be, but he loved the sport and the training. He was a Fairtex lifer: He'd been there for twelve months some time ago, and when I was there, he was planning on staying for another year. He was seriously overweight—I would put him around 250—though the weight was sloughing off him in the heat. He was primarily there to lose weight; the first time he'd come to Fairtex he'd lost more than fifty pounds. Blue was one of the nicest guys you could ever meet, without a mean bone in his body. The Thais loved him, both for his gentle demeanor and for his persistence in the face of his physicality.

You had to give Blue credit. He wasn't there to fight, and he didn't have much form, but he tried. There was a trainer for the Lumpini fighters who in all my time there never spoke to me or looked at me once; he didn't have any time for or interest in the silly *farang*. But he would talk to Blue. Blue had won them over by nearly killing himself training, by a show of heart. Now, at my fight, he had his hair carefully styled and looked nervous as hell.

"Sam, you warm," Yaquit said, as I climbed to my feet and began to shadowbox, staring at the floor. There are two schools of thought about where your eyes should be when fighting: You stare at your opponent's eyes and let your peripheral vision cover his body like a membrane, or you stare at your opponent's midsection. I was of the latter school. The eyes are for mind games, and intimidation, and distractions, and tricks. I don't do any of those things. I just want to hit, to get through and make good connections, to be there in front of the other fighter and to find a way through him. I don't care about him one way or the other; I don't know him.

There was a commotion where my opponent was warming up. He'd drawn a crowd, but I ignored it. I later found out that he was putting on a real show, dropping ax-kicks and flat-punching the brick walls. He'd also taken off his shirt and pants to reveal a body covered in deep, serious tattoos—demons and snakes and fish. The Thais loved it and were screaming, "*Yakuza!*" Traditionally, a member of the Yakuza, the Japanese mafia, has tattoos covering his entire body, except on his face, neck, and hands. Another Yakuza tradition is to cut off a finger to show regret if you disappoint your boss. I can't prove that my opponent was Yakuza, but he was sporting about five thousand dollars' worth of tattoos and he did show up with four or five burly Japanese guys (of course, they could have been friends from his gym or dojo). I learned later that he was missing half of his left pinkie. Maybe he wasn't Yakuza, but the Thais certainly thought so.

I put on my cup and fight shorts and went over and got my gloves. Yaquit tied them on. The gloves weighed ten ounces each and felt like nothing. At Harvard and Fairtex, I had used regular boxing gloves, the sixteen-ouncers, so I couldn't believe these things. Once a fighter puts on those lobster claws, he's good for only one thing.

Yaquit spoke to me very intensely. "Sam, elbow," he said, making an elbowing gesture. I could see he was worried. From the way everyone avoided my eyes, I was getting the sense that they were concerned for me.

Then it was time to go.

I step into the ring, and stand facing my corner, hands on the ropes, waiting for the music to start the *wai khru*. My pulse begins to race. I avoid looking at my opponent. Finally, I am really nervous.

The music comes up, and we begin our walk. I move around the ring counterclockwise, with my inside fist up and outside fist on the top rope. This is a way to learn the ring, to feel it. I bow and say a prayer in each corner, ostensibly to placate the spirits of the corners. I read somewhere that the way to win a fight is to take control of one corner, and then another, until finally you control the whole ring. So I mutter to each corner as I stop and bow my head, "This is my corner."

Then the *wai khru* begins. I learned Apidej's *wai khru,* as is proper. I walk in small spiraling circles into the center of the ring and carefully get down on my knees, kowtowing toward my own corner, my back to my opponent's corner. The *wai khru* is the time to think about your parents, your family, and your trainer. I do, and it works. It centers me, reminding me of why I am here and who I am.

I sit up and bow three times, swinging my arms wide and curling them up to my face as I arch back. And then a slow climb to the feet, the *ram muay,* turning and stepping lightly, deliberately, dancing to the beat like it's an Indian rain dance. I stare at the ground, intent on learning every square inch of the canvas, of knowing the dimensions of the ring. It's all mine.

The music ends. I bow to my corner and go over to Yaquit. He removes my mongkol and says something in Thai—which I don't understand and doesn't concern me—and crosses himself; he's Catholic. Later I found out he had said, "Sam, have a cool heart."

I go back to the center and touch gloves with my opponent. He is trying to glare me down. I'm not interested in a staring contest. The referee holds both our gloves and says something in Thai, warning us. We both nod, even though neither of us understands him.

I return to my corner and the bell rings. The pipes trill, and we come together. I have my game plan and I'm not going to deviate from it: *Take it easy the first round, kick low and hard at his legs, and feel him out. Nobody kicks high until the third round. Don't clinch.*

I kick him first, a low right-leg kick, and a few seconds later land a weak left-leg kick. I fight traditional, or orthodox, stance, which, like boxing, leads with the left, so my stronger kicks are right-leg kicks. The lead-leg kicks require a quick shuffle step that telegraphs. My opponent comes back with a heavy, strong leg kick. He is a southpaw, a lefty, so he uses his right hand to jab and his left to power punch. He begins alternating between leading with his left and leading with his right, a very karate thing to do, to try to confuse your opponent. His stance is shallow, though, and his shoulders are nearly parallel with mine, so it doesn't make much difference; the angle and speed of his blows don't change much whether he is leading left or right. After a few more punches, he throws a heavy kick to my right side, low, just above the waist, and I think, *Hey, maybe I can kick to the body too.*

I'm not really thinking out there; I'm just trying to stay with him, stay in his face. There are moments when the ref is yelling, "Pick it up, Red!"—referring to my red trunks—which kind of throws me, as my world has shrunk to my opposition and nothing exists or makes sense outside of our intense dialogue of punches and kicks. I just want to keep up my end of the conversation.

My opponent keeps landing heavy kicks on my lead leg, on the outside of my left knee. They don't really hurt, but I know that it's not good for me. For some reason, I can't block them shin on shin.

Suddenly I'm on my ass, scrambling to get to my feet. I can't tell if it was a punch or kick that put me down, I think probably a kick. I just want to get up, to get on with it, to get back in front of him. I don't even take my standing eight count to catch my breath, which surprises my opponent a little; he's already walked over to his corner. He comes back warily and we touch gloves. He should jump all over me, but he doesn't, so I take those few seconds of rest. Then I start punching, and he stumbles and slips and goes down on his own.

I am exhausted, but I hear Blue calling through the haze, "He's through! He's through!" and I think, *Shit, Blue's right. He's all done.* I just have to keep on him, not let up, and he'll run out of gas.

He keeps swinging for me, going for the big knockout punch, but I keep my hands up and he never lands one. I chase him around and he turns and grapples with me, and I hear someone yell, "Knee!" I throw a knee, just a little one. I feel it smush into his gut, into the softness underneath his rib cage, and to my astonishment he collapses, just goes straight down. The ref steps in and I stand over my opponent in amazement. Finally, I walk over to a neutral corner, unable to believe what is happening. I watch him try, still on one knee, to pick up his mouth guard, and I think, *Don't get up, don't get up.* Then the ref beckons me over, so I start back, squaring myself up, getting back onto my toes. The ref looks back at him, and he still isn't really on his feet. He is doubled over and pawing weakly for his mouth guard, swaying unsteadily. The ref waves him out. First-round KO.

I was relieved, but I didn't quite know what to do. I went down on one knee next to my opponent, who had collapsed again, touched his gloves, and said something like "Good fight," and he nodded. He was fine, just a little winded. We walked over to his corner, and it didn't seem like I was going to get a drink from his guys, so I went back into the middle of the ring and bowed to the judges and the crowd. It was a little anticlimactic. Usually after a fight the winner and loser will go arm in arm to both corners and have a drink of water from each trainer. I had been killing myself with Apidej for months to be ready for five rounds, and all I got was one?

I walked back over to my corner, and from the way Anthony hugged me and the expressions on his and Blue's faces, I realized they had thought I was going to get creamed. But I still wasn't ready to leave the ring. I wanted at least three rounds, just for the sake of experience. I couldn't believe it had ended so quickly. Anthony brought Apidej over for the cameras and I tried to get down on my knees to bow to him, but he caught me and held me fast, laughing. It was my first fight and I got lucky, fighting an older out-of-shape guy. Apidej knew it wasn't a big deal.

I ran into my opponent afterward, in the showers. I thought, *Oh shit,* because in here, on the slick tile floor, he could do some karate and really mess me up. But he was a perfect gentleman, polite from start to finish, and he shook my hand as he left the shower. I felt a little bad for him. He'd flown in from Tokyo just for this, but he hadn't had enough time to acclimate and rest, and then he warmed up too much. He was definitely a better fighter than I was, but muay Thai is a young man's game. Whoever is in better shape wins. It's that simple.

I was lucky, but in a sense, so was he. I didn't follow Yaquit's advice and wade in throwing elbows; it might have turned into a bloodbath if I had, because I doubt my opponent would have been ready for those, either. And if the fight had gone into the later rounds, he wouldn't have gotten any less tired.

Afterward, Blue, Anthony, Apidej, a few others, and I walked down the street to a little curbside restaurant and drank Elephant beer and ate salty snacks. I gradually became jubilant and thought I might never be tired again. Apidej told me a story that really stuck with me. He had been in a bar with a bunch of friends as a younger man, when he was the best fighter in Thailand, and a friend of his had become very drunk and tried to pick a fight. Apidej had just quietly gotten up and *wai*'d respectfully, and high, but his eyes deadly and calm behind his gesture, and backed out. The *wai* is the gesture of greeting respectfully and also for giving thanks, hands in prayer to the forehead, elbows out, a slight bow—I do it all the time because it engenders politeness. But when Apidej acted out for us the way he had done it, bowing before his aggressive friend, I could see in his eyes the pure and tranquil knowledge of victory. This is a guy who kicked so hard that if you blocked with your arm, he'd break it—and yet he had the utter control to not be baited. That's what I admired, more than anything. Apidej is a devout Buddhist, and he meditated often, and I was curious about that. Something in that attitude seemed like the real warrior attitude, secure in self-knowledge, aware of things that don't matter and untroubled by them.

I left Thailand a week later. My visa had run out, and to be honest, I was sick of training, bored of no booze and no girls and the monotony of hitting the pads and pounding the bags. Norman Mailer captured the tedium of training in his book *The Fight,* an account of the legendary Ali-Foreman "Rumble in the Jungle":

> Just as a man serving a long sentence in prison will begin to live in despair about the time he recognizes that the effort to keep his sanity is going to leave him less of a man, so a fighter goes through something of the same calculation. The prisoner and the fighter must give up some part of what is best in him (since what is best for any human is no more designed for prison—or training—than an animal for the zoo). Sooner or later the fighter recognizes that something in his psyche is paying too much for the training. Boredom is not only deadening his personality but killing his soul.

A few weeks before I had to leave, my friend Quentin Oram had e-mailed me from Australia and asked if I would help him and his girlfriend (also a great friend of mine), Florence Bel, take his '38 Hans Christian cutter across the Indian Ocean. We had all met working on a yacht in the Caribbean.

So I flew back to Darwin, and we spent five months crossing the seven thousand miles. Quentin is English and Florence is French, and they refought the Hundred Years' War during the passage. We touched in Durban, South Africa, and I happily got off the boat and wandered around for four months. It was restful after the long, tedious anxiety of the passage, except for being chased by a young bull elephant near Kruger and stroking the fin of a great white shark off the southern coast. When I was alone and unobserved, I would shadowbox a little, and my unused limbs would flash and spin. I missed fighting, and I thought about how much better I'd be if I were still training and competing. I would sometimes talk about it, but people's reactions were weird; they didn't know where to put me, or whether they believed me.

Finally, I flew back to the States and started temping in Boston, a little panicked to be twenty-six years old and without a career. But I felt like I was in disguise wearing a tie on the subway, like I was pretending. I hated my job. I worked at a law firm and found myself turning into a nihilist, an anarchist, hiding files, sleeping in closets; soon I would work half an hour and then take an hour break. I asked my brother-in-law, a computer systems manager, to write me a virus, and he clapped me on the back and laughingly shook his head. I wanted to tear down the financial district. I worked out and found some guys to hit Thai pads with, but I was so far out of fighting shape that it felt like a joke. There was a black guy with a wicked lead-leg kick who had fought in New York, and he was surprised at how good I was for just six months of training. "You might be something if you put in a few years," he said.

When people asked me about my muay Thai experience, the stories began to feel distant and dreamlike. Friends shook their heads (usually affectionately) or gave me puzzled looks. I guess it was a strange thing to go do, although at the time it didn't seem that way. I was frequently asked, "Why? Why fight?" I could argue that the fear of fighting drove me to fight, but I'm not afraid of being hurt, and the thought of getting knocked out doesn't faze me. What I am afraid of is being made a fool of, of dishonoring myself.

But that's not all of it: I am afraid of confrontation. I don't like it when anyone gets mad at me, and I try to avoid angering anyone. It's not big scary men, or women, or anything in particular. I don't like pissing anyone off. I am afraid of the anger of others.

By doing something repeatedly, though, and understanding it, you can diffuse and defuse the fear. This is true for sailing, riding motorcycles, asking girls out—even getting hit in the face by a man who wants to kill you.

I thought that I could walk away from fighting, having taken the test. But fighting is never over. I hadn't been tested, I had been given an easy victory without any kind of struggle. I hadn't *learned* enough to be done. I had the problem all boxers and fighters have: They never want to quit, they always are looking ahead to the next fight, when they'll do better. I was broke, though, all the sailing money long spent. I didn't have the background to be a professional fighter—I started too late and wasn't a genetic freak who could get away with it—and I wasn't sure that just training was enough stimulation.

In the summer of '01, I nearly joined the Marine Corps again, this time to fly helicopters, and I was breaking in my boots for boot camp when, on some desperate whim, I took a job doing construction for Raytheon in Antarctica, at the South Pole. The National Science Foundation pays for the operations there and contracted out to Raytheon; they were building a huge year-round station to hold the large numbers of scientists and visitors that the Pole gets these days—around two hundred in the summer and thirty to fifty people in the winter.

Ahh, Antarctica. You had to be there. It was 70 below zero without windchill the first week down there; with windchill it hit 118 below. That's brisk. We were working outside for ten hours a day, and even during "summer" it was usually 20 below.

I remember when summer ended and the temperatures began to drop again, one of the crane operators said to me cheerily, "There's a nip of fall in the air today." It was 50 below. When I wasn't working, I lifted weights and ran on a treadmill, and there was a heavy bag in a little gymnasium that I would pound on. I felt like I had just scratched the surface of fighting, and the depths beckoned, but I needed money.

While down in Antarctica I met Cheri Dailey, a beautiful, tall, strong girl who was one of the few female smoke jumpers in the world. I thought smoke jumping sounded about right. I asked Cheri how I could be more like her, and she hooked me up with her old hand crew (a twenty-person firefighting team) in Washington State. I couldn't have had a better recommendation. There is a legend about Cheri Dailey, and it goes like this: One of the fitness tests that smoke jumpers take is humping a hundred-pound pack for three miles. Out of a class of about sixty, Cheri came in first, beating all the men—and these guys are Division 1 football players, total badasses. Cheri smoked them all. She also had a tongue stud.

I left Antarctica in January as winter was settling in, the sun beginning its monthlong set, and traveled around New Zealand for a month before coming back to the States. I bummed around L.A. and New York again, then headed out west in the spring to join a firefighting crew.

The Ahtanum 20 was a state crew where the average age was about twenty-two. I was twenty-seven and made a conscious decision to "out-young-man" the young men on the crew; I would be more enthusiastic, run farther, work harder, race around more. It was the best way I could see to handle the situation of being the old guy who was a rookie. We had a good time, fighting fires and roaming Washington, which is a heartbreakingly beautiful place. I was the weird old dude who hung punching bags in the trees around camp and hit them barefoot. The Ahtanum 20 was a type-2 crew, which meant we couldn't do certain dangerous jobs that called for type-1 crews, called Hotshots. I remember watching Hotshot crews head into the worst parts of the fires and thinking, *Man, I got to get on with those guys.*

In the winter I came back east to get my EMT certification, and the following spring I headed out to interview with Hotshot crews. I drove all over the country and was picked up by the Gila Hotshots in New Mexico. It was a considerable honor to be hired by them, as Gila is considered one of the best crews in the country. Up at the camp, high in the Gila National Forest, I found a heavy bag and hung it with some carabiners, to pound on in the afternoons. At the time, I wouldn't have said I was going to fight again, but the idea still lurked.

Fire, especially big fire, is awesome. Sometimes when we were doing big burnouts on gnarly fires, working in and among acres of flames, seeing clumps of trees torch out fifty or a hundred feet into the sky—there's a lot of adrenaline there, too. When the heat hits like a wall and drives you back without conscious thought, the straps of your backpack so hot they burn you through the Nomex shirt—we all suffer from a touch of pyromania in the business. Our primary weapon against fire is fire, and burning was my favorite job. Being on big fires at night, watching the behavior of intense heat and flame, can be indescribably beautiful.

After the season, I applied for a position with the North Cascades smoke jumpers in Washington State and got a new tattoo on my left forearm, a tattoo of my life, with the motto *"Mundis Ex Igne Factus Est,"* which means "The World Is Made of Fire" in Latin, a quote from a Helprin book (*A Soldier in the Great War*) that I had read maybe five years earlier. It captured the idea that life is born of struggle and striving, that true joy and understanding do not come from comfort and safety; they come from epiphany born in exhaustion (and not exhaustion for its own sake). Safety and comfort are mortal danger to the soul. No good painting ever came easily to me: The good ones were battles. I got the tattoo so that I would always see it there and be reminded.

Though I had applied to be a smoke jumper (and got hired), somewhere, in the dark wilderness of my heart, I still wanted to fight. I had promised myself when I went to Thailand that I would get ten fights, and then stop; because ten fights would be enough to know what fighting *really* is. I had quit after one—and I had never been tested. If only I could find a way to get it to pay for itself—that's how I had done all my traveling before. It's a part of my philosophy: You can always get it to pay for itself somehow.

Fighting is a way to feel, an anti–video game, a way to *force* something to happen. That's what brought me back to it, because when I've fought someone, I know something has happened. How many days of your life pass you by that you could take or leave? When nothing really happened?

During college, I had lived and studied at the Slade School in London for a year, and I became involved in the trance club scene— the Fridge, Escape from Samsara, Return to the Source—and what became apparent was that these thousand kids tripping balls on ecstasy just want to *feel* something. They just want to feel as though everyone in the room understands them, and belongs, and that they belong, and, most important, that something is happening.

All those experiences—sailing around the world, Antarctica, firefighting—I chose them because they were the best options I had going. All I am is persistent, and willing to entertain many ideas. I've done drugs; and I used to drink like it was my job. I wasn't a college athlete; in college, I was a painter who smoked two packs of cigarettes a day. I've done things that maybe I should be ashamed of, but I'm not.

You have a specific responsibility to existence, to God if you like, to taste, touch, and smell what there is to experience. You have to do everything. If given an option between doing something and not doing it, you have to do it; because you've already done the "not do it" part. This can be juvenile and dangerous, I realize, and there are a lot of things I have chosen not do, for a million reasons. I was raised polite. I've never hurt anyone, except guys I was sparring or fighting with. And I don't take needless risks. The idea is to make it through intact; "safety" is my middle name. But I feel that you owe it to the world to be curious. Somebody asked me if I was looking for something. I am looking for *everything*.

Part of my responsibility, while I am strong enough, lies with fighting—not just to get as good as possible, but to understand it, and I maintain that to understand something, you have to do it, and do it more than once. I thought I had closed the door on fighting when I left Thailand, but I hadn't. Four years later it was still there.

So I set out to explore and explain the world of fighting, to myself and to anyone who would listen—not everywhere in the world, and not everything, because that would never end—to try in some small way, with some logical progression, to understand it.

2

RULE NUMBER SEVEN, FIGHT CLUB

Sam fighting in Springdale, Ohio, May 7, 2004.

It's not something he can do anything about, being a bleeder, any more than a guy with a glass jaw can do something about not having a set of whiskers.

—F. X. Toole, *Rope Burns*

It started when I walked into the back room of the Amherst Athletic Club in Amherst, Massachusetts, a little college town in pastoral New England. I was back at home, visiting my mom after a fire season with the Gila Hotshots. December and January in Massachusetts were record-breaking cold, down in the negative 40s at night.

The Amherst Athletic Club had a dark, small room with mats on the floor and rows of gloves and shin pads and various martial arts training gear. The Sheetrock was caved in with human silhouettes where people had been mashed into the wall. I was curious. I asked around, and started training a little bit there, and was shocked to discover how far Mixed Martial Arts had come.

Nearly everyone has heard or seen clips of the Ultimate Fighting Championships (UFC), started in the United States in 1993, held in the infamous Octagon, a high-walled, chain-link octagonal cage for the fighters to battle in. Ultimate Fighting was marketed as the answer to the questions that had persisted since the karate boom in the sixties: Which style was more effective? My tiger-crane kung fu is far deadlier than your Okinawan karate. Well, now you could prove it. Who wins when a good boxer meets a good kickboxer? When a wrestler fights a

41

kung-fu expert? We can answer those questions by fighting with "no rules," evoking old gladiator contests, and satisfying the crowd's bloodlust. Since then, the UFC has moved through various incarnations and venues, has added some basic rules and the use of a referee, and has come under political fire and had management problems. For a while it wasn't even on cable TV. But the UFC survived due entirely to a grassroots fan base that also trains, and more important, fights.

This is a fan base that fights. It is interested in and drawn to fights, fistfights, action movies, who's the toughest?–type questions. It is considered "white trash," and, judging from the crowd shots at the UFC, it is primarily white, male, and tattooed—the disenfranchised, burning to test their manhood, angry at their father or situation or *something*— in short, my people.

The first UFCs were dominated by a slender Brazilian named Royce Gracie, who won by taking the fight to the ground and using Brazilian jiu-jitsu to control his opponents. Royce and his family's jiu-jitsu stood the American martial arts world on its head. All these guys who had been doing karate for twenty years, who had their own schools, suddenly realized they had a glaring weakness: the ground. If a fight went to the ground, and they often do, their vaunted kicks and punches were ineffective. People scrambled to learn Brazilian jiu-jitsu. What evolved was a style known as mixed martial arts, or MMA, where practitioners "mix" the various martial arts to make a complete fighter. You mix boxing and kickboxing and muay Thai with freestyle wrestling and jiu-jitsu, maybe a little judo, whatever you want. Just make sure it all works.

Though I knew the UFC was still around—I'd occasionally catch ads for it on television—finding it in my hometown in western Massachusetts was hard to believe. I soon discovered that it was everywhere. There are several hundred all-amateur events a year in the United States. This isn't like amateur boxing with headgear; this is serious. Your only protection is a mouthpiece, a cup, and some little fingerless gloves so you can punch your opponent in the head and not break your knuckles but still be able to grip and wrestle. This is real fighting, and you can get pounded in there. Although it is sometimes called NHB for "no holds barred," there are some things you can't do: head butting, eye gouging, fishhooking (when you hook a guy's mouth with a finger or two), punching the back of the head. Other than that, it's pretty much all fair game; you can knee and elbow, you can choke, you can crank his ankle until he submits.

For weeks, trapped in the deep midwinter freeze that gripped New England like an immense, airy python, I kept coming back to the idea of an MMA fight. I'd had my taste of fighting in Thailand, but it hadn't been enough; it was over too quickly. I hadn't learned enough; my fighting was still weak and flawed. Training and fighting in MMA would be a chance to round out my skills as a fighter. I was still afraid that there was so much I didn't know and wasn't comfortable with. I had just sold the Thailand story to *Men's Journal,* and I realized there was a way I could maybe get someone else to finance my training: by writing about it. I decided to approach an editor with some ideas to see where it got me, and surprisingly, he was enthusiastic. He asked me why I was so interested in learning enough to fight in a cage. I told him I wanted to learn the skills, to learn how to fight without rules, but there was more.

MMA fighters are scary in a way that boxers and kickboxers aren't. They are savage. When you go to the ground, there is a desperation in the struggle for dominance that fuels a ferocity that you don't get in other sports. I find these fighters frightening in a "monster-under-the-bed" scary way. Shaved heads, bulging muscles, and, above all, anger, eyes snapping with anger. There is no letup; you pour it on until you win. You hit him, he falls back, and you swarm him. And whoever wins the fight, the unspoken signifier of victory is *I could have killed you.* There are no excuses in the rules. If we were alone, in some back alley or on a deserted island, and we fought without all these people watching, then I could have killed you.

I was lured by the siren song of violence, the dark-faced coin of masculinity. Could I find my own rage? Could I tap into it?

The co-owner and trainer at Amherst Athletic was an African expatriate named Kirik Jenness, a tall, lean white guy who has made MMA his life. He runs the largest MMA Web site in the world and has been training and fighting for thirty years. He had a long list of contacts, but when I asked him where the best place to train might be, he said, "Probably Pat Miletich's place in Iowa. He's got some of the best fighters in the world there, and there's nothing else to do in Iowa but fight."

I called around and thought about Florida, and Oregon, and some other teams; but what I kept hearing about was Team Miletich in Iowa. I spoke with the legendary Pat Miletich on his cell phone. I was nervous, talking too loud, and he was unconcerned and enthusiastic. "Of course, it'd be fun, bro," he said. Unhesitating.

So I went.

* * *

I drove out to Bettendorf, Iowa, across a snowy wasteland and crashed in a no-frills motel in the middle of town. Bettendorf is one of the Quad Cities, four little towns that sit on the Mississippi in eastern Iowa and western Illinois: industrial and blue-collar, with the Big Muddy flowing frozen and brown and sluggish as molasses down the middle.

The next morning, I found the Champions Fitness Center. Right as I walked in the door I exchanged nods with a medium-height, broad-shouldered man. He had a wicked set of neatly cauliflowered ears and a pleasant, battered face that maintained a boyish air. Pat Miletich.

Pat Miletich, the "Croatian Sensation," was born and bred in Iowa (there's nothing Croatian about him but his name) and became one of the most successful fighters in the UFC—winning five titles at 170 pounds—by being the most technically proficient fighter in the game. He understood before anyone else the need to diversify and borrow from different disciplines, and as a result he is now widely recognized as probably the best MMA trainer in the world.

Pat also has a reputation for being a good guy; as Kirik said, "the nicest guy in the sport." He shook my hand and gave me a quick tour of the brand-new gym, fresh white paint and new equipment everywhere. We walked under the cardio machines and out into the giant weight room and took a hard right into the heart of the gym. Pat cocked an eye at me, smiling. "You've got some size on you," he said. "What do you walk around at?" He meant weight.

"Something like one ninety-five," I said.

"Good, you can cut to one eighty-five easily then." We chatted a little about a piece I was planning on writing for *Men's Journal* about MMA, an introduction to the sport. "It's not for everyone," he said with a slight pause, a tiny raising of the eyebrow. I got it.

I rented an apartment across from the gym's parking lot, filthy and decrepit but three hundred dollars a month and the shower got hot. One of those modern indoor flush toilets—what else do you need? I even could see a tiny brown strip of the Mississippi, and Illinois across the bridge. I had no furniture, so I rented a bed and bought a folding chair and table from Wal-Mart.

That night, a Friday, I started training. "Sparring" just means practice fighting, standing up, usually three-minute rounds with thirty-second breaks or five-minute rounds with minute breaks. You wear headgear and big sixteen-ounce gloves, and a cup and mouth guard and shin protectors, and bang on each other. We kicked, punched, clinched, and on Mondays we went for "takedowns," in which you take your opponent to the ground in such a way that you come down on top. The headgear keeps you from getting cut, but there were still knockouts and plenty of concussions and bloody noses to go around. Miletich's place is famous for the hard sparring on Monday and Wednesday nights (Friday was light sparring), and I thought I was doing okay until Pat grabbed me and said, "Hey, Sam, come spar the heavyweight champion of the world." What could I do but say yes?

A minute later, I found myself sparring with Tim Sylvia, six foot eight and 260 pounds. He was so big and strong I couldn't really get near him, and the few times I did hit him it was like punching into a tree. He was taking it so easy on me that I could actually see and think, which was very nice of him. I knew a little bit about Tim, that he was from Maine, so I tried to talk about Maine between rounds to keep him in a friendly mood. It was a key strategy, because he could have destroyed me easily, if he just decided to let a few body punches go hard. He wore no headgear. His head was massive, forbidding, like a stone statue with jutting brow and craggy jaw. He was a nice guy; he thumped me some, but nowhere near as bad as it might have been.

After practice there was a warm glow in the gym, the air like a sauna from twenty or thirty guys sweating and bleeding their hearts out. People flopped down on the mats, discussing in groups of two or three their sparring mistakes, or fights seen recently on TV. The atmosphere was excellent; although I wasn't a part of it, I could sense the camaraderie. It made me just a little lonelier as I packed up and limped home across the parking lot and up a set of rickety wooden stairs.

The water out of the tap in my hovel was foaming and leggy, and left a serious rim of scum in the glass. Didn't taste too bad, though. The light in the kitchen didn't work. I stumbled around in the dark and showered (that shower was the only good thing in my life for weeks) and made a plate of beans for myself. I forced down a few bites but was too tired to eat.

I was already beat to pieces. *This is going to be rough,* I thought to myself with a tinge of despair. I hadn't trained like this in years. I had the suspicion that twenty-nine was going to be way different than twenty-five. Still, I was committed—I was going to fight, so I better get ready.

I tried to get into a routine as quickly as possible. Monday, Wednesday, and Friday were sparring days (Monday with takedowns), and on those days I ran and lifted a little in the mornings, while my Tuesdays and Thursdays were devoted entirely to grappling: a basic class at nine, another basic class at five-thirty, and then advanced from five-thirty to six-thirty, when the experienced guys repeatedly tied me in knots, yanked my arms out, cranked my neck.

There is nothing so frightening as being on the ground with a guy who really knows what he's doing; it's like being in the water with a shark. You're struggling, desperate, trying to escape, and suddenly you can't breathe, you're smothered, and you can't see, your arms are getting twisted off, and you "tap" and then it's all over. "Tapping," a light tap on your opponent, or on the mat, is how you concede the fight. He's caught you in a "submission." A submission is when you get your opponent in an arm-bar, or a knee-bar, or a choke, or a thousand other things, where you essentially threaten your opponent with a broken limb or being choked unconscious. He can tap instead of actually having his arm broken or losing consciousness because you're pinching his carotid arteries.

Submission fighting is a huge part of ground fighting. It is at the heart of MMA and one of the reasons the sport has a small, educated following. It's sometimes hard for uneducated observers to understand that while the two guys were rolling around, one guy could have broken the other guy's arm and the other guy admitted it. A submission can happen in seconds; the "ground game" is extremely technical and about position and outthinking your opponent; it's a lot like playing chess.

Having done muay Thai and some boxing, my "stand-up" fighting was okay—not good, by any means, but at least I had a clue as to what I wanted to do. My ground game, however, was nonexistent. I never even wrestled in high school. People sometimes wonder why one of the best MMA gyms in the world is in Iowa, but when you realize that some of the best wrestlers in the world come from Iowa, it starts to make sense. I came to dread the grappling days, and on the mornings afterward I would wake up with my whole body in agony. I started calling this "car-wreck-itis," that feeling of having been in a car wreck the night before, where everything is strained and black-and-blue, including little muscles you didn't know existed. Getting out of bed took ten minutes.

The only other time I've been beat up like that was after branding. During college I worked a summer on the largest cattle ranch in

Montana, and I helped brand for three days, wrasslin' calves, late in the season when they were getting big. Those calves would run all over you and kick you to shit, like you'd been put in a blender.

During those first two weeks, I often left sparring to stanch a bloody nose, a common occurrence at Pat's. Somebody was always dashing to the paper towels. People laughed, yelled in faux anger, "Clean up your mess!" and Tim delighted in crowing, "Sam can't hold his mud." I sparred with several different people, but far and away the worst was Tim; every time I threw a rear-leg kick he trapped it and dumped me, without fail. His hands were like sledgehammers, and if he had landed some hard body shots, I would probably have died. I hovered between trying to hit him and not wanting to piss him off. He trapped me in a corner and my tiny life flashed before my eyes as I scrambled. He once threw a turning back kick at me, and I leapt aside and it hit the wall like a wrecking ball.I gave him a dirty look and almost stopped sparring: *Are you trying to kill me?* Afterward, someone told me I was the same height as Andrei Arlovski, Tim's next fight opponent.

I felt a little like the new kid in school. People were watching me. They wanted to test me out, although I wasn't very good, so that didn't last. Several times during my stay I saw outside pro fighters come in to spar, and everyone lined up to beat their asses. People just got pounded; it was a rough place and you didn't just walk in there and start sparring because those guys would slaughter you.

A few days into it, I met a guy named Marshall Blevins, a manufacturing engineer about my age who'd been with Pat for two and a half years. Marshall fought amateur kickboxing and has won regional, national, and North American titles, but he joked that he still got nervous before a Wednesday night. He was an easygoing guy with a laconic manner, and very helpful, giving me some pointers. "It doesn't take long to get pounded out of a Wednesday class if you don't want to be there," he said.

"I remember sparring with Jens [Pulver] for the first time; he knocked me out with a head kick. A lot of these guys you don't want to show them you're hurt, but you get booted in the head, hit the wall, and slide down. . . . Well, you shake it off and bite down on your mouthpiece and start swinging again. Most of these guys are like that—you hurt them, they'll come back twice as hard." He smiled and laughed.

Though I think they went easy on me mostly because Pat introduced me as a writer, it still was pretty rough. I got hit particularly hard one night and could feel blood running in a thin stream out of my nose. The next day my whole face was swollen. Pat looked at me and laughed. "Did you break your nose?"

"No, no, it's just bruised," I assured him. I didn't break it. No way. Pat looked doubtful.

I have heard critiques of Pat's gym, that the sparring is too hard, that people get hurt and don't learn enough. It is a hard place to learn, and you become averse to taking risks and trying new things when you're getting beaten on. However, MMA is a rough, rough sport; toughness is critical. You need to be tough, to have overall body toughness to succeed. That night my face in the mirror looked deformed, a tremendous swollen bulge over my nose and between my eyes; the blood settled in a few days to give me two black eyes, like makeup under the skin.

Because I didn't know any better, I kept at it. I continued to get pounded and thrown around by Tim, by the other heavyweights. I ended up on my ass all the time, but once, halfway through the week, as we were all leaving and I was dazedly collecting myself from the floor, Pat remarked with a laugh, "Sam, you're going to be tough as hell in two months," and my heart swelled. I knew he was just trying to keep my spirits up, but it worked.

Team Miletich, or Team MFS (Miletich Fighting Systems), is Pat's stable of fighters, one for each weight class in the UFC. His team reads like a who's who in mixed martial arts. Jens Pulver, "Little Evil," at 155 pounds, is a five-time world champion. Matt Hughes was and still is the dominant 170-pound fighter after Pat vacated the slot, winning six titles; Jack Black and "Ruthless" Robbie Lawler also fight at 170, and with Matt they're three of the top ten welterweights in the world. Tony "the Freak" Fryklund was a badly underrated 185-pounder, and Jeremy Horn is one of the best in the world at 185 or 205. Of course, Tim Sylvia, the former champ, is still a serious heavyweight (under 265) contender. There's a second tier, under those guys, of about ten or fifteen pro fighters who are all up and coming, guys like Spencer Fisher, Rory Markham, and Sam Hoger, with impressive records and lesser titles. Of course, the team is a revolving concept, with players changing as their standings go up and down—this was all in the early part of 2004.

It's a little like walking into a boxing gym where Trinidad, De La Hoya, Roy Jones Jr., and Lennox Lewis all train together with ten of their friends. It's intimidating; the guy you're going to be sparring with is on a poster on the wall. And the second-tier guys are so good, it's like Tony says, "You can't get a break," because anybody in there will give you a hard time, anybody in there on Wednesday night can be a handful.

Pat has somehow welded all these fighters together. They sought him out and moved to Iowa to be with him.

Pat grew up wrestling and playing football and battling with his brothers. He wrestled in college, after his dad, the football coach, died, and moved into kickboxing and boxing afterward. He was lucky in that Davenport, another of the Quad Cities, had an excellent boxing gym; some great pros have come out of it: Michael Nunn, Antoine Echols under Alvino Peña. Pat boxed professionally, studied Brazilian jiu-jitsu with Sergio Monteiro in Tampa and muay Thai with Long Longley in Illinois. He wasn't just mixing his training; he was finding the best trainers in the country. He was revolutionary in that he combined these fighting elements better than anyone had before. In the UFC, before Pat, people would stick to their one discipline and try to use it for everything, or maybe be able to do a few things well. Pat was one of the first to be able to do everything: He could box, he could wrestle, he had submissions, and he understood how to put them all together— especially the transitions between them, which in my mind is perhaps the most important part of professional MMA. He could find a weak link in any fighter he met. And coming up at a time when MMA in America was in its infancy, he was a self-made fighter. He had to bring the elements together on his own, mixing up in his own "laboratory" the stand-up and ground fighting he liked.

I had two little black eyes, and my whole body was in agony. Often I woke up with my legs, trunk, back, shoulders, biceps, and forearms all screaming.

After grappling one night, my biceps hurt so bad that I thought I might faint. I couldn't hide the pain; I was "guarding" (that's an EMT word for unconscious protective behavior, when people with broken necks from car accidents, for example, walk around cupping their neck with both hands). People asked if I was okay, if I'd hurt my arms. There was a lot of camaraderie, but I wasn't admitted yet. Instead, I eaves-dropped and soaked up what I could from the outside. I talked to Pat about my aching biceps and he looked thoughtful and massaged my arm a bit and asked, "Are you sure it isn't a case of wuss-itis?" and laughed with me. Pat is just so naturally tough—in all his fights he's never gone down from a punch to the head—that he doesn't quite understand mere mortals.

Pat did a training program for law enforcement called Controlled FORCE with some police officers he met through MMA. Tony Grano, a policeman and martial artist, was training and cornering a fighter opposite Pat in an MMA fight, and they hit it off. Tony saw that MMA was a considerable resource to tap into, as everything in it had been tested and retested, and discarded if it proved to be impractical.

I flew down to Austin, Texas, to attend a training session with Pat, Tony Fryklund, and the two police officers who run the program, Tony Grano and Donni Roberts. These guys, lifelong martial artists, were teaching a weeklong seminar at Lackland Air Force Base for military police and instructors.

Pat began teaching by saying, "I can't teach you what I would do in a certain situation, because I'm a fighter who's been training his whole life. Instead, I'm going to teach you a series of techniques that a 115-pound woman can do to a 250-pound man, provided she executes the technique properly."

The problems with training police officers in the use of physical force weren't what you'd expect. Pat said, "It used to be that they didn't really want to train police officers too much in martial arts because they were afraid of them going around beating people down. The reality is the opposite; a trained officer is relaxed and able to cope with a physical situation without the panic and adrenaline that an untrained officer might fall into, which leads him to beat someone down." *Black Belt* magazine agreed with him in its March 2004 issue: "Untrained officers, when threatened physically, are three times more likely to resort to deadly force. . . ."

In Controlled FORCE, there are no strikes, only mechanical locks, so only leverage is used. There aren't any "pain" compliance techniques. The officers learned a series of locks: ways of holding and controlling a suspect through pressure and leverage on his arms and shoulders. The techniques had to be simple—easily remembered without daily training—and effective without actually hurting a suspect. Fat cops who don't exercise needed to be able to execute the techniques. The training had to take into consideration liability issues and lawsuits. There are no strikes in the basic course; in the advanced survival course there are open-hand strikes because they won't break your hand, and they look better for the Rodney King video. How much force do you use? The least amount necessary. The instructors stressed having options, locks to fall back on: "These locks are going to fail, but when they do, you'll be ready to go for the next one, and if that one fails, you can keep going until you get something." The important thing was to keep moving, keep your perpetrator off balance, and flow from one lock to the next. So you grab his arm and twist it one way, and when he fights it by pulling the other way, you switch and go with him, using his force against him.

It was fun to be part of the team. We kept up a constant banter, everyone basically abusing everyone else, physically and verbally. Pat and Donni wrestled so hard in the van that Pat tore Donni's ear up and he bled all over the place, and Tony had to yell at everyone. It was a little like being a freshman and hanging out with the cool seniors in high school; everything was a big rough joke and I couldn't stop giggling.

One morning, at Denny's over coffee, Pat looked at me and just laughed, a short dry bark.

"What?"

"You broke your nose, you know that? It's crooked."

"It is?"

Everyone started laughing. "Yeah, it is," Pat said.

Back in Iowa I was sicker than a dog, having developed a sinus infection—probably from the busted nose. I'd been there for about a month before I left to spend a week with Pat and the boys at Lackland, and I was supposed to be around for a few more weeks and then fight. Pat had got me a kickboxing match, "to get the ring-rust off," but on the night of the fight I was coughing, crying, stuffed up, and I hadn't slept in three days from the infection, so I bowed out. My MMA fight was moved back more than a month by the promoter, a move I was all too happy to accept because I hadn't felt good in weeks. I went on antibiotics.

My small brown room became a haven. I went to the Bettendorf library and got books and retreated to my bed, under my sleeping bags, and read and watched the clock inch toward the next practice session. This could be torturous on a Wednesday afternoon, when at four-thirty I was just sitting around waiting for six-thirty, watching the minutes crawl by. But afterward, coming home, having survived a Wednesday night was a great feeling, and there was the luxury of getting in the shower for as long as I wanted, then climbing into bed with a good thriller, NPR burbling cheerfully in the background. I listened to so much public radio that I actually gave them twenty dollars when they started their fund drive.

I had two dingy pull-down blinds, which stayed down all night, as a bright halogen street lamp yellowed the night right outside my bedroom. First thing in the morning I snapped them both up to let in the gray light of day. I made coffee and tried to write every morning and waited for the first class at ten. The antibiotics worked and I got better.

I lived on Pat's "fighter diet," of which the main rule is no carbs after twelve noon. I boiled chicken breasts and ate them with tortillas and peanut sauce, and I ate salads (a lot of broccoli), and oatmeal. That was it. It was hard to eat at night after grappling or sparring. I was just too tired to even chew my food; even a meal-replacement shake took some doing—I had to muscle it down.

My hovel was a cold, lonely place. One of the two windows had a gutted air conditioner still in place, and a family of birds nested in it; I could hear them stirring before dawn like giant rats in a cage.

Around the time my grappling began to develop, I started to make friends with a few of the up-and-comers, the young pros and dedicated amateurs.

Champions Fitness is a serious place. The weightlifting was run by Dale Ruplinger, a former Mr. America, Mr. Olympia, Mr. Universe. The pretty girl behind the front desk, Emily Fisher, with the ponytail and a southern accent, had fought seven times and beaten three guys in MMA. Her husband, Spencer Fisher, was one of the top non-UFC fighters at the gym, with a 10-0 record as a pro, and they were the first husband-and-wife team ever on the same MMA card at the International Cage Competition in Minnesota. The chiropractor, Dr. Mark Schmall, grappled and was starting stand-up fighting when I arrived. I rolled with him sometimes, and he delighted in tying me in knots from the bottom.

I got to know Tony "the Freak" a little better and found out we went to the same junior high; my mom was even one of his teachers. Tony is a character, and there is a notorious image of him from a cage fight in Canada, in which he is covered in blood, raging. He had taken an elbow to the forehead, it bled so badly the ref stopped the fight, and Tony went temporarily insane. He was so emotional he blacked out and didn't remember rampaging around the ring until Pat and Matt Hughes dragged him down into his corner and covered his face with a towel, like an animal. "I could fight fine," Tony said. "If I had trouble seeing, that was my problem, you know? It was cosmetic, a scratch on the hood. You don't throw away the car just because a windshield wiper is busted. . . . I was so emotional that now I can understand a temporary insanity plea." He had also been running a fever of 103 and had been puking the night before the fight.

Tony was one of the older guys at thirty-three, and he'd been down a long road to get there. He was in the U.S. Coast Guard as a rescue diver and an EMT; he'd been a safety officer on the Big Dig and a stuntman before his constant training in martial arts eventually took over his life. He fought in UFC 14 and won the first round but lost the second. It took him five years to get back to the UFC (because losing, to Tony, means that you are dead—your opponent has killed you). Eventually, he went down to Atlantic City to watch Jens Pulver fight and met Pat and asked if he could come out to Iowa to train. He busted his ass on the first day, and Pat invited him to be on the team, one of the best things that ever happened to him. Team Miletich isn't just a word or a gig to these guys; it is an integral part of their identities. As Tim Sylvia said, "A lot of these fighters are from broken homes, and Team Miletich is their family." For all of them it was a huge point of pride and honor to be asked to be a part of Team MFS. They all have stories about coming to Iowa and the intimidation and fear they felt, but there were no hazings or bad beatings, like the Lion's Den and other camps are infamous for. Being a part of Team MFS is much more about chemistry and the intangibles: Does Pat like you? Are you showing him your work ethic? Can you get along with the other guys?

Tony, like many fighters, is without reservation when talking about himself. I think the nakedness of fighting publicly, the exposure for all to see and judge one's "quality," makes fighters good interview subjects. They'll talk about anything. For Tony, "The martial arts are about respect and discipline, knowledge. Fighting is different. Fighting is about ego. When we're fighting, I'm going to fuck you up. Prove me wrong; prove to me that you're tougher than me." And for Tony, ego isn't the negative "Oh, look at me" ego, it's more about self-knowledge and total dedication to testing and pushing yourself as far as possible, a way to know everything about yourself.

One Wednesday night, Tony was sparring with a promising amateur named Kenny, and Tony was getting pissed off because Kenny wasn't coming hard enough. So Tony would throw his arms wide open and let Kenny tee off and hit him flush and open and unprotected, and then close and punish Kenny until he turned away in fear and hesitation. Then Tony would open up again, half taunting and half enraged, until finally he took Kenny down hard and slammed him in the guts. Then he pulled Kenny back up, embraced him, and they talked a little.

Later I could overhear Tony talking about it and he said, "Kenny's got the speed, the technique, everything, but he lacks a little in confidence. . . . I've kind of taken that kid under my wing and am trying to help him. It's all right if we beat the shit out of each other in here as long as we never lose to anyone outside this gym." That was the prevalent attitude: You kill each other in the gym, and then the fighting elsewhere is easy. I heard again and again from other amateur fighters that the people they sparred with in the gym were ten times tougher than anyone they ever met in the cage.

Justin Brown befriended me in a grappling class, because he remembered what it was like to walk in and not know anybody. "People in here were nice to me and took me under their wing, so now I try and help some of the new guys out."

Justin was twenty-seven and is 4–0 as an amateur, just getting started. "You gotta have your shit together or you get your face ripped off," he said, laughing. He was divorced with two kids, five and seven, and held down two jobs—as a manager at a local Hy-Vee (a supermarket chain) and a bouncer at Daisy Dukes, a strip club. He had a very strong sense of the Miletich team and the honor it was to be associated with it. He didn't want to street fight because it might hurt the gym's credibility. Justin was from Des Moines and said lightly that in Iowa, the mentality is "fuckin' or fightin'." "If you're not getting laid, you might as well find somebody to fight. You'd be sitting around a bar and someone walks up and says, 'Let's go outside and fight'—well, okay."

The gym was a remarkably egalitarian place, and once you'd been accepted, it was friendly and helpful. Everyone gave tips to everyone else; if you saw something, you mentioned it. "Keep those hands up," Tim might call from the sidelines, watching two amateurs spar on their own time. Fighters of all skill levels were in there at all different times, depending on their schedules, and much of the training was done by peers. The pros would stop you and come over and grapple with you—to show you something or give a little lecture on footwork.

It is one of the more interesting facets of MMA: the democracy. In MMA, there are no grand masters, no belts, no fixed ranking system. Knowledge is shared, so good strikers work out with good grapplers, and they teach each other. Far superior fighters like Tony gave me help all the time, and then, sometimes I would tell him about something I'd seen Thai fighters do in Thailand, and instead of dismissing me, he and the others listened carefully. They were willing to take knowledge from anywhere.

The grappling nights were the best examples. The gym was rife with judo black belts, under Coach Humphries, but the judo guys all came to the grappling nights to expand their knowledge. Nearly everyone in there had trained elsewhere, and everyone contributed to group knowledge. There were Iowa state champion wrestlers, Brazilian jiu-jitsu black belts, and everything in between.

Let me try to explain a few of the principles of the ground game, as I understand them. Everyone, more or less, can understand "stand-up" fighting. It's boxing and kickboxing and muay Thai. You punch, kick, elbow, and knee. Then you lock up and go for a takedown, much like in high school wrestling, often by dropping down, "shooting" in, and snatching up ankles or legs.

Once on the ground, each man works for position. You always want to be on top; your weight is working for you and you have much more control, although some fighters skilled in ground fighting actually prefer to work from the bottom. The bottom man wants to keep the top man "in his guard," which means the bottom man has his arms free and his legs around the top man's waist. It looks a little like the missionary position, but it's safer for the bottom man because he can control the top man's hips, the key to the ground game. The top man can punch and look for submissions, but he doesn't have a decisive advantage. So he looks to "pass guard," which means he wants to somehow maneuver his legs over the bottom man's legs until he is "mounted," or off to the side in "side-control."

"Mount" is exactly like what the grammar school bully used to do to you; sit on your chest with his knees under your armpits and rain punches down. It is very dangerous for the bottom man, as the top man can punch with impunity and easily set up submissions. The bottom man has to squirm, buck, and scramble to either reverse the position or at least get back into guard. Side-control is more stable and versatile, and pretty much equally bad for the bottom man—he has to get back to guard.

When he's in guard, the bottom man has a lot of submissions he can go for, chokes and arm-bars. He can use his legs to set up a "triangle" choke, where he catches the opponent in a triangle between his legs and uses them (plus one of the opponent's own arms, pinned helplessly) to cut off breathing. In an arm-bar, he tries to hold one of the opponent's arms straight and in such a way that he can break it if the guy doesn't tap out. He can try a "guillotine" choke, a kind of head-lock where he exerts direct pressure on his opponent's windpipe. Those are just the basics and the ones you see most often; there are hundreds or thousands of variations and methods. And some fighters don't even try for submissions, they just work for position and try to beat their man into oblivion, the "ground-and-pound."

Other fighters prefer to stay on their feet, as it's a little more ex-citing for the crowd and they feel more confident on their feet; so those guys just fight standing and train hard to avoid being taken down, called "sprawling"; when a man dives for your legs to take you down, you kick them out backward, sprawling away from him, and land on top of him with your hips, driving him into the mat. This style is sometimes called "sprawl-and-brawl," and it's what I was trying to learn.

I needed to learn to move my head. I would feel the hard stinging impact that jarred my world, the rushing in my ears like I'm underwater, and then I could feel the blood gushing from my nostrils, the droplets spat-tering my gloves and shirt. I would rush outside to the paper towels, and the gym rats, lifting weights, would stare with a mixture of pity and chagrin. I joked with Pat that I was going to bleed all over my opponents to scare them. And then I mopped up the blood, put my headgear back on, and tried to get back in there, until I got popped again and repeated the whole process. Sam can't hold his mud.

I didn't talk to Jens Pulver much, but he is one of the fighters I most admired, devastatingly heavy-handed for 155 pounds, and he moved like a pro boxer—he had won a few pro boxing fights. He said to me at one point, "You got to find a way to survive in here. We all did. We all found a way to survive in here sparring on Wednesdays, on the Hill, during grappling nights."

The Hill. I'd heard about it for weeks now, and finally one morning Pat grabbed me as I was coming to work out. Along with Mike White-head, an up-and-coming heavyweight and a national champion wrestler from Oregon, and Tim Sylvia, who had a fight coming up, we headed out to the Hill. I still had a persistent, hacking cough, but this was going to "blow out" my lungs, said Pat. We parked on the top of a windy, steep little hill and Pat stayed behind as the three of us headed down to start. There was a slight sense of dread, of imminent doom.

The Hill is a killer because it is not so long and steep that you can't sprint it; you can. It just about kills you to sprint it, but you can, just barely. And then you jog to the bottom and do it again, a total of six times.

So you start pounding up the steep paved road, and you feel okay, and then it twists a little, and you keep pounding, because there's the corner, and then if you can make *that,* it teases you, because there's the finish line, so you "sprint" through (in reality just a short, choppy, painful jog by now) and stand there gasping like you have asthma, wheezing with a high note in your chest. The third one felt like it should be the last one, and during the slow jogs back down the hill my hamstrings and ass were burning like someone had injected the muscles with a syringe full of poison. The fifth one felt like I should be dead, or maybe puke a little, but then there's just one left—anyone could do one more. . . .

I ran the Hill once a week, and I was supposed to pyramid up, to do eight and then ten and then twelve the week before the fight. Pat once ran it sixteen times. "I've never gotten tired during a fight," he said. "The one thing I always knew going in was that I had prepared better and harder than my opponent, that I was in better shape. I wasn't going to get tired, and when a fight runs to twenty-five minutes, that's really something." I was reminded of the adage I'd gleaned from watching muay Thai in Thailand: Whoever's in better shape wins.

Pat watched me running and dying, and somehow that was where I earned his interest, a little bit, because I left everything I had on the Hill. It wasn't very much, but it was everything I had, and I noticed from then on that Pat somewhat accepted me into his family.

After about a month and a half, I fought an informal boxing match down at the local bar's Friday Night Fights. One could drop in around eight p.m. and sign up to fight. They asked me if I'd fight a 220-pound guy, and I looked at the guy and said yeah, because he looked big and soft and had been drinking. Three one-minute rounds, fun for all, headgear and gloves. Tim and Tony were there and cornered me enthusiastically, but the guy was a spaz and came out swinging and I stood there and flailed away with him; he caught me and I caught him, but my punches were straighter. Tim between rounds said, "Now you see why a spaz is hard to fight," and it's true; very unconventional fighters can pose problems to amateurs like me—you get sucked into their spazzy world. "Don't trade, jab," said Tim (meaning don't stand there and trade punch for punch with him, but work the jab instead). I started doing that the second round, and the guy quickly ran out of steam and waved me off.

Later that night, as my nose swelled again, I realized I still had no head movement. I'm not seeing the punches coming, and I'm leaving my head still. I sat next to a cute twenty-year-old student chiropractor who wasn't listening and said, "I don't think I have the violence in me for this."

But in a sense, I was kidding myself. I knew that I would probably fall into the trap of humanity: naked rage fueled by self-preservation and ego, the opposite of empathy, closing oneself off to the pain of another.

The following Wednesday night I stayed away from the heavyweights and sparred the little guys and did much, much better. Because I'm tall, I would always stand with the heavyweights, but they all outweighed me by thirty or forty pounds. So instead I sparred with lighter guys and towered over them, but, hey, that made my life easy. I could survive; my nose didn't bleed. I started keeping people on the end of my jab, where Pat wanted me to, too far away to hit me back.

Afterward, after eight three-minute rounds, we jumped rope, and I felt a little bit like I belonged, like I could stay there and train forever.

Two guys from Team Miletich were fighting in the next UFC in Las Vegas, Robbie Lawler and Tim Sylvia. Tim was making his big comeback after being stripped of the title for testing positive for steroids, and Robbie was a heavy favorite.

I flew into an overcast Vegas on a Thursday afternoon and went to the hotel and found the guys. We took the long walk down to the Events Center. People would first stop Tim, and then they'd grab Matt and Robbie as they recognized them. All of Team MFS navigated their minor celebrity with natural, unforced grace, shaking hands and taking pictures and enjoying themselves without getting too slowed down or frustrated.

The weigh-in was crowded, several hundred people around, and the ring girls and the announcer, Michael Buffer, and some rowdy fans. Over the P.A. I heard that Tim was not going to fight. He had trace elements of banned substances in his system and his most recent test hadn't come back yet, so the Nevada Gaming Commission wouldn't let him step on the scale. No scale means no fight. My mouth hung open. I had planned on shadowing Tim for the night, but now that was out. Luckily, I still had Robbie Lawler, a welterweight (170 pounds) contender and one of Pat's prodigies, twenty-two years old, explosive, heavy-handed, and a heavy favorite (5–2) over Nick Diaz. Robbie was a UFC fan favorite, because he threw bombs—heavy, knockout punches—which makes fights exciting. Robbie looked good at the weigh-in, muscular and heavier than his taller and slimmer opponent.

Tim was disappointed about not being able to fight but not crushed. I asked him if he was coming out for a few beers and he shook his head, "I'm in great shape. Why would I come drinking now?" He'd be able to fight again in two months. In a way, it was as though he hadn't quite accepted the fact that he wasn't fighting, or his body hadn't. His body and spirit had been bent toward that fight for so long that it would take them some time to disengage, even if his mind acceped it. Tim is intelligent and remarkably sensitive—not that he cries at sad movies, but he is aware of his surroundings and the people around him and how they are feeling. During training he can be a bully and will punish you if you stand up to him, but outside of the gym he's friendly and open.

As for his steroid use, he must have gotten some bad advice. In his statement to the press, he said he wanted to look better on TV, and I believe him; it's the kind of thing that would secretly bother him. The night after the weigh-in, the night of the fight, his test results came back negative, but it was too late.

Afterward I found Pat and the boys and we jumped in an SUV limo to go to break Robbie's weigh-in fast at Olive Garden, creeping through Vegas rush hour. Any UFC fight fan would have given his arm to ride in that limo, with Pat Miletich, Jeremy Horn, Matt Hughes, Tony Fryklund, and Robbie Lawler. It was fun being with those guys and seeing them recognized for the stars they are, by fans in the know. In Vegas, around fight night, they were mobbed for autographs and photos just about everywhere, and they dealt with it well, smiling and shaking hands and taking photos. Their patience seemed endless, and they had fun with it. A drunk kid accosted Pat and said, "I'm coming to live and train in Iowa with you guys. I've got twenty grand and six months." Pat laughed and said to him, "Make sure you buy a round-trip ticket 'cause you won't make it through two training sessions," and burst out laughing, *with* the kid as much as at him.

Dinner was lively, everyone talking and laughing; ribald and blasé humor abounded. The guys were laid back and friendly and willing to be entertained; they asked me about firefighting, and everyone weighed in on movies and girls, occasionally breaking into extremely technical and detailed discussions of fights that had happened here, or in Japan, or in Korea. Except for the scar tissue, they could have been mistaken for slightly dangerous frat boys on a break, but there was an air of professionalism that would make you question that conclusion. You could see people trying to figure them out, slightly wary of their confidence and roughness. In the limo, someone farted, and there was much yelling and hallooing and covering of faces with shirts, gasping theatrically out of open windows at the gritty Vegas air. It was that kind of night.

Robbie was probably the quietest, and not just because he had a fight, but because that's the way he is; he's not a loud talker. He's solid and dark—he looks Filipino but is only half. He was relaxed and happy there among his friends and brothers. Team MFS is like a band of brothers with Pat as a sort of father/uncle/eldest brother who is expected to know everything—a role Pat occasionally resists, as he just wants to be a kid sometimes.

Matt Hughes, on my right, was well known and a six-time UFC welterweight champ, an Iowa farm boy who struck me as the most professional and relaxed of anyone there. He seemed unflappable and confident. Sure, he's lost fights, you could hear him say, but that stuff happens. He's still one of the toughest guys in the world.

Jeremy Horn, across the table and recommending the Tuscan sausage soup, was perhaps the most interesting of Pat's boys, because of his record (something like 112–6, an unreal number of fights) and his poise. He fights all the time, every month, anywhere against anybody. He'll fight at 205 pounds or 185, although 185 is a little more natural for him. Most guys who fight at 205 walk around at 230; Jeremy probably walks around at 210. His ground game is considered one of the best in the world; he's fought the best fighters and beaten some of them, and I've watched him spar and bang with Tim without any problem. What's so funny is that he is the most unassuming and normal-looking guy in the crowd. If you ran into him at a bar, you wouldn't look at him twice; he looks as if he could be selling Bibles or running for student council. Yet listening to people talk around the gym, most are more afraid of him than anyone else, and most people say he's the best guy they've ever rolled with.

I kept maintaining to anyone who would listen that this sport is being marketed wrong. They try to spectacle it up, make it like pro wrestling with smoke and fireworks, when really they should be emphasizing the technical aspects of it. The blood will sell itself; everyone knows how rough it is. What should be sold is the technical side. It's perceived as a pro wrestling type of thing, when in reality it is a very serious, technical sport. It can be hard to watch because the ground fighting can be slow and methodical, each man extremely careful, as any tiny slipup can mean the fight; it's similar to how cautious heavyweight boxers can get with their constant clinching, because any punch can be a KO.

The bloody part is incidental; you have to look at it as a part of a greater whole. Noses and lips bleed when they get hit; it's not a big deal. The guy on the bottom getting pounded and getting bloody isn't necessarily in a great amount of trouble. He can be bleeding, yet most of the blows are meant to distract him and keep him from thinking while the man on top sets up either more serious blows or submission holds. The tiny gloves mean knockouts and bad cuts happen all the time, and one slipup and a good jiu-jitsu player will have you in a submission and tapping before you even know what happened. Yes, it's a rough sport, especially now, when many people grow up so distant from fighting and blood. But it wouldn't have been considered rough a hundred or two hundred years ago, and before that, MMA would have seemed mild and overly refereed.

After you watch the fights for a while, you start to see how amazing some of these guys are, not just as athletes but in their composure and their technical thinking. Of course, Pat's right: It's not for everyone. But there can be no denying that it is a legitimate sport, a contest of wills, an arena for excellence on a par with any sport in the modern world. Fighters go into the arena stripped to their core, naked for the world to see and judge. They go in the face of a highly trained man whose goal is to break them down and destroy them.

After the Olive Garden, Robbie went to bed and everyone else went out; and we fell or were picked off by the Vegas evening, one by one, until we were all gone.

Fight day in Vegas was rainy and grim, and no one stirred before noon. Around four o'clock that afternoon we came together to walk Robbie down into the arena. He was quiet and relaxed; the rest of us were a little more keyed up. I overheard Matt saying that he finds it more stressful to be in the corner than to fight.

We headed through the cool, quiet, carpeted halls and into the dense casino. The crowd was thick with fight fans in black T-shirts and tattoos calling after Robbie, and we tried to keep moving. Robbie stopped sometimes and shook hands or signed, but we moved quickly, across the casino floor and into the dark depths of the Events Center.

We found our private locker room, and Robbie sat in the corner. I went to find some water and took a look out through the heavy black curtains. My press pass was a shield against the angry glares of the ushers and security guards. The Events Center was a steep stadium, not huge but with seats for twelve thousand, and it was maybe half full before the preliminary fights began. I found my name printed on a seat at the press table, just like a real journalist. I headed back to Robbie.

Barbara Ehrenreich's book *Blood Rites* is a fascinating attempt by an admitted layperson to understand some of the roots of violence and its "nobility." She posits a gem of an idea: *Homo sapiens,* for most of his evolutionary history, was prey. He's weaker, smaller, slower, and without natural weaponry like fangs or claws. His natural inclination was probably toward group survival, like the monkey's: throw rocks, keep watch, and run and hide up trees when predators approach.

As Ehrenreich writes, "No doubt much of 'human nature' was indeed laid down during the 2½ million years or so when *Homo* lived in small bands and depended on wild animals and plants for food. But it is my contention that our peculiar and ambivalent relationship to violence is rooted in a primordial experience that we have managed, as a species, to almost entirely repress. And this is the experience, not of hunting, but of being preyed on by animals that were initially far more skillful hunters than ourselves."

However, *Homo sapiens,* with his big brain and his tool building, has become the ultimate predator on the planet, by a thousand times. Ehrenreich argues that this is a social and learned change, as opposed to an evolved one. Man learned to hunt in packs, to build better and better tools. He has moved to the apex predator spot relatively recently, yet his "wiring," his natural inclination, is to act like prey.

Fear is part of our lives—fear of the dark, the unknown, of strangers—especially at a young age. Fear of being eaten is the rudimentary evolutionary concept that we all share. All of the old gods required sacrifice, forms of which exist today: *Thus the ritual of sacrifice reveals an almost universal attribute of the archaic deity to whom sacrifices are offered: He or she is a carnivore.*

What Ehrenreich argues so interestingly is that man has to undergo a change; he has a euphoric release from fear (it's hardwired in) as he realizes his place as predator. This euphoria is what leads to the sacralization of war. She talks at length about initiation rites and "manhood" as boys become hunters. It's all about realizing that you're the predator, not the prey, and the savage joy of survival. Why do little boys always play with guns and swords? Because they contain in themselves the schematics to overcome the prey status.

Joyce Carol Oates explains in *On Boxing* that "man's greatest passion" is not for peace, it's for war. Men, as the evolved protectors of the tribe, are wired to be more passionate about war than peace because the more warlike men were more successful in the darker ages of human prehistory.

Sporting events reflect this learned change from prey to predator. When a boxer wins a fight, he thrusts his hands into the air and the crowd goes wild. He has proved himself to be the predator, not the prey, and the crowd is vicariously identifying with him. How many sports fans, when talking about the team they support, identify with it to the point of saying "We"? As in, "We had a shot at the Super Bowl but had too many injuries."

I always feel like saying, "What 'we,' motherfucker? Are you on the team?" but the fan's emotion is an honest one. Everyone wants to be the predator and feels ecstatic emotion when the predator status is confirmed. It boils down to a refashioning of "We will not get eaten today." It's a survival mechanism that is out of place in the modern world, where survival is not threatened on a daily basis. So it finds a fit with sporting events, and it fits the best with fighting.

The backstage private locker room was small and white concrete, with several showers and little lockers and free soap and towels. Robbie was very calm, and Jeremy and Matt maintained an easy flow of conversation. We had time. A couple of Nevada Gaming Commission inspectors in red jackets joined us and sat watching our little TV and talking about free food and how to get more from the caterers. About forty minutes before the fight, an older black man with an event uniform vest came in and taped Robbie's hands with professional ease. He'd been taping boxers for a hundred years. The taper asked Robbie something, and Robbie said, "Don't worry about the grip, I'm not trying to grab," and everyone laughed. I asked the inspectors what they were looking for, and one of them told me a story from a year back, when a fighter was caught with several pounds of tape on his fists, essentially turning them into clubs. The taper signed Robbie's wraps, smiled, and went to the next dressing room.

The mood was light. Another photographer commented on it: "Man, you can tell a winner's locker room," he said. "Some of those other guys are acting like somebody died." The ref came through, and there was a brief discussion of the rules. We were getting closer, and Robbie shadowboxed, sometimes commenting to Pat, "If this one lands, it's a life-or-death situation," and "I think this is the right he might walk into." Matt and Pat pulled his gloves on, a tough struggle with the little gloves that protect the hands and allow fighters like Robbie to throw big punches.

Now we were almost there. Robbie hit the focus mitts with Pat, sparred a little with Jeremy, did some standing grappling with Matt called "pummeling," to warm up and loosen up. They were careful not to tire him, as soon, essentially, he'd be fighting for his life. Only two cornermen, Pat and Matt, could walk out with Robbie, so I left to find my seat.

The crowd presence hit like a wall, a massive entity in itself. The place was dark and crowded, a narrow canyon of teeming humanity. It was a warm monster that surrounded and buffeted us with its heat and noise and mood; it actually breathed a hot wind on us. My front-row press seat was amid a sea of journalists and laptops. I edged past and through to my seat, annoying the journalists, and pulled out my two-inch notepad and pen and tried to look professional.

The music was deafening, different death metal for each fighter. Nick Diaz came out first—a slender, dark-haired, goateed kid with an aristocratic Spanish face. He didn't look nervous. The music changed and Robbie was making his entrance, and with a roar the crowd let us know who the favorite was.

The fight took place in the Octagon, a wide arena fenced in with a high chain-link fence that at first seems campy but is actually important. When fights go to the ground in the ring, there is always a danger that the combatants will spill out. In Japan, where the Pride and Pancrase fights—also MMA—are held in rings like boxing rings, the referee has to stop the fight, bring the fighters back into the center, and try to restart them from the same position, which not only disrupts the flow but gives a winded fighter time to recover and can change the fight. Conversely, fighters in the UFC can use the cage as a weapon—something that certain UFC champions have excelled at.

Robbie and Nick bounce and eye each other across the wide space, the corners shout last-minute advice, and the ref gives his final instructions. Suddenly, the fight is on and the crowd is roaring with anticipation. They want to see Robbie knock this kid out with his trademark ferocity.

Robbie begins backing away, looking for an opening, letting Nick pursue him, and angling to land big—somehow he's a little hesitant. He's been so confident up to this point, but suddenly, maybe, there is some doubt in there. He had hurt a rib two weeks before, rolling with Matt, and since then he hasn't done anything but work on his cardio. He claimed it wasn't bothering him, but the first thing I think when watching him back away is that he is hurt.

The first round is pretty good, both guys swinging and hitting, and Nick surprising everyone with his boxing and stand-up fighting. Before this, he had been known as a submission specialist who would be better off if the fight went to the ground. He pursues Robbie with confidence and even starts talking shit, taunting. Robbie looks furious, and they both seem to hurt each other some. It's not decisive, but I would have given the first round to Robbie.

Just seconds into the next round, the unthinkable: Robbie swings and misses and Nick, with his slight reach advantage, throws a light, crisp hook that catches Robbie right behind the ear, and Robbie is out. He goes down like a poleaxed steer, his body stiffening in the air, out on his feet. The ref leaps in and Robbie tries to get up and stumbles back against the cage and goes drunkenly down again. The crowd erupts and Nick can scarcely believe it. He's KO'd Robbie Lawler, the guy who was going to kill him.

One of the big things that separates MMA from boxing is there is no standing eight count or ten count. In MMA, if you cannot "intelligently defend" yourself—if you are stunned or badly shaken, even for a few seconds—the referee will stop the fight.

Robbie begins to recover and realizes what has happened, and his face is agonized. He can't believe it, his emotion is running riot all over him. The fight is over. I can see him silently screaming at himself, at the world, tearing around the cage, which is filling with people.

I got up, annoying the real journalists again, and beat Robbie back-stage. He was desperately unhappy. He yelled "Fuck" a few times but was already subsiding when Matt, the six-time UFC champion, said to him, in a quiet, controlled voice, "Listen, we all lose. Pat's lost, Jeremy's lost, I've lost twice to the same guy, once in seventeen seconds," and Robbie seemed to hear him. Pat finished it with, "Now we move on. It's water under the bridge now." Robbie's eyes were dark and wounded, his distress all over him, but I could see him gathering strength from his teammates.

I went back out toward the ring and watched the rest of the fights. There were some good ones, especially Chris Lytle dominating Tiki Ghosn through the force of his will. The main event was a much hyped bout between Tito Ortiz and Chuck Liddell (light heavyweights at 205), and Chuck, the underdog, won by KO in the second round, which delighted the crowd. There was a tremendous amount of tension during the first round as they both felt each other out, but in the second round, you could see Chuck suddenly realize, "Hey, I can hit this guy," and he relaxed his shoulders a fraction and started letting his hands go and pretty soon he knocked Tito out.

There was a lot of postfight discussion and analysis from the journalists, but it sounded a little false and tinny to me. I felt slightly superior to them; at least I *tried* to do this stuff, as opposed to just watching. I waited to talk to Pat and Tony and Tim to venture my opinions. "Tito's always been a little scared to stand up with Chuck, but he did, and I give him credit for it," said Tony. He thought that the UFC protected its special fighters, like Tito, too much for his liking. Even though he lost, Tito made more than twice what Chuck made for that fight. "Tito's chin," he said with finality, "is suspect."

It was raining hard the next morning; one of the three days it rains all year in Vegas. Pat and I were flying out together, and Pat said to me in the cab over the squeak of the wipers, "Every time I come here it takes a year off my life. I hate going through all this and then having one of my boys get knocked out."

I asked what he was going to work on with Robbie, and he smiled.

"He's got to keep his hands up. He's learned he's not invincible; it happens to every fighter at some point in their career. They run into somebody they can't steamroll through, they take a shot that hurts them. Robbie got caught—it happens to everybody. He's got to keep his hands up."

Pretty simple.

* * *

Another editor from *Men's Journal* had been developing a piece for the 2004 summer Olympics in Athens, a sort of "workout" piece involving three different Olympic athletes: a swimmer, a decathlete, and a boxer. He wanted me to work out with one of them, and no, it wasn't the swimmer.

So I flew out of the Moline, Illinois, airport (one of the world's great airports; you just park and walk, like going to the mall) to San Francisco and drove across the filigree of bridges into Oakland. I was there to cover Andre Ward, one of the U.S. Boxing Team captains, a much hyped "speed merchant" who was blitzing his way through tournaments without getting a single point scored on him. He was going four rounds with other top amateurs and they weren't hitting him *once*.

A twenty-year-old amateur light-heavyweight (178 pounds), Ward hadn't lost a fight since 1997. A rattlesnake strikes at eight feet per second; a decent pro boxer throws a jab at eighty feet per second. I didn't bring a radar gun, but I can tell you that Andre was fast. While some of his speed was natural, some of it had to do with his trainer, and godfather, Virgil Hunter, who had been with him since he was nine years old. Andre had lived with Virgil in Oakland since his early teens.

I met Virgil on a beautiful Oakland morning at a coffee shop by a park. At first glance he seemed young, in his thirties, but eventually he told me he was fifty.

Virgil Hunter had been involved with boxing and training fighters since 1966, when he was taught the sweet science by his uncles in the kitchen. "I'd been training fighters for twenty-some years, but with Andre I decided to reassess the whole thing. I could develop him from the ground up, from the root to the fruit." Virgil incorporated Pilates and Acceleration and tailored Andre's workouts on a day-by-day basis. "It varies depending on what he needs," said Virgil in his quiet drawl, resplendent in a Team USA Boxing jumpsuit. "What did Andre look like yesterday? What does he need to work on? There will always be shadowboxing and mirror work, but sometimes he'll spar three rounds and go straight home, and other times he won't spar at all. It depends on him, really."

Virgil's watchful eye was Andre's greatest asset. Virgil was calm and quiet and observant, and never haranguing. I rarely saw him give instruction to Andre at all; it seemed as if Andre could sense him watching and knew what he wanted. In two days, he muttered into Andre's ear once, for a few seconds, or maybe twice; nonetheless, he was always watching, a reassuring presence. "Sometimes as a trainer you won't say anything for days, just watch, just so you can be sure you've seen something. You [the fighter] are lying in bed at night, thinking about what kind of fighter you want to be, and you begin to apply it, without discussion, in training. You show me what you can do and I see it, you teach me to teach you." The feel of professionalism is so different here than in Iowa, a more weary, workman feel. These guys are in it for the money and because they were born into it. But they still love fighting—don't get that wrong. Boxers may be a lot of things, but the good ones love to box.

Virgil, a probation counselor in Alameda County, was also a juvenile hall counselor, and he remarked how it was always harder to restrain the smaller, more wiry, and slippery kids than the big kids with muscles. Virgil was not interested in free weights and big muscles, he was interested in speed and power and core stability. Power, the grail of boxing, comes from speed, not muscles.

"In boxing, speed throws you—it makes you so vulnerable you lose your ability to fight. You need to stay lean to generate velocity, and I train Andre from the inside out. He's powerful in his movements. You get a big muscular guy in there, you make him work, and all those muscles suck up the oxygen in his blood. You fight to keep him from doing what he wants to do, and then you are whupping his ass." Virgil laughed softly.

"In the later rounds, you let him try and do what he wants to do, but now you know what he's trying and you're fresh and you can destroy him—because he's finally got you where he wants you, but now it's better for *you*."

Andre's training breathed this philosophy throughout. At the NovaCare rehab center in Castro Valley we did the Acceleration program, which was a lot of sprinting on a frighteningly steep treadmill. Amateur boxing goes for four two-minute rounds, so it's very quick and explosive; a two-minute round can go by in a heartbeat. Sprinting builds up that short-term endurance and, most important, quick recovery time, that oxygen-debt relief between rounds. Afterward we did some medicine ball throwing for core strength and explosiveness, and shoulder stability drills. We didn't even look at free weights, although Andre has done them in the past to build strength.

On alternate days there was Pilates in a clean, upscale gym on pretty wooden machines, again focusing on the core and shoulder strength and stability. Virgil discovered Pilates himself when he was rehabbing an injury, did some research, and found out that its creator had been a boxer. I was slightly skeptical, but Andre had been at it for eight weeks, and he said it had made a big difference in his strength and flexibility.

After lunch and siesta (Andre swears by the afternoon nap, and I am a fervid supporter myself) we met again at King's Boxing Gym, on Thirty-fifth Avenue in downtown Oakland. This was a real boxing gym, clean and well worn and crowded with fighters and bags, the walls covered with fight posters and pictures of boxers, the feel of old sweat and blood. It's quite a contrast to the Pilates and Acceleration places. Old school. Real fighters eyed me in a way that is not hostile or even curious but just appraising.

No one in the world is a better judge of a man than an experienced old boxing trainer; he can judge deep into a fighter's flesh just by watching him move, watching him do a few things. Old fight trainers are like horse-racing trainers in their appraisal of flesh, teeth, and bone, with the added advantage of having *been* the horse, knowing the horse from the inside out.

I felt vulnerable in front of those watchful eyes. My weaknesses were going to be exposed for all to see. Andre was stopped for handshakes and smiles and conversation. Virgil was going to take him out of here to Texas soon, away from all these distractions.

I watched Andre shadowbox and there was an inkling of his capabilities; every now and again, in his relaxed shuffle, there was a jab that was faster than thought and crisper than a brand-new hundred-dollar bill. He was light and graceful, and his hands gently knifed the air, carving through hooks and uppercuts, effortless. His face was smooth and open and guileless, and he looked young; but when he spoke, he seemed mature, unflappable.

I asked him if he'd ever been hurt in the ring.

"Naaw, not really," he said. "It's been a couple of years since anybody's landed a clean shot on me. My older brother and I used to get into wars during sparring, but he's taking a few years off boxing right now. Nobody's ever hit me as hard as he did."

Andre sparred a young welterweight before me, a kid who made it to the nationals in 2000 and now fights pro, and Andre handled him with an ease that could be called contemptuous if there was any contempt in him, which there wasn't. To me, what shone were his feet and his explosive quickness, the springiness in his bouncing; his body was under the total control of his mind. If he wanted to bounce one way and then flash back the other, bobbing and weaving and then—bing-bing-bing—flashing through three long punches with his glowing white gloves, he did it, and so fast it was very hard to understand what had happened.

Finally, it was my turn and I climbed through the ropes clumsily, no longer conscious of the other eyes in the gym. We began sparring and I was hesitant and awkward, and Virgil yelled, "Hold on a second. Sam, get over here." He was laughing a little. I ran over to the corner.

"Sam, would you hit him? He can protect himself. Now, *hit him!*" Virgil's voice was high and amused. I nodded and turned around. For the next two rounds, I went after Andre and tried to tear his head off.

It was instantly apparent how good he was, and how great the difference between us in skill and speed was. Andre zipped me twice and then basically stopped throwing punches; instead, he worked on his defense and his movement, and I went after him and missed by miles. I threw hooks that started off aimed at his head and ended up faltering in the air feet from where he was. I got him in the corner and threw a barrage, a dozen punches, and he blocked and bobbed and shifted and not one punch got through, and then he dipped and spun away. He didn't punch me because if he had, I wouldn't have been able to do anything. He jabbed me once or twice and I was hit before I saw him move. If he wanted to knock me out, he could have done it in seconds.

I heard the guys in the gym yelling, "Let your hands go" (meaning start throwing more punches) at me and "Don't let him hit you" to Andre. He blocked punches before I even threw them, checking me as I started to move, waiting patiently for my hands to get going.

In all, I threw, I don't know, maybe sixty punches and I caught him once, my pathetic little triumph, a glancing hook as he danced away. He threw three light jabs before he stopped punching entirely, and they all were on the money. My mouth guard had a little blood in it, nothing new there. He thanked me for the workout, and I thanked him for not murdering me.

Both Andre and Virgil were really *nice* guys. You got the sense almost immediately that there's no bullshit, no overt ego, just confidence and competence and a game plan for Andre's career. They were looking far past the Olympics. Andre knew his style would work well in the pros, with more and longer rounds and less focus on points. He knew how dirty boxing could be; he'd had friends go pro with the wrong trainers, get thrown in with pro fighters with fifty fights and get beaten badly. Andre wanted to be out of boxing and rich by thirty—with his brain intact. He had a wife and two children, so I asked him if his wife worries about him, and he smiled. "She used to, but then she started watching me fight and she sees I don't get hit much and now she doesn't worry."

After sparring, Andre and I stood around the ring, covered in sweat but relaxed in the easy camaraderie of men who had just fought and now could be friendly again. We talked about the routine, and the dangers of boredom with training, and I said something silly and clichéd like "You gotta stay hungry."

Andre laughed. "Hungry? You gotta be *starving, man.*"

I had an extra day, so I ate lunch with Virgil, and we walked around one of his old haunts in Oakland. He took a little interest in me as a fighter when I told him about what I was doing.

"That's just brawling, that stuff," he said of the UFC, and he was right, to a point. The stand-up fighting is often brawling. He told me that if I spent a year working out in a boxing gym, I could be a bad-ass and make money as a sparring partner, which was very flattering, if unappealing. Life as a punching bag.

Virgil was a "gunslinger," something he doesn't talk about much. He fought in unsanctioned bouts coming up because the money was often better. I started pestering him for advice. I asked him which school he belonged to, look at your man's eyes or his body. Virgil is of the latter. "He ain't going to hit you with his eyes," he said with a chuckle. "In the ring, I can make you look at what I want you to look at."

He was very unhappy that I didn't know anything about my opponent; that was just foolish. How can you prepare for something you don't know? He told me to make a quick assessment of the opponent and to watch the enemy trainer. Is he calm? Is he talking to his fighter all the time, making him nervous? Does the trainer have no confidence in his man?

"Truth in observation, that'll win a fight," he said.

Back in Iowa, summer was on its way, and I had about a month of hard training left without interruptions. I started doing "the circuit," an exercise routine Pat lifted from a women's magazine, in which you do two exercises for each body part and then run hard for eight minutes (increasing the speed every two minutes), and you do this whole thing three times, before practice.

I started to feel strong. I had friends. I played chess with Sam Hoger, the "Alaskan Assassin," a twenty-two-year-old pro heavyweight, from Alaska by way of Panama and Germany. Sam was getting his MBA and was dead set on Harvard Law; luckily, I beat him at chess, because he could have surely kicked my ass. He wore flashy suits and was an environmental lobbyist as well as a student. He was a big, dusky, well-coiffed fellow, a little larger than life, jolly and loud and intelligent and calling out, "Hey, girl," to nearly every girl we walked past in a friendly, nonaggressive way, half self-mocking and half curious. That was something Tony did, as well: "Hey, baby . . . Then, sotto voce: "Your name is Baby, isn't it?"

There was a little bit of *Fight Club* when hanging out with these guys. You'd walk into a restaurant with four or five muscular bald guys with black eyes and scarred eyebrows, and sometimes people got a little nervous. These guys had a lot of fun, and they did what they wanted. Sam was fond of quoting the film to me: "When you start fighting, the volume on everything else in your life just gets turned down."

Fighters have a lot of downtime. They train hard, but they still have to rest quite a bit to recover, and you can't really train more than six or seven hours a day. Drinking will kill you, especially when you are trying to pyramid up to fighting shape, so either you go to bars and drink OJ and water, which Tony and Tim did, or you stay home.

I remember in Thailand, when I had been gearing up for my fight, I took a weekend in Bangkok, just to get out of the camp after a few months, and I had three beers one night. Those three beers set me back about three weeks in my training (easily measured by the pad rounds). That's the fine knife's edge of fitness you walk; that's what they mean by "fighting shape." So for their downtime, fighters don't drink and are often forced into cleaner pursuits like watching movies and surfing the Internet.

It is slightly comical, all these fighters combing the Internet for references to themselves, and often feuds will start. Someone will say something in an online interview and someone else will respond, and suddenly everyone is enraged and calling one another out. It has a tinge of junior high school, parading gossip. No one is more sensitive to insult than "tough guys."

One of the *Fight Club* guys I hung out with was Brandon Adamson, who fights at 155 (and has a thirty-inch vertical) and was making the transition from amateur to pro. He was in Jens Pulver's weight class and he usually had black eyes from Jens pounding on him, but he was game as hell.

Brandon was twenty-three and had a wife and two children and was getting his bachelor's, as well as working as a security guard at a local hospital. He wanted to teach ADD kids, because he himself had serious problems with ADD in high school and "could have really used the help." That's one thing about Iowa: There are a lot of guys younger than me with one or two kids. Brandon moved here from California and then Minnesota, and his desire to fight was just growing stronger, his interest deeper. He was 1–1 as a pro, 6–4 as an amateur, and day care cost him four hundred dollars a week, but somehow he held it all together.

I asked him why he fights. I ask a lot of people that—and it's where you start to verge into the territory of what fighters don't talk about. We're all here for very different reasons and yet there is something we all have in common, and I'm not sure what that is. For Brandon, it's not about money. "It's about clout," he says, and he keeps hold of that word; there is some deeper significance that I am missing. He goes on a bit, about the rush, and adrenaline junkies, and a love of training, but I can tell he feels he has said it all when he says "clout." He means respect. F. X. Toole wrote in *Rope Burns,* which became *Million Dollar Baby,* that fight fans think it is about being tough, but "the fight game is about getting respect." For Brandon, respect has not been given—he's had to take it.

Sam and I went to the fights in Wisconsin, and I saw Brandon fight an epic battle, with many reversals, but he finally prevailed with a guillotine near the end of the third round. He walked away at the end of the night with a face that looked as if it'd been hit with a baseball bat and a trophy that was larger than himself. His face and eyes were swollen and cut like a side of meat, blood and tissue exposed everywhere.

Watching the crowd react and surge to its feet, I can see that this isn't just a fight; it's a celebration of courage. The crowd lives vicariously through the fighters and loves even the losers as "honorable warriors." The crowd has some kind of cathartic experience through the ordeal of the fighters.

This particular crowd is so knowledgeable, they cheer before I can even see what's happening, as when someone goes for an arm-bar (even if they don't get it), and there is respectful applause when a beleaguered fighter who was mounted finally regains his guard.

* * *

I still had car-wreck-itis, but by staying away from the heavyweights, I did much better on Mondays and Wednesdays. Then one Wednesday night came the event I had been dreading.

I was sparring some kid (never seen before or since) who was just boxing. He was strong and nervous but not great, and I had him bleeding into his mouth guard when he landed a hard body shot on my floating ribs and knocked the wind out of me. We paused, and I caught my breath, and then we kept going and I kept jabbing him, but a part of me went *Oh shit.*

I have a recurring injury to my costal cartilage, the stuff in between my ribs on both sides of my chest. I am prone to separating and straining the stuff. It first happened badly when I was working construction at the South Pole. Four guys and I were flipping over an end wall to a large Quonset hut, and it came down on me and folded me in half. I tried to hide it for about a week. I was hanging Sheetrock, but eventually I couldn't even lift my arms. The doc there wanted to evac me, but I begged and stayed on light duty for six weeks. Then, about a year later, I was in L.A. boxing for a couple of days at the La Brea Boxing Academy, and my first day sparring I got a little excited and was chasing around a guy who was much better than I was, and he settled me down with a good body shot. Again I tried to pretend it was just bruised, but it wasn't, and I nearly missed the summer firefighting season with the Gila Hotshots.

Basically, when you injure your ribs, you're screwed, you can't do anything for about four to six weeks, sometimes longer. Almost any motion you do involves flexing of the ribcage, and it hurts just to breathe. I had two weeks left till the fight. It was a situation very similar to what had happened to Robbie. I had suspected, at the back of my mind, that this might happen at some point and was just hoping for the best, hoping to get through with a little luck and not tweaking it. But now I was hurt.

I took a day off to mope. What should I do? Robbie had gone through with his fight, but he was a pro. I didn't have to fight. So I debated with myself over a weekend. I wrote a long letter to my editor at *Men's Journal* explaining the situation but never sent it.

Pat brought me some Celebrex, a prescription anti-inflammatory, the next night, and I was in a kind of fantasyland, hoping against hope that I would be okay. We went out, driving around Bettendorf. Pat wanted a few beers, and I kept him company. We stopped by some bars, Pat dealing with his celebrity and shaking hands. He told me a story of a couple of years back, when he had nearly gotten into a fight with some guys in a parking lot, and one of them said to him, "Do you know who I am? I'm Pat Miletich!" and Pat gave the guy a look, pulled out his driver's license, and showed the guy his ID. Everyone was so disgusted with the lie and being found out that the situation was totally defused—no one wanted to fight—and everyone just went home.

Pat's fondest wish was to climb Everest. He had read George Mallory's book when he was a kid, the first book he ever finished. We decided to plan on it in four or five years, when we're both rich. Pat is known as the nicest guy in the sport, and it's true. He is charismatic and friendly and just a pleasure to be with. He makes everybody feel good, and yet he has a wicked sense of humor. He has a few false teeth he likes to pull out without telling anyone, and then he gives you a big, gap-toothed, hayseed, "I'm a country idiot" grin. He pretends he wants to name one of his kids Slobodan. He tells stories of street fights and shenanigans from his younger, wilder days that would turn your hair white. His charisma is unmistakable, as is the strength of his character. I just liked him instinctively.

Later that night, I had a eureka moment. When Pat asked me why I was doing this, without thinking I answered, "Because I'm not very good at it." That old answer again, but essentially the truth. Pat laughed a little and said, "Well, you've gotten a lot better." I wasn't convinced, though.

The next day I ran the Hill eight times, to my astonishment. A fat guy on a golf cart asked me why I was doing that. I've got a fight, I told him. Are you with those Ultimate Fighters? he asked. Kind of, I said, that's the type of fighting I'm doing.

I thought so, he said, I could tell by the tattoos, and your facial expression when you were sprinting.

That grimace of agony must look tough from a distance. The next morning, a Saturday, I was significantly worse. It hurt to open the window, to drive, any twisting motion. I wasn't even going to shadowbox for a week, just run. I was depressed, and I coughed lightly and a twinge shot through my whole body. I had just a few days left to decide if I was going to fight, and those days became a series of separate incidents, erratic moments.

I was hanging out at Tim Sylvia and Tony Fryklund's place, watching TV and talking to Tim about *Chute Boxe,* in Brazil. "I wouldn't get in there with those guys," I said, and Tim snorted and said, "Why not? You're a tough kid." He didn't really mean anything by it, just that if I could hang with any of the Miletich guys, I could hang with anybody. That is, he wasn't trying to compliment me, he was saying, Don't be a pussy, you can do it. And because he wasn't trying to compliment me, it was a huge compliment.

I talked to Pat about not fighting, and he laughingly asked me, "Are you faking injury to get out of a fight?" and I wasn't, but there was a door, a way out. Always a door. Always a way out, with some honor intact. I wished it was just in my head, but it wasn't. It was outside of my control. Was it worth fighting hurt?

Tony and I met Brandon at Barnes and Noble, and Brandon was full of enthusiasm for my fight, despite the injury. He was all fired up to be my cornerman; he said that he'd get me crazy before the fight. "You gotta fight, man. It's the warrior way."

I would still go to the gym. It was murder to have to sit there at night and not be able to work out, not be able to get in there and hit and be hit. Everyone agrees that coming to practice and not being able to work out, which is what you are supposed to do if you're injured so at least you can learn through osmosis, is the worst part of getting hurt.

Tony was moving into the final stages of his fight psychosis. He had a big fight coming up on the same night as mine, in Hawaii, possibly the biggest fight of his career, against Matt Lindland, the number one 185-pound guy in the world. Tony talked to his sparring partners as if they were Lindland; he gave the imaginary Lindland the finger after knocking him out, walking away sneering, leaving his fantasy enemy crumpled in the dust. He'd dyed the tiny stubble he had left on his head blond. He looked ripped, his stamina was up, and he was kicking ass. He was talking to himself all the time.

There is something that reeks slightly of madness in this approach to violence, the premeditation of a scheduled fight. You watch the days and hours shrink toward a guarantee of violence, and it does something to you. Your contract with society becomes slightly more tenuous.

It tortured me, watching everyone else train and knowing I couldn't. I could feel myself slipping out of tip-top shape (which I was never really in), wondering if I was too old and slow and weak.

Pat tried to take me in hand those last days, working fundamentals such as footwork, but we were both frustrated by my injury. It's a fact of life, and these guys fought hurt all the time. When you train this hard, there will always be something.

Tony and I went to the sauna, trying to cut a little water weight. I weighed in at 194 (having just downed a lot of water) and Tony kept referring to me as being "a little portly." We put Vicks VapoRub on our chests and poured water laced with eucalyptus oil on the hot rocks.

Just eight days until the fight, and I woke up at three forty-five and couldn't fall back asleep. My mind was twisted up like a pretzel. All I could think about was dashing elbows in my opponent's face, scoring hits, putting together combinations, knockouts.

Another day, Brandon came down to hit mitts with me. In a kind of boxing workout, Brandon held focus mitts and I chased him around punching them, a strict hands-only workout but about all my ribs would allow.

With four days left I decided to fight, despite the rib. I was depressed and yelling at inaminate objects in my apartment again. But I fell back on those immortal words at the base of all good decision making: *Fuck it.*

I ate just one real meal a day. I had been running and my cardio was pretty good (I actually ran the Hill ten times), but I hadn't been able to roll with anyone for weeks. I was going to have to stay off the ground above all things. I sat on the edge of my bed and thought for a long time while I watched the cars across the river shimmering like droplets in an IV tube.

I couldn't have walked away anymore—I would never have felt right about it, partly because I'd worked too hard. I was going to learn what it's like to fight hurt. That's something everyone should know.

All I had left was to make weight.

On my last workout day, I went in and hit mitts with Pat, something invaluable, as his close personal attention was extremely helpful. Pat's style was the short, strong man's game—slip and hard shots on the inside. He had about fifteen fighters he was training and a gym he was starting up, so he was busy as hell. (And he was going to Hawaii to corner for Tony. Matt Lindland had beat Pat when Pat tried to move up in weight; there was history there.)

I even "sparred" that night, worked on my offense with Rory Markham while he worked on his defense. He didn't throw anything at me; I chased him around for three rounds. I felt pretty good, able to find angles, which is what Pat had me working on.

I had thrown some kicks the day before, and when I woke, my rib was twitching but felt okay, and I'd done nearly everything I could do. I'd run the Hill, trained hard, I had taken my licks—*So I'm going to go out there and do my best*, I thought. *If he's good, or he takes me down, I lose. If he's just decent, I have a chance.*

I weighed myself that morning and I came in at 186, which was wonderful, and I could relax. My legs were still a little sore, and I just wanted them to be fresh, so coming in at 186 with two days left was a godsend.

I did some hand fighting that night and I felt good, not great. My sprawl wasn't instantaneous like it should have been, because of my ribs, but it was as good as possible.

Tony and I went to the sauna and cranked it up to ten and made our medicinal steam. It descended on my shoulders, scorching my ears, burning my nostrils if I breathed through my nose.

That Thursday, at five a.m., the day before the fight, I woke up and couldn't fall back asleep, so I went over to the gym as it opened and checked my weight. I was starving. I carefully pulled off my clothes and weighed in at 188. *Fuck.*

The weigh-in was going to be the same night as the fight, so I would need to be walking around at close to the right weight. Professional fighters have the weigh-in the day before, so they can dehydrate and "cut" the six or seven pounds of water that all athletes carry, weigh in, and still have twenty-four hours or more to put the fluids back in. I didn't have that option, I was weighing in just a few hours before the fight.

I got my "sauna suit," a cheap, disposable track suit made of trash bag–type material, and put my sweatshirt on over it and went back to the gym. I rode the bike for about ten minutes, sweating heavily, and then I went into the fight room and blasted my music and shadowboxed for three rounds, feeling a little bit like Rocky. Then I skipped rope for three rounds. I didn't really want to be working like that the day before a fight, but I had to know if I could make weight.

I showered and went and weighed in at 184 and laughed with relief. I had a dream in which my opponent kicked me in the nuts and broke my cup. I dreamt of tearing my ribs to shreds and still trying to fight, with my left arm pasted low to my body, shielding them.

* * *

The next day, I drove the five hours down to Cincinnati with Ben Lowy, a freelance photographer *Men's Journal* had hired, and watched him eat Subway sandwiches. I was never a high school wrestler, and I'd never had to "make weight" before, so I wasn't that experienced with my own body. I didn't know for sure how much I would have to sweat off before I weighed in. That night, at the hotel, I shadowboxed for another three rounds in the sauna suit and felt pretty crisp, although my legs were hot again.

Basically, I made a trade-off. I gave away being totally rested and fresh for what I hoped would be a decisive advantage in reach. I'm six foot three, so anybody I fight at 185 will almost certainly be shorter than me. I was going to jab, stay outside, and throw punches in bunches. I had no ground game, so I was counting on my stand-up to carry me.

I planned on weighing in at five p.m. and then eating (PowerBars and stuff like that) and rehydrating until the fights started, at around eight. At that point I felt like maybe it was a mistake to fight at 185, but I had told Monte Cox, the promoter, that that was what I wanted to fight at, so I was going to show up weighing 185. I wasn't going to "cheat" and come in over and just say, "Whoops, sorry, you still gotta fight me."

The day of the fight, Friday, I sat around the hotel all day, after a light breakfast of cereal and some fruit, and I didn't drink any water at all. I watched TV, husbanding my resources. Around three-thirty, I got in the sauna suit and went down and rode the hotel exercise bike for ten minutes, then sat in my bathroom with the hot shower on for fifteen minutes, and then showered and went to weigh in. If I was over, I'd be pretty close, and I could make it by skipping rope for fifteen minutes at the weigh-in, I figured. I still hadn't had anything to drink all that day. I felt a little funny but more or less rested.

Ben and I drove through Springdale and found Tori's Station and went to weigh in. Come back at six, they told me. It was a big pink venue that sometimes had concerts and sometimes had weddings, seats for maybe two hundred people. Nothing fancy, but there was a big white mesh cage, which was exciting just to see.

We came back at six, and Monte told me that the weigh-in doesn't matter. "If you're anywhere from 185 to 190, you should be okay," he said. *Thanks a lot for telling me now, Monte,* I thought, and weighed in with clothes on at 185 pounds. So I was probably down around 183.

My corners, Brandon and Ryan, were driving down that day from Iowa and were still on the road; they got there as we were helping Josh, also from our gym, get ready to fight. Josh, a muscular, broad guy who was maybe five foot nine, was blond and blue-eyed and originally from Zimbabwe. He was fighting a black guy. "Probably Monte's idea of a joke," Josh said lightly, "to have the white African fight the African American." Josh was also fighting at 185, and I had rolled with him quite a bit. He was really strong on the ground. He was strong, period, but his stand-up wasn't great. Josh had been very, very nervous, although he had gotten better since a few days ago. Now that his fight was here (his first), he was remarkably calm.

Josh was taken down in the first round, but he maintained his poise and never took much punishment. In the second round, he mounted and was raining down punches, and they stopped the fight. He came out with a big smile and said, "That's a different kind of rush." It felt inevitable, Miletich guys are winners.

Brandon taped me up, and I Vaselined my eyebrows, nose, and inside my nose, all to help avoid cuts. Mouth guard, cup, fight shorts, wrapped hands, and the fingerless MMA gloves. I was ready to go.

I started warming up and felt good, loose and crisp, my punches felt sharp, and then I threw the left hook and it barely twinged my rib at all. I was going to be fine. My legs still were a little hot, and I knew they weren't fresh like they should be, but that would be okay. I was going to tower over this guy anyway. Josh had fought at the same weight, and the guy he fought was about five-six.

I shadowboxed hard, hit pads a tiny bit, and then, as we were close, just paced, shaking my arms slightly. I felt good. I was mentally ready to beat the shit out of someone. Brandon did an excellent job as a corner; he realized that my mental state was strong and left me alone.

Then we were nearly there. I saw my opponent backstage, and I thought, *Man, he looks big for 185.* I wasn't going to have any real reach on him—he was probably six-one or six-two. Oh, well. Nothing to be done now but go out there and see what happens.

I paced around, just kept moving, and again took stock. I wasn't 100 percent fresh, as I had been dehydrated all day, but I was good. I'd been drinking water since six and was finally pissing again. The "Why am I doing this?" thoughts had come and gone. This is what we do.

* * *

Over the P.A. system they announce the next fight: "Weighing in at two hundred and five pounds . . ." and I don't hear the rest. Wait a minute, this can't be my fight—someone must have given me the wrong fight order. But then I hear the end of the announcement, ". . . his opponent from Amherst, Massachusetts, Sam Sheridan, one hundred and eighty-five pounds." I could scarcely believe my ears. Two hundred and five! *Are you shitting me?*

I first think of all those lovely meals I'd skipped the last two weeks, all those nights going to bed on a protein shake with my stomach rumbling. *Man, I could have eaten like a king these last two weeks and been fine.* I am giving up twenty pounds.

My mind flashes back to Thailand, and I think, *They've done it to me again. The promoters have fucked me again.* I can see Brandon's angry face, and he is arguing with the promoter, but I'll fight anybody right now.

Then I am up in the cage and aware of my opponent. He is a little bit shorter than me and not bulging with muscles, which is something. He isn't overly nervous, though; he's calm and ready to go, watching me back without animosity.

The ref, Rich Franklin, a fighter I recognize from the UFC, checks me out, asks me if I have a cup on, and then it's time to go. I come out and offer my opponent an outstretched glove and he blinks, and we touch gloves (to show respect) and it's on.

The first exchange is clear; we trade hard jabs and I think I hit him a little harder than he hits me. And then it's into the swirling maelstrom.

I pursue him around and take plenty of hard shots to the head for my troubles, but they don't hurt at all. Here's the secret: It's fun. You don't feel any pain, adrenaline takes care of that—you're just getting into it. I am having a blast, but I am also eating punches.

I hit him, he catches me. We go into a clinch a couple of times and I land a few knees and so does he, but I barely feel his knees. When my knees go into his soft stomach, I think, *Go down, go down!*—like the guy I fought in Thailand had gone down.

This guy is tough, though. I rock him with a hook and blast a kick into his side and he actually goes down, and I step forward to try to finish but he's back up, and I realize two things: He's tougher than I want him to be, and I am running out of gas already, in the first round. In just three minutes.

As the round ends, I know I am bleeding from the nose. I walk over to the corner and Brandon is talking to me, but it doesn't really matter; I am breathing too hard, I am already "gassed." He offers me some water, but I can't take it. I bend down to listen to him and he tells me to punch my way in, and I'm not crisp enough, my legs are gone and I'm already in survival mode—and the only way I know to survive is to attack.

The round starts back up, and I go after him again. He catches me with a few good shots, and I am staggered this time. I go backward and manage to get him in a clinch, but I lose my mouth guard. He's rocking me, though I never feel like I'm in danger of getting knocked out.

I am trying still to get through to him. I can hear my own grunts as I throw knees in the clinch, and they sound as if they are coming from someone else.

Then the ref stops the fight to look at me, and the EMT comes out, and I can hear them conversing right in front of me like I'm not there. I feel nothing. If they let the fight go, I'll keep fighting. If they stop it, I'll stop. I know I'm bleeding a lot, there is blood on my chest.

"His pupils are different sizes," says the EMT, and that makes the decision for the ref. He waves the fight over. I can hear them announcing my name and that I am a journalist as I leave the cage, and it's embarrassing: He's not really a fighter, but look, he tried.

I was dully furious about the weight difference, though not about the fight. The fight was fun. The other guy deserved to win. I had fought stupidly and not dodged or slipped a single punch as I had been training to. Instead, I'd come straight at him, whether from anger or frustration I don't know. I think I have a fatal flaw; when I get hit, I just want to hit back, without rhyme or reason.

I walked into the bathroom and looked at myself, and it made me laugh; I was covered in blood, like something out of a horror movie. As I was taking stuff off, the local paramedic came and checked me out, and he pronounced me okay, and told me not to worry about the pupils until tomorrow morning. I wouldn't need stitches.

One of the promoters came by and said to me, "That was a great fight. Anytime you want to fight in one of my promotions, as an amateur or professional, you let me know," and I looked at Brandon with confusion: Did he just offer me a pro fight?

It turned out I was something of a crowd favorite, basically for bleeding all over the place and standing in there and taking my licks.

People kept telling me it was the fight of the night, things like that. As my eye started to swell shut, I thought, yeah, well, great. I still lost.

Monte tried to explain the weigh-in mistake as a miscommunication and hoped to make me feel better by telling me what a good fight it was, but I just stared at him. I believed him that it was an honest mistake (Monte had a bunch of other shows going on in different cities, he was working with other promoters, and he was careless), but it still annoyed me to no end. He said, "It'll be a great story for the magazine," and I thought, *Don't do me any more favors, Monte.* The bottom line is that promoters don't care about fighters; they just want asses in seats. As a fighter, you trust the promoters, and it makes you vulnerable. I think Monte just had no idea of my real abilities, and I know he didn't know anything about my opponent. Monte figured I was working out with Pat, so I must be a badass.

The vendor gave me a free hat and T-shirt, and various people shook my hand as I drank my beer. I watched the rest of the fights and realized what a terrible venue this was; the lighting was horrible, and the white cage made it extremely hard to tell what was happening inside. Only the fighters and the ref could really tell what was happening in there, which I guess is the way it is anyway.

I chatted with my opponent, Jason Keneman, while we watched the fights and drank a few beers. He was a nice guy. He'd done some muay Thai, and this had been his first MMA fight. He hadn't wanted to go to the ground at all, and neither had I because of my rib. The rib . . . after all that mental anguish, it had barely bothered me during the fight, even though he'd landed a long body shot right on it. I found out Jason had been training for four years; he had a record of 9–1 in muay Thai. I thought he had seemed pretty calm out there. My one muay Thai fight was nearly four years ago, I had been training about three months since then, and I gave up twenty pounds and had still given him a decent fight—at least I'd pushed the action. That's what training with Pat's guys can do for you—it can make up for a lot.

I hadn't been knocked out or anything. They'd stopped it, and I had definitely been losing on points anyway, even though I had done some damage and had him down once. Getting my mouth guard knocked out . . . that's not good. That means you're getting the shit kicked out of you.

The dilated pupil that had frightened the EMT turned out just to be a "bruise" and was normal a few hours later. The doctor I spoke with later—who was also a fight referee—said the fight never should have been stopped. In medical terms, the mechanism of injury—a punch—isn't going to cause the brain damage that would result in different size pupils. That would take a car accident or big fall, a more serious impact. He also gave me grief about keeping my hands up while he stitched my eyebrow (he disagreed with the paramedic).

What was most interesting was how much fun it had been. Being in there, bouncing around, pasting him, getting blasted, whatever—it had all been remarkably fun and exciting. Nothing hurt. I didn't feel any pain at all during the fight. Sure, you know things are bad, like, *Oops, that shot was bad,* but it didn't hurt. It was the week, the day of the fight that had really sucked. All that starving and worrying and dehydrating for nothing.

For that, more than anything, I was pissed at Monte and the show. Because I felt that if I had been fresh, and 194 pounds, and crisp . . . well, who knows? It would have been a better fight. As it was, I pressed the action the whole time. I chased him around. When he inadvertently kicked me in the nuts and the ref gave me time to recover, I didn't take much because I knew my opponent was more tired than I was (I wasn't hurt at all; the cup had worked fine). I think if I had been going strong into the third round, I might have been able to get to him. It's all wishful thinking, but it's the way I felt. Of course, that's part of fighting, you've got to hold on to your ego, win or lose.

What embarrassed me wasn't losing the fight, it was coming back to Pat's looking like I got my ass kicked, even when I didn't. My face was all swollen up, my eyes were bruised; driving back, when we stopped at gas stations, people would fastidiously avoid looking at me, like I was a burn victim. I dreaded walking into the gym because my fighting credibility was gone—I was just a journalist "having an experience." That's the feeling I hated, that I was playing, and I got my hand slapped for it. And no matter what people might say about how good a fight it was and that I gave nearly as good as I got, it doesn't really matter, because without a win I felt like I besmirched the Miletich name. That's why I didn't put on my Miletich T-shirt after the fight; I didn't want to associate losing with MFS. I let Pat down. One look at my face and he'd know I fought a stupid fight, that I didn't do what I was supposed to do, which was slip and move and stay outside. It was written all over my battered face: Here's a stupid fighter, betrayed by a stark inability to move his head.

* * *

My ribs were killing me. Sharp shooting pains. I certainly reinjured them. I found out about four months later, when I finally got an X-ray, that there was a "healing fracture" on the floating rib.

I thought about how much happier the homecoming would have been if I'd won. Sure, I was giving up twenty pounds in the fight, but Tony had done that and won. Mike French, another friend from the gym, was 147 and beat a guy who was over 190. Pat fought a guy who weighed 260. And won. That stuff just happens, especially at the amateur level in MMA.

I got out of Bettendorf fast, as I was embarrassed to be walking around the gym. I had some good friends there, but now I didn't want to face them. I had learned a few things, like what was needed for a knockout; neither Jason nor I had put together enough punches. And that MMA is not a place to learn to fight; I should have ten amateur boxing and kickboxing fights before I get back into the cage.

It was fun. All those blows, the ribs, everything. At least I'd been in a real brawl, finally. And I hadn't gotten killed. The fight had been stopped, I hadn't been knocked out. Who knows what might have happened if we'd been on a desert island? I might have outlasted him in the end, all those Hills might have borne fruit.

Driving home, through a steaming Chicago, Tony called to see how I was doing. I asked him how he was doing, as he'd lost a decision in Hawaii to Matt Lindland that same night, and we had been commiserating. He was fine.

"It just sucks to lose," I said.

"Yeah," he said, "but there's a lot more to it, to doing what we do, than just the fight. If the fight was all there was to it, then it wouldn't be worth it."

I thought about what Brandon and I had talked about at length on the drive home from Cincinnati, the meaning of *clout*. It's not really about the admiration or respect of others; it's about self-respect. We have an innate hatred of fear, and we climb into the cage and prove to ourselves that it is nothing to be afraid of. Even this extreme situation, this death match in a cage in front of screaming fans, is nothing to be afraid of.

After I got home Pat sent me an e-mail. He said, "I just wanted to let you know you can fly our colors anytime you want. You showed a lot of heart and 90 percent of the fighters who come here do not last as long as you did." He closed by saying, "You are without a doubt a fighter."

Pat Miletich said that about me.

3

THE RIVER OF JANUARY

Brazilian Top Team. Kneeling, left to right: Bebeo, Murilo
Bustamente, Zé Mario Sperry. Standing in the center is Antonio
Rodrigo Nogueira, to his right is his twin brother, Rogerio.

At AABB Gym, Rio de Janiero. From left to right: Milton Viera,
Zé Mario Sperry, Eduardo "Mumm-Ra," Emerson "Sushiman,"
November 2004.

Extravagant fictions without a structure to contain them.
    —Joyce Carol Oates, *On Boxing*, referring to fighters

Rio de Janeiro is a city unlike any other, improbably built into cliffs and mountains and around the lagoons and beaches of a wild tropical forest. The urban sprawl, *Zona Norte* (the North Zone), stretches away in mile after mile of rough and vibrant city, decaying and rising from the decay. From the top of Sugarloaf, one of the rock promontories that rear like titanic fingers from the sand of *Zona Sul*, you can see everything. The sheer cliff mountains that emerge from the hotels and apartments look like God's chess pieces. The *favelas*, the slums, have crept up the sides of the steep mountains like moss, and at night they twinkle like stars.

In the heart of *Zona Sul*, on the edge of the lagoon, Brazilian Top Team trains. They train to fight *vale tudo*, "anything goes" in Portuguese— the same thing as MMA—and Top Team is one of the most famous teams in the world.

The gym is luxurious, filling a city block, with swimming pools, tennis courts, workout rooms, and restaurants under a leafy tropical bower. The sun beats down through the giant trees and vines and cuts stark patterns on the mosaic floor. The gym, the Athletic Association of Bank of Brazil (AABB), is a gentlemen's club, and it is an indication of the high social standing of jiu-jitsu players.

Inside the main training room, just a big padded space, about thirty men of different colors and sizes (but a similar overall powerful shape) are grappling and sweating in the tropical heat. The mats swim with sweat as bodies flow and twist against one another,

89

sinuous as snakes. Everyone has *orelha estourada,* the wickedly cauli-flowered ears of lifelong jiu-jitsu enthusiasts, and most wear mul-tiple tattoos and knee braces. They are all training for *vale tudo* fights, but a select few are also training for Pride, the biggest MMA event in the world, held in Japan.

Martial arts have always been rife with mythology; warriors will boast, and men will make legends of their heroes, teachers, and fathers. Every martial art has its own path to victory, to invulnerability, to freedom from fear. If you study with this teacher, and practice the moves ten thousand times, no one can defeat you; you will never need to be afraid again. The secrets of the ancients, the death touch, the one-inch punch; stories of mystical teachers who can move people without touching them. It's hard not to walk out of a Bruce Lee film feeling as if you could fight fifteen guys at once. Mysticism and martial arts go hand in hand, and every school mythologizes its instructors.

Modern MMA has been a testing ground for those myths, a stepping-off point for thousand-year-old traditions; as Pat Miletich said, "Every-thing gets better, cars get better, watches get better, computers. . . . Why should fighting be stuck in the Middle Ages?"

In the United States, before the inception of MMA, karate and tae kwon do had been dominant—fueled by the "karate boom" in the six-ties and seventies, itself fueled by the chop-socky tradition of Chinese filmmaking. The highly stylized kung fu movies from China were cult fads that influenced mainstream ideas of fighting and martial arts. The Olympics had developed judo (since the turn of the century) and tae kwon do into very sporty forms and distanced them from "real" fight-ing. Boxing had evolved into a beautiful, elegant war of attrition.

In 1993 Ultimate Fighting, with its "no rules" cachet and promise of blood, was a pay-per-view hit in the niche market between boxing and pro wrestling. The contests were organized in part by Rorion Gracie, a Brazilian jiu-jitsu expert who was intent on bringing his family's art and style of fighting to the United States. These *vale tudo* fights had been happening in Brazil for nearly a century, and Rorion's slender young brother Royce Gracie, with the benefit of all that experience, won three of the first four UFCs. He won those fights by bringing his opponents to the ground and submitting them off his back—something the American audiences had never seen. The achievement was real. Royce was a tre-mendous fighter, and the point was not lost on the U.S. viewers: Ignore ground fighting at your peril.

Ultimate Fighting was pretty much an extension of the "Gracie challenge" that had already existed in Brazil: Bring all comers and the Gracies will defeat them. Carlos Gracie, to promote his fledgling school in the twenties, took out an ad in *O Globo,* the major national newspaper: "If you want your face smashed and your arms broken, contact the nearest Gracie jiu-jitsu school."

When Commodore Perry opened Japan in the 1850s, Americans and Europeans were exposed to both jiu-jitsu* and sumo wrestling, and competition between European boxers and Japanese fighters must have existed. From the turn of the century on, Japanese wrestlers would travel to fight exhibition matches, sometimes against other wrestlers and sometimes against boxers.

"Let us link the start of *vale tudo* with the entertainment industry typical of the early industrialized world, in contexts such as Victorian London or the Belle Époque of Paris. In all these venues there were for decades challenging activities, but all that gave place to purely theatrical fights, while in Brazil real fights were practiced for all of the twentieth century, with the accompanying development of technical sophistication," says Carlos Loddo (who is writing his own book on the history of *vale tudo*), addressing this early phenomenon.

We have all heard of those old circuses that would travel around and invite local farm boys to fight the veteran strongman (who would know all the tricks and work them over): It's the same atmosphere in which John L. Sullivan would travel to a new town, walk into a bar, and announce, "I can lick any man in the place." In the rest of the world, these exhibitions split into prizefighting (boxing) and professional wrestling (meaning "worked," or fixed, fights). In Brazil, that never happened.

Mitsuyo Maeda, a Japanese fighter and ambassador for judo, came to New York in 1904 and lectured under his master, Tomita, at West Point; he had some success and continued to travel and put on exhibitions. Eventually Maeda turned to professional wrestling, "muscular theater," in which the outcome was rarely in doubt, for money. He wrestled all over the world, in London, Belgium, Scotland, and Spain. He wrestled in Cuba and in 1909 in the bullfighting rings in Mexico City. Finally, he

---

*The spelling of jiu-jitsu can be called into question. It appears to me that "jujitsu" is the traditional Japanese art, and "jiu-jitsu" is what the Brazilians started doing, and the differences between traditions are great enough to warrant a whole different name. If you want to argue about it, contact Carlos Loddo.

ended up in Brazil, with its large Japanese immigrant population, and it was there that he met the Gracie family and began teaching the young Carlos Gracie jujitsu.

Maeda taught Carlos for about five years, then left him to his own devices. That was for the best, for Carlos had grasped the ideas behind Maeda's technique, and after being left alone, without the rigid Japanese structure, he and his brothers started to create. Carlos brought in his younger brother Helio, who was small and skinny (Carlos at first thought him too frail to train). Helio was forced to turn away from power and look for other ways to win—by attacking an opponent's arm with his whole body, instead of pitting arm against arm. With his drive he became the chief innovator of the family. Together Carlos and Helio began Gracie jiu-jitsu, a martial art in its own right. Carlos also became interested in the connection between food and well-being, and nutrition was a pillar of his family's success.

Ironically, it was Helio who became the big fighter out of their school, and he began achieving notoriety as he fought Americans, Japanese, and other Brazilians all through the thirties. In 1948, Helio and Carlos started their famous school in Rio, on the Avenida Rio Branca. Rio's richest playboys trained there, and Helio's celebrity continued to flourish. In 1950 he challenged Joe Louis to fight for a million *cruzeiros*, but Joe never accepted. Helio continued to fight, and in 1951 he fought a Japanese fighter in Maracana Stadium, the largest soccer stadium in the world. The Gracie school consisted of lawyers, judges, and the crème de la crème of Brazilian society. The Gracies were also fiercely protective of their sphere. Loddo writes that "anyone who would teach fighting in Rio, if claiming too loud that such practice was an efficient method for self-defense purposes . . . would end up, sooner or later, having to put the practice to test against the Gracies' jiu-jitsu."

Brazilian Top Team was born under Carlson Gracie, a famous fighter and teacher, and became arguably the most successful MMA team in history.

I had decided to go to Brazil to learn jiu-jitsu and meet the greatest ground fighters in the world. It was a logical step; the biggest influence on MMA in the States was without a doubt Brazilian jiu-jitsu and *vale tudo*. I would try to fill the gaping hole in my fighting; I had a little tiny bit, a glimpse of the ground game, but I needed more.

When I thought back to my cage fight, it seemed ridiculous that I had gone in there without a ground game at all. Just stupid. If I had

had any kind of confidence in my ground game, I could have tried to take my opponent down when the stand-up was going all his way. It's what Pat would have done; if you're getting shelled standing, put him on the ground. I had gone into that fight without knowing a single takedown. Now, my stand-up was okay, good enough to spar with decent people and not come out too badly, but it wasn't anywhere near good enough to be my only thing. I needed options; it was just foolishness not to have a complete game. If I went to Brazil, the home of jiu-jitsu, and I stayed and trained for four months at Top Team, I would *force* myself to have at least the basis for a ground game.

I also needed a way to finance it, so I somehow sold a proposal for the book you are reading. This had the added benefit of access: Now that I was a writer, I had an in with the fighters.

Brazilians fight in *vale tudo,* but the big time for them is Pride in Japan. Pride fighting, a promotion like the UFC, is big money and giant stadiums with ninety thousand people.The fighters get the respect and treatment that top professional athletes in the United States receive. Bob Sapp, an American ex-NFL lineman who fought in the K-1 (a huge kickboxing event that has branched out into MMA) and who also has competed in MMA, made millions a year and appeared on the cover of *Time*'s Asian edition and in countless Japanese advertisements. He was not a technical fighter but a monster at something like 355 pounds and 10 percent body fat—a black Godzilla—and the Japanese love him. Japan is one of the only places where MMA fighters can make serious money. The UFC, by far the dominant promotion in the United States, takes care of the top guys, but the undercard payment is brutally low.

I knew the fighters of Brazil Top Team from watching Pride fights; they were legendary, bigger than life. Zé Mario Sperry, perhaps one of the greatest ground fighters ever, led the team out from under Carlson Gracie after Carlson left Rio to come to the United States. Sperry and Murilo Bustamante, the other team leader, are among the living legends of the sport.

I was particularly interested in Antonio Rodrigo Nogueira, or "Minotauro," as they call him, a Pride fighter who had pulled off submissions on people I had thought couldn't be submitted. I wanted to see the modern MMA world at its apogee. I decided I would see if I could follow Rodrigo into his training and through a fight in Japan.

While training in Iowa, I had met a grappler named Danny Ives, and we had talked a little about Brazil, where he visited often. "Just come on down and I'll hook you up," he said. He told me about a guy named Scotty Nelson, who ran a Web site, OntheMat.com, and I called Scotty one day around three in the afternoon and woke him up.

"Yeah, man, just come on down and we'll work it out," he grumbled at me. So I flew down a few days later. A lesser man might have questioned the wisdom of going to Brazil to train with the greatest ground fighters in the world with a "healing fracture" on his floating rib. But not me, genius that I am.

Scott Nelson is a blond, blue-eyed California gringo who looked like a surfer kid with badly cauliflowered ears. He was thirty-five but seemed twenty-five, with a hint of the weariness and seen-it-all attitude of the seasoned expatriate, a Graham Greene character in the MTV "Jackass" tradition. He'd been in Rio for about three years, running Onthe Mat.com, the definitive site on jiu-jitsu in Brazil and in the States, and his Internet business supported his gringo lifestyle. He competed, as well, and had a whole bucketload of medals and honors from various competitions: gold in the 2001 Brazilian Team Championships, first in United Gracie in San Francisco (Team), third at the World Grappling Games, second at the U.S. National. He was not a top, world-class jiu-jitsu practitioner but a dedicated lifelong enthusiast, and he'd practiced, or "rolled," with some of the best people in the world for seven years, in both the States and Brazil.

Scotty is incredibly generous and open to both foreigners and locals. He invited me to stay at his house, where there are always fighters in transition or foreigners in from the States, for a few weeks of training. When I arrived, a bunch of jiu-jitsu guys from Boulder, Colorado, were just finishing their stay, partying and chasing girls and eating like kings; they were training at Gracie Barra, the local branch of the Gracie Academy. They had nicknames like "White Rabbit" and "Green Giant."

Scotty said I could train anywhere I wanted, as a gringo (and a beginner); but don't talk about it, and try not to let them catch you training at competing schools. Even for foreigners, training at several different schools can be problematic. If you go from one gym to another, it is viewed as a betrayal, a stab in the back. At first this seems silly, archaic, and juvenile, but the deeper I went into the fight game, the more I came to understand and sympathize with it. The fight game consists of relationships, of reputations: between fighter and trainer, trainer and manager, manager and promoter. They all have to trust one another to some degree, and because the fight game is often involved with the shadowy edges of society, that trust is sometimes abused. There isn't much money to go around. Reputation is life for a trainer, manager, promoter, fighter: Can you deliver the goods? If the word on the street is that you can't, your career is in trouble. Your reputation is your livelihood and in some sense what you fight for, in all facets of the game.

And, of course, it's all tough guys, and no one is as sensitive to perceived slights as tough guys.

I moved into Scotty's back room when the other guys moved out, and I hung out with him and did core training for my ribs. I figured I'd spend a few weeks there, getting my bearings and taking Portuguese lessons, then make the transition to Top Team and get my own place. Scotty had mats on his balcony, and we would sometimes train out there. He was a big help to me because he would go lightly on my ribs.

I wanted to fight, or at least compete in some grappling tournaments after I'd been there for a while, so I was running and skipping rope and not drinking, while Scotty was basically partying, smoking weed, and hanging out. It was thanks to him that I became aware of the subculture ties between surfing and jiu-jitsu. Most fighters also surf, some professionally. Renzo Gracie (another world-famous Gracie, who now runs a school in Manhattan) was a pro surfer, and at Top Team a big-wave rider with the world's biggest wave under his belt, Rodrigo "the Monster" Resende, sometimes showed up. The weed smoking is another part of it. There is a whole contingent of jiu-jitsu players all over the world who self-medicate with THC.

Even training on Scotty's balcony, I was struck by the democracy of ground fighting. The people teaching ground fighting aren't untouchable professors; they are other fighters, older and more experienced, but because you "train" with them, they teach on a very friendly, face-to-face level. "Training" in Brazil means more or less full-speed and strength-submission grappling, with gi or without. A gi, or kimono, as the Brazilians call it, is the thick white judo uniform that stands in for clothing you might wear in a street fight. Though early fighters perfected their ground games with a gi, now most vale tudo fighters practice without it, as most MMA fights will not allow it.

Grappling is a discussion, it's an open forum. The way you train is with a bunch of friends sitting around watching two guys grappling, and trying various things at half speed, and then going for it nearly full speed. At Scotty's house, out on the balcony, various gringos and Brazilians would smoke weed and roll. It was there I met a somewhat famous fighter named Tony DeSouza, who was ranked pretty high in the world, had fought in the UFC three times, and was living in Brazil and Peru.

Tony was thirty, a Peruvian citizen who had grown up in the United States as an illegal alien. His parents had come to Southern California when he was ten years old to make a better life and to get away from the violence in Peru. He had gone to high school in San Marino and attended Cal State Bakersfield on a wrestling scholarship, all as an illegal alien. "I hate lying, and I had to lie all the time," Tony said. When I met him, he looked like an *indío,* a bushman with a thick head of curly hair and a giant bushy beard, with flat, dark brown eyes and a battered nose.

Tony was a wrestling standout and did very well as a freshman and sophomore in the Division I Pac-10 (he was voted most outstanding) and was rated in the top twelve in the country, but his interest started to flag and he butted heads with his coaches, who were overtraining him. He failed to qualify for Division I his senior year, even though he beat several Division I all-Americans. Anger filled him up: "I just went out there to hurt guys," he said. "My last fight I had the guy crying. I lost by fifteen points." He did a lot of street fighting. "Bouncers," he said to me, and then rolled his eyes as though that said everything. And in a way it did. Tony's not a big guy, maybe five-nine and 170 pounds, and he is not physically intimidating despite his battered visage and gnarled ears.

He drifted and worked in Vegas, and got into jiu-jitsu almost by accident. Within a few weeks he was living in the gym, and within six months he had his first MMA fight. Soon after, he was in the UFC. He fought three times in the UFC (he went 2–1) and in a few other places, before moving back to Peru and starting his own gym.

Tony had come to Rio via the Amazon; he'd spent a month on the river. He'd left Peru with about a hundred dollars U.S. and had pretty much bummed his way down, sleeping outside. When I met him, he had just fought Luiz Azeredo in Meca, the big Brazilian *vale tudo* event, and beaten him. Luiz was arguably the best Brazilian in his weight class. Tony had him in a finishing move, "the Twister," but it was so technical that the referee didn't recognize it and stopped the fight and restarted them standing. Tony shook it off like it was nothing.

During the fight the crowd starting chanting "*Mendigo,*" meaning "the bum," at Tony, because he resembled a famous homeless TV character. He did look like a wild man, and he was sleeping on the mats at his gym in Centro with about six other penniless jiu-jitsu fighters when I met him. He was an extreme example of the new breed of fighter, taking the ground game to higher and more rarefied air, traveling like an old journeyman boxer, seeking out new teachers and opportunities to fight.

One night, Scotty and I went to see Darryl Gholar, an American wrestler who had changed the face of *vale tudo*. We drove through the warmth and glow of Rio, past street kids congregated on mattresses in the center of the tunnels, right in the exhaust and in the eyes of the thousands of cars streaming by. It was so strange, to see these kids in the middle of the tunnel, but then you realize that for them it is safe. The constant stream of cars and headlights doesn't concern them, although it flows by only a few feet away; they are deep in the cave and safe. Nobody is going to walk the thousand feet either way in darkness, in that narrow hell, to get to them.

Darryl Gholar had come to Brazil to teach takedowns. The wrestling takedown is an essential ingredient of the ground game because it is a way to control the fight and end up on the ground in a better position, on top. A main reason American wrestlers have been so good at *vale tudo* is their powerful takedown ability, learned from a young age.

Darryl Gholar loved Brazil and had been there for several years. He was in his early forties, a world-class freestyle wrestler who at his peak had beaten people like Randy Couture at wrestling. Darryl had suffered a brain aneurysm, and Scotty had pretty much been the only one who had gone to see him in the hospital, bringing him food and comfort, as well as dealing with some con artists who told Darryl's mom that she needed to wire seven grand for an operation. Scotty asked around and found out that that was horseshit. He had passed the hat on his Web site and raised two thousand dollars for Darryl, money to buy him a ticket back to the States.

Darryl had recently been led astray by Wallid Ismail, a famous fighter who began on the same team as Zé Mario and Murilo Bustamante, under Carlson Gracie. Darryl had been Top Team's wrestling coach, and Wallid had promised him a lot more money to leave and come to the team he was starting. When Darryl showed up with his bridges burned at Top Team, Wallid had no money and no team. Wallid had done this to some other famous fighters, as well. Now the wrestling coach at Top Team is a Brazilian, Jefferson Teixeira, a three-time national champ and former collegiate coach, a diminutive figure with perfect form. They do two hard wrestling workouts a week at Top Team, because the takedown (and its defense) is one of the most important aspects of the ground game. (Since my trip, Darryl has gone back to Top Team and is coaching again—and the Top Team fighters are taking everyone down at will.)

Darryl's dad came in to help him, for although Darryl seemed healthy, he still moved gingerly, and there was a sense of tension and fragility about him. His father had been a pro boxer, and we talked about Thailand. He'd lived there in 1962 and '63 in the service and had loved it. He was trying to tell his son how it compared to Brazil. There was something of a similar feel, hot-country jungle and third world. They were interested in my book and wanted to talk about it. "Do you ever watch animals, horses and cows and birds?" asked Darryl's father, a tall, thick, distinguished man with an open, handsome face and gray hair. He made the motions of jostling his elbows for space, for position. "It's natural, everything fights."

Copacabana is a bustling, dense city, hovering between third world and first: street kids and homeless alongside professionals and couples walking with grocery bags and briefcases, shadowed by obvious criminal types, skeletally thin and strung out, giving you the hairy eyeball, kids begging and sniffing glue from rags, every big fancy building secure behind glass and steel curtains and doormen.

Scott, Lincoln, Nick, and I piled into a jeep one afternoon and blasted through a dense, heavy, overcast city to the north, to see some *vale tudo*. Nick, the "Green Giant," was a large, gentle guy from Colorado, where he worked as a barista and took his jiu-jitsu very seriously. He was about as gringo as they come, lily-white and red-blond. Lincoln was a skinny punk with tattoos and wild red hair and a slightly goofy air, who had worked in carnivals and freak shows (I think he wrestled midgets at Lollapalooza), and was down here for some months, grappling at Gracie Barra. He made the joke "I'm like Jason—they keep killing me and I keep coming back." I liked him because he wore a T-shirt that said, "The Clash is the only band that matters," and you can't really say it better than that.

We flew through the twisting canyons of Rio, past the famous slum City of God, and over a huge bridge spanning an endless bay with the pride of Brazil's navy loitering around the base, and cranes and oil rigs like dinosaurs or monster robots in a science fiction set. It's the longest bridge in the world, or in Brazil, depending on whom you're in the car with. We lanced out into the deepening gloom and the jungle, seeing occasional fires along the road.

It took a little doing, but we found the venue at a fairground, complete with stalls of prize Brahman cows, some fancy new tractors, food and beer, and a huge soundstage set up for a concert. The fights had been scheduled to begin at around eight p.m., which is when we got there, but a light drizzle began and there was no crowd, so they put them off for two hours.

The fighters—instantly recognizable by their bulk, the *pite-boys* (from "pit bull," pronounced "pitchey-boys") with heavily snarled cauliflower ears, battered noses and eyebrows, and thick heavy shoulders and hands—and their respective teams were milling around. One guy was absolutely immense and dark black, with arms like separate people attached to his shoulders, a steroid wonder, with bloodshot eyes in a handsome, chiseled face. A lot of black and olive skin, skullcaps, eyes searching one another out. Being with Scott and the other gringos, it was as if I didn't exist because I was so obviously not a fighter, or at least not one to be concerned about.

They call them *pite-boys,* somewhat like the motorcycle guys are called moto boys. It's almost a fashion thing, but the *pite-boys* are a little more extreme. They often show up to a club or party and if they aren't let in will kick everyone's ass in the line, or pull the tent down on the party. They are essentially social terrorists. There are stories about how poor street kids will sometimes take rocks and mash up their own ears, in order to look tough, like *pite-boys.*

"Once you get pretty good at jiu-jitsu, beating up someone who doesn't know any jiu-jitsu is pretty fucking easy. So you get this whole power trip," was Scott's explanation for the phenomenon. *Pite-boys* were notorious throughout Rio. "They've got a gun and you don't; and these guys abuse the power." Most *pite-boys* were upper class, with the freedom from legal persecution that privilege affords in Brazil.

While shaved heads, tats, and cauliflower ears are the uniform, some of the most notorious *pite-boys* don't quite fit that stereotype, like Ryan Gracie and Georginio. And it's usually not the best fighters who are the bad *pite-boys;* for instance, Murilo and Zé Mario aren't out in clubs beating people up.

There were some particularly infamous incidents, such as one battle between Ryan Gracie and Macoco that destroyed an entire sushi restaurant in São Paolo. Now just as every dog bite becomes a pit-bull attack, every public fight is blamed on *pite-boys.*

Luta livre just means "wrestling," but it has come to stand for a different tradition from Gracie jiu-jitsu, a competitor. It was "no-gi" from the beginning, as the students were too poor to afford the uniform. The essential difference is class, *luta livre* being the no-gi wrestling of the poor in the *favelas,* and jiu-jitsu being the art of the rich and powerful of Rio. *Luta livre* became its own style of submission wrestling.

The two styles clashed, somewhat inevitably (this is South America and machismo is the rule), in Rio in the early eighties, probably on the beach, where so much Carioca life happens, and evolved into a Hatfield and McCoy–style enmity. There was an attempt to end the rivalry by a series of *vale tudo* matches. In the first series, Eugenio Tadeu and the other kickboxing guys did surprisingly well (they had just started learning *luta livre*), but their leader, Flavio Molina, an excellent kickboxer, was destroyed.

In the early nineties, representatives of the two traditions fought again. This time the Gracie jiu-jitsu people were better organized and included two of Carlson's students, Murilo Bustamente and Wallid Ismail, and they won all their fights. There was talk that the Gracies had their students do all their fighting for them, but the focus of the Gracie family at that time was on the United States, where they were starting the UFC.

We found our seats in the increasing drizzle as the fights finally got under way. The intensity of the clashes was ferocious and intoxicating. It seemed suddenly incongruous that there were about five hundred human beings and two of them were locked in the ultimate effort, while the rest were at rest.

The crowd and the venue were far more upscale than I would have thought, with a real ring and remote-controlled light show, although some poor bastard had to go up and crawl around on the frame and cover the fancy lights with trash bags as the rain increased. There were little kids around, sitting on their parents' laps and dancing to the violent, profanity-filled American hip-hop and screaming. Compared to Thailand, though, these people were rich; they had cell phones and cars and clothes and girlfriends. There was nothing third world about it. The fair where Johnny Deroy had fought four years ago in Thailand had been in another universe.

The fights were pretty straightforward, with few submissions or submission attempts. It seemed that everyone was so well versed in jiu-jitsu that ground-and-pound, holding the other man down, in his guard, and beating him through a slow, steady, heavy constant pressure and battering was the safest and most effective thing to do. You avoid taking risks, you don't look to "finish" with a submission attempt, as these, when they fail, can leave you out of position. It's safe, but it's not a crowd pleaser. It's boring and is sometimes called "lay-and-pray," because you lay on top of the opponent and pray to win by decision.

The rain came spitting out of the dark sky and swirled in the brilliant TV-ready lights (there was a substantial film crew there), and the fighters slipped and slopped and sprawled on the wet canvas. There was a pretense of civility; fighters were forced to shake hands and embrace after a fight.

In the second *vale tudo* fight, a Gracie Barra fighter was beating a slightly smaller *luta livre* guy, and he had him down and kicked him in the face, which laid the *luta livre* guy out. This is against the local rules, to kick someone who's on the ground when you are standing (though you can do it in Japan), and everyone freaked out. Eugenio Tadeu was yelling from his corner. The *luta livre* guy stayed down, and although he stirred and moved, the ref wouldn't let him up, and a stretcher was brought and the huge black guy and his buddies manhandled the *luta livre* guy onto the stretcher and away.

There was a famous *vale tudo* match in Rio that was on TV, when a young Renzo Gracie was fighting Eugenio. Before the fight, the *luta livre* supporters had taken all the good seats, and they began to grow rowdier and rowdier as the fight started. A riot broke out, the power went down, and in the darkness, Renzo Gracie got stabbed.

For the rest of this night, there wasn't much carnage, just a lot of decisions or quick stoppages. I thought about trying to fight here and figured I might be able to stand with these guys but there was no way I could go to the ground with anyone. It would be a lot smarter to learn something and try a few grappling tournaments first.

The rain finally stopped, and we milled around with the other fighters and congratulated a few winners. The lower-level fighters all eyeballed one another and posed and looked tough, but the top professionals, the few that were around, were smiling and greeting one another, members of an elite club. They only fight for money; there was no animosity, no aggression, just friendliness.

A few weeks after I arrived in Rio, I finally went up to Lagoa to train with Brazilian Top Team. I was pretty nervous. I had my first *gi* in my backpack and was uncomfortably aware of its crisp white starch.

I wended my way across cool stone patios, through the vines and shrubs, between pools and tennis courts under massive tropical trees and made it to the gym at around ten forty-five, thinking class started at eleven, as advertised. Of course, this was Rio and these were *cariocas* (the slang term for Rio dwellers), famous for being late, so class didn't start until almost an hour later. Scotty would say, when we were waiting for someone who was from Rio and the wait turned into hours, "We're being *carioca*'ed."

I reluctantly put the *gi* on and felt like I was posing. I didn't have a belt, and as I stood around stretching, waiting for class to start, I realized that because no one could see what belt I was, there was some speculation. Jiu-jitsu has a belt-ranking system—white, blue, purple, brown, black—and achieving a black belt is a serious accomplishment that might take seven to ten years. Your teacher, or *mestre,* decides when you are ready and has a lot to do with your pedigree. For instance, someone who is a Murilo Bustamante black belt is probably a lot better than someone who is a black belt from an unknown in the United States, because Murilo is stingy with his black belts. And your teacher will reflect stylistically in your game, as well. There's an artistic sense to all this, the way you play your game.

The head instructor, Olavo, came after me with questions, even after I asked him for a white belt, yelling, "You are good, no? Professional?" and laughing that I was being modest. I got my white belt and tied it on; I had learned how from Scotty the night before. Everyone felt better once I had a belt on.

The training didn't seem too bad. We warmed up and started trying out moves, and I sweated and strained and felt okay for a white belt. I had the four months of no-gi at Pat's place to help me, but anyone other than a white belt slaughtered me, just had their way with me like I was a child. The *gi* is a mystery; it chokes and pulls and twists around your body. It controls you: By controlling the *gi*, you control the man inside it.

While I was rolling with a purple belt, a guy with maybe two to three years of constant study, he got me in something very deep that exerted pressure on my left shoulder—no pain, just pressure—and I waited for a few minutes for something to happen. I wasn't in much pain and didn't think he had a real submission; I wanted to see if he'd let it go, but he didn't, so I tapped. We reset and kept rolling, and I thought nothing more of it until later.

I got thrashed around for a while longer, and the session ended, and we all bowed and clapped and shook hands on the way out. There was a no-gi training session next, just submissions, and I was invited to join it. I felt pretty good, but my left shoulder was tingling, pins and needles, so I declined. *Better take it easy,* I thought. Little did I know the damage I had done.

On the steps outside, I talked to Fernando, also known as Margarida, a famous jiu-jitsu player who had won the 2001 Mundials and slaughtered everyone in his way; he was enormously thick and still quite young, in his early twenties. He told me how he hated all the evil in the world, how he wanted to kill all his enemies and then vanish. I told him he should be like Gandhi, forgive your enemies, and he laughed and said, "Look at your shoes, your clothes, you have money, you have no problems."

I had run into this line before; there was a common sentiment among the jiu-jitsu players that we gringos were playboys, that the foreigners were all rich. They would give us crap, but these are guys who have always had maids, who have never mowed a lawn or made their own bed. They've always been in society's upper crust and have never had a menial job like washing dishes.

That night I sat alone in the house fighting off an encroaching sense of dread. I knew what lay ahead: a lot of getting beat up. My shoulder was tingling in a weird way. I had a neat row of blisters along my fingertips, from grabbing the *gi,* which I carefully slit and slathered with antibiotic cream.

The *gi* was my new nightmare. After three days in a *gi,* I knew it was a whole different universe. I was a total beginner, getting swept and ridden by every blue belt on the mat. *Gi* grappling is all about the *gi,* you grab it at every turn, pulling pant legs, twisting sleeves, gripping and pulling the belt, the lapels, untucking your opponent's *gi* and twisting the loose ends around his body to turn him, to choke him. The cloth controls the body underneath, and the body controls the cloth and breaks grips.

It is interesting and much more technical than no-gi because of all the cloth gripping; for instance, when someone gets you in an arm-bar, there is almost no chance of escape because he has a hold of the sleeve on your *gi.* If you're grappling no-gi, the sweat and slipperiness of your hands give you a decent chance to escape with a strong whipping pull; there is a lot less to hold on to. So the pace with *gi* seems slower, more deliberate, more thoughtful—punctuated by seconds of desperate movement, muscles straining, attempts to surprise your opponent. In no-gi, the movements and straining and changing positions are endless.

I was the punching bag of choice; guys came to me because I made them feel good about themselves. I strained and strained, and they still easily reversed me, swept me, flattened me out. I just had no idea what I was doing, so I helped them sweep me by holding the wrong thing, pushing the wrong way. Everyone gave me his back because I didn't know what to do with it—except for a few of the other white belts, who didn't really like me because I was stronger and bigger than they were, and so I pushed them around but lacked the technique to finish them. "Taking the back" means climbing onto someone's back, and it is perhaps the most advantageous position in fighting, but an experienced guy can handle someone on his back and escape or reverse the position.

Afterward, my left shoulder would glow with pain, twitching and spasming, while I sat and watched the pro fighters go through their no-*gi* workouts.

I found an apartment in Ipanema and moved to be closer to the gym, within a ten-minute walk. I was paying six hundred dollars a month, which was still a gringo price, for two rooms and a tiny kitchen a block from *Posto 10,* on Ipanema beach, arguably the nicest beach in the city (although *Posto 9* had better girls, it was too crowded on the weekends). Ipanema, in the *cidade maravihlosa,* is a truly beautiful place. Wide leafy streets, sunny and hazy and bright and hot, with European taste but a unique world. The sidewalks are all the same—cobblestone, pounded into a concrete sand and then set to harden—and everywhere there are huge gaping ruts and shattered piles of stones. It is lovely in a gecko, sun-dappled way, with patterns of different-colored stones and large fish shapes set into the boardwalk. Everything reeks of the sea and the beach and heat and the jungle.

The main street is luxury commercialism: Louis Vuitton outlets, jewelry, ridiculous high-end sporting gear, H. Stern precious gems, and giant pharmacies. There are stands on every corner where fresh fruit juice is available for a pittance; Brazil has about five fruits that you've never heard of, unique to its jungle. I asked friends about this or that fruit and got, "Oh, there's no translation in English." I ended up hooked on *acai* and *morago,* a kind of thick shake of a dark, richly textured fruit mixed with strawberry *(morago). Acai* is supposedly wonderful for you, twenty grams of protein and trans-fatty acids and vitamins. It is relatively new to Rio, from the north; Wallid Ismail brought it south with him. Eventually, like most people, I made the switch to *acai* and banana, as it's a little less sweet.

The street kids seemed remarkably happy, smiling and playing, making up games all the time, remaining children. They juggled for the cars and slept in lazy packs like dumped luggage, strewn in haphazard piles on the pavement. *How nice not to be one of them,* I thought as I walked home with a thousand reals burning a hole in my pocket, as I had to pay the landlord in cash. *Why not just hand it to some kids, hand the whole stinking wad to them, right then and there? Just do it.* But I didn't. I turned hurriedly and shook my head as they came babbling to me with soft, high voices. I didn't understand the words, but I understood the plaintiveness, the note of sadness, of hunger, of human commonality— Help me please. . . . I am you and you are me, so why should you get to have all the fun? Why do you get to eat?

It was the only thing that distracted me in this beautiful, golden jungle city on the lip of the blue blue sea. The street kids bothered me less and less the longer I stayed, until I didn't even see them, like everyone else. I lived for the most part in *Zona Sul,* the magic place, the richest part of the country, a fantasy world.

I had hurt my shoulder much worse than I could have possibly imagined. The pain increased day by day, and I took a few days off and then tried to train when it felt better, and it invariably got worse and worse until it would be hanging off my side like a chunk of driftwood, throbbing and tingling by the end of a training session. It felt as if it were held on by my *gi.* I began to panic, thinking that I'd damaged the rotator cuff. I couldn't have come all this way to get hurt.

First, I tried self-medication. I went wandering and got an injection of cortisone at a quiet little mom-and-pop pharmacy from a tiny old man with glasses who seemed to understand me perfectly. *Cortisona. Eu achuego mi hombro. Sim, sim.* Boom, he gave me the shot of cloudy liquid into the meat of the shoulder. It made no difference at all.

Most people would have been ecstatic to be on vacation here in Ipanema without being able to train, but I was miserable. I had nightmares—my dreams were filled with snakes—and would wake up at five and drink coffee and fret. I had already been down here for a month; I was missing valuable training time.

I would have done anything to be healthy, for a magic pill to heal my shoulder. I would look covetously at all the other guys, consumed with shoulder envy.

It wasn't only that I couldn't train; it affected everything about me, about how the friendships went. Fighters will talk very differently to someone who works out with them, to someone they've been sparring and struggling with. There is an instant intimacy; fighters are friends after they fight because they have tested and know each other. As males, their respective status is known. Without a chance to prove myself as at least a willing beginner, I was a perennial outsider, tolerated instead of welcomed.

After a month of training off and on, I realized I had to go to a doctor, and I went to see Zé Mario's and Rodrigo's doctor and got an MRI for about $150. I had inflammation and edema, little balls of white fluid building up in the tissue, but fortunately no muscular or bone damage. The doctor told me that maybe in fifteen days I could resume training. He was sadly, egregiously wrong: Four months later it was still screwed up, and a doctor stateside would decide that I had an umbral tear to part of the rotator cuff.

As I waited in vain for my shoulder to heal, I continued to go to Top Team every day to sit and watch for two or three hours, trying to educate my eyes, trying to understand what was happening. Slowly, I managed to make the internal adjustment that I wasn't going to be able to train for a while, if at all; but it was bitterly disappointing. Such an opportunity lost, one that would never come again. However, I had to find the positive side; that is an aspect of jiu-jitsu. Look at Helio, one of the founders; he was considered too small and weak, so he was forced to turn from power to technique and became one of the major champions of the art.

Jean Jacques Machado is a famous black belt in jiu-jitsu who has a birth defect; one of his hands is badly deformed, so he can't make the *gi* grips like the other black belts. Despite this, he became one of the greatest technical grapplers of all time. He was forced to use his hand as a hook and grab not the cloth so much as the body and limbs of his opponent; as a result, in the no-*gi*, he was way ahead of everyone else. It turned out to be an advantage. There is a Brazilian word, *malandro,* that conveys something of the essence of a crook but also of someone who turns a disadvantage, a potential setback, into an advantage. Maybe I could do the same, learn by being forced to watch and study. So I watched every day, until my eyes glazed over.

It's been said that the main obstacle to jiu-jitsu ever becoming an Olympic sport is that it is impossible to watch without at least some experience. To the uninitiated, it is a total mystery. Even after a little familiarity, I knew I was not seeing half of what was happening. I was failing to appreciate the skill and cleverness on display. The strength

of boxing and muay Thai is that even the unschooled eye can appreciate the fights to some degree. You could say that at any pro boxing match
there are maybe ten people in the whole stadium who really *understand*
what is going on, but everyone in there can appreciate a war. With
ground fighting, with or without the *gi,* that isn't the case. To the un-
informed observer it looks strange, slow, and, as a friend put it, "oddly
intimate."

One day I took an afternoon off from watching Top Team to meet with
a famous *capoeirista* on the edge of Lagoa, in a park. Spring was ending
in Brazil, and the clouds hung low over the bowl of mountains, muddy
and threatening. Capoeira is the only martial art native to Brazil, and,
although I don't trust it as a strictly fighting art, it provides terrific
strength and agility training, and the good practitioners are strong and
graceful. The *mestre* I met with was João José da Silva; probably in his
late forties or early fifties, he is known as João do Pulo, the Jump Man.
He was an aging, slight black man with a handsome, clear-eyed face
and a neat mustache. His hair was still dark and curly, and he generated goodwill and warmth. He was born in Bahia, but came to Rio with
his parents, who were small farmers, when he was eleven years old and
began to play capoeira.

He fought *vale tudo* when he was sixteen, or at least fought other
capoeiristas, and became famous for entering it so young. He laughed
and said that he had been knocked out a few times and gone home with
his face covered in blood.

We hunkered in the rain in the park in some dingy concrete pa-
vilions that smelled vaguely of piss, and out of the corner of my eye I
watched the lightning crown and wreathe the mountains around the
city and the slow spread of water across the concrete floor. There was
supposed to be a session that afternoon, and maybe thirty students
would show up if the weather was good. However, rain depresses the
Cariocas, and they probably wouldn't come, at least not in numbers.

The legend goes that capoeira was developed by slaves, who hid it
from their masters by turning it into a dance whenever a white man drew
near, and there are antecedents in Angolan foot fighting. *Capoeiragem*
was a very violent street game in Rio at the turn of the nineteenth century, and the police tried to crack down on it. Today, capoeira is highly
popular in Rio, although as a purely fighting art, it doesn't seem to do
particularly well in the ring. There is some capoeira that has a ground
game, but the stand-up is a little too stylized to compete directly with

boxing and muay Thai. A lot of fighters at Top Team had done some capoeira; it is a social activity, fun, and terrific for power and timing. In Rio, the girls do it like they do tae bo or cardio kickboxing in the United States; it's a little trendy.

João had had some horrible accidents. He'd fallen off a horse working at a jockey club; he had destroyed his knee in two places in '89 during a samba school dance; and he'd been in a terrible car crash in '94, which had kept him from capoeira for long periods. He said that destiny (and doctors) tried to keep him from capoeira, but he fought back every time. Now he had a disease, I couldn't understand what it was, but the veins on his arms were swollen and black and hugely heavy, and when I touched them, they fluttered tentatively. I could feel the blood underneath the tissue-thin skin pulsing, vibrating like a bird's heart in an endless, delicate shudder. It was killing him, and capoeira may have been accelerating the process, but his need was great. When he played, he forgot all his problems, and he had to forcibly remind himself that he couldn't jump like he used to. There was no drinking or drugs; capoeira was his only solace.

I asked him about fighting and other arts. He gave me a look—he knew that many fighters felt that capoeira was a dance and not a fighting art. João had studied some boxing and muay Thai and other things, but he said, "If the snake doesn't bite me, I will kill it"—it's not the technique or school that is important, but the action of the fighter.

There was something about him that reminded me of Apidej. Something in the gentleness, the knowingness, the completeness he wore around him. As the rain increased, he and the dozen students who showed up decided they would just play instruments and sing, as the music is as important to capoeira as the actions, and one's rank inside the system is as much about skill with the instruments as it is about physical ability. When they started to sing a slower song, in the Angolan style, I could hear the sounds of Africa, and for the first time since coming to Brazil, I really felt the weight of a foreign place.

I had noticed that many jiu-jitsu players had some kind of special relationship to pit bulls, to fighting dogs. They would often have tattoos of a favorite dog, and many gyms and gis had a cartoon of a pit bull on them; it was the old symbol for Gracie jiu-jitsu. I asked Scotty about it one day, and he put me onto a friend of his, Escorrega.

A small, slender Gracie Barra black belt with excellent English, Escorrega had been Scotty's original connection in Brazil. He had spent a lot of time in the United States and was working on his "extraordinary person" visa. He was also an expert on cockfighting and dogfighting.

Escorrega's family was from Minas, a farm town to the south, and for five generations they had been breeding cocks; Escorrega himself had been in dogs for ten years. There are two basic types of cocks, just as there are two types of dogs (although there are endless bloodlines and families): One hits harder and tires more quickly; the other has endless stamina but doesn't strike as hard. Escorrega, in dogs and cocks, always preferred the ones that hit harder.

Escorrega's real love is not the cocks but dogfighting, and he educated me for hours, his English fluent and filled with "dudes." He got angry with how fighting dogs are demonized: "Fighting dogs are not dangerous to humans, dude." When a dog fights, he explained, there are usually three people in the pit, the two trainers and the referee; and if the dog wants to bite a person, it will leave itself open to the other dog and get killed, or the handler will kill it. Fighting dogs who bite people are not bred on. Of course, there are always assholes and drug dealers who get good fighting dogs and torture them and teach them bad habits, but that's not a true fighting dog, and those dogs don't fight well. "Anything in a bad person's hands can be a weapon," he said. But the trainers, the real ones, are good people, and have regular lives and kids in college and baseball practice and church.

The international centers for dogfighting are in North America, in the southern United States and in Mexico. Escorrega was careful about using real names, but he told me that he lived with one of the greatest dog breeders in the world in the United States. The dogs are bred in attempts to find that perfect balance of hard biting and stamina—but the most important trait for a fighting dog, a trait that can breed true, is *gameness*.

Gameness is a critical term to dogfighters, jiu-jitsu players, and fighters. It can be described as heart, as willingness to fight—a love of the fight stronger than a love of life. Some dogs don't last for ten minutes in a fight before they want to quit, and some dogs will die before they quit. I mentioned an acquaintance whose family in Louisiana had been in fighting dogs when he was a boy. This person said that he was always looking for a dog that would fight past forty-five minutes.

Escorrega nodded enthusiastically. "Not only heart, not just big lungs—what your friend was trying to say. People think we force the dogs to fight, but that's not true. The dogs are not created in laboratories— they are bred from dogs who love to fight. They train and run and swim in a pool, work on a treadmill, bite rawhide pull toys to develop the neck and bite and shoulders. They have a good diet, good carbohydrates, good fats, protein, creatine, vitamins, massage."

He smiled knowingly. "What your friend was talking about? All this care, you must love the animal, and if the animal loves you back, you will get a dog that fights past forty-five minutes, an animal with gameness. If there is love, the dog will fight to the death. Like everything, dude. Without it, the dog will not show heart. That's why the crazy assholes, the bastards that mistreat their dogs, don't have good fighting dogs. They have no love for their animals and no mercy for what they do. If you are fighting for something, you have to fight for what you love. If he doesn't love you, he's gonna quit. No one, no dog in the world, will fight for more than forty-five minutes without love and heart."

That's the secret: It's about love.

Olavo Abreu was the black belt who ran the *gi* classes at Top Team, although there were five or ten black belts who regularly showed up. He was a well-built man in his late thirties with unbelievably bad ears— the worst cauliflower of anyone I've seen. They looked like they came off the set of a Spielberg film. He was handsome and black-haired with a little gray creeping in, and swaggering and tough and spoke perfect English, peppered with profanities. It's funny how the *gi* makes you swagger a little, like a samurai in a Kurosawa film.

Olavo became my fountain of information, somewhat against his will, because I just kept coming in. Even though I couldn't train, I sat on the mats next to him, watching and asking questions: Who's going for what? What hold is that? Is that guy winning or losing that position? Olavo was a dedicated lifelong player, but he was not the best black belt around; in fact, there were a few blue and purple belts that gave him fits. He'd been teaching since he was a purple belt and had always liked it.

"I am not so good, man, there are a lot of guys better than me, but I understand jiu-jitsu, how to teach it," he said. He was dedicated— he was a brown belt for nine years before he got his black, and a great taskmaster, which is perhaps more important for this team. The *Cariocas* would sit around on the mats and chat for hours without him there to harangue them. The morning *gi* classes at Top Team were for those who compete in the *gi* and were hard core; they were all really good, even the lower belts. Strong and fierce and always attacking, on the move. They usually just needed a motivator, someone to yell at them to get back to training, and Olavo excelled at that.

The classes started with a warm-up, and then broke into groups, usually along belt lines, and went over a few different positions, perhaps a new sweep or a defense; and then quickly it became a sparring session. Everyone paired up, all belts with all belts, and went at it for five-minute rounds, sparring for forty-five minutes, an hour. Sweating, spinning, flipping, faces calm and unflappable, sometimes with eyes closed. Gripping and sweeping, an endless battle to control the hands through the sleeves, to grip and break the grip on the collar. Because there is no punching, just wrestling and submissions, a lot of fighters "pull guard" because they prefer to work from the bottom. You get points like in wrestling (two points for a sweep—reversing someone or taking him onto his back). When I was able to train, the trick was getting everyone to show me how they had just killed me, show me the defense, instead of just getting tapped every thirty seconds without trying to learn something.

Olavo was thirty-seven and a two-time Brazilian champ who had won a lot of other awards, but he had also suffered egregious injuries. He had his whole bicep torn off the bone in a bicep slice, a move that is now illegal. The doctor I visited knew him, and when the doctor told me I couldn't train for a while, I looked so despondent that he laughed and said that when he told Olavo to take two years off to rehab, Olavo cried, tears streaming down his cheeks. Jiu-jitsu was critical to Olavo's identity, and he took immense pride in his position and skills.

"Jiu-jitsu is like being a Jedi knight. . . . The knowledge is with you all the time—you dream it when you sleep, you can see it walking, it surrounds you. You go out alone but you are not alone because you have jiu-jitsu."

Every year, Olavo went to Abu Dhabi to teach jiu-jitsu to a sheik who had become a grappling enthusiast and some of his fighters. He'd spend three months living in a hotel and just training, all the time; the boredom was vicious, but the money was good. When he stayed abroad, away from his family, jiu-jitsu was his company. The name Abu Dhabi had become synonymous with the biggest grappling contest in the world, sponsored by that same sheik, with the best grapplers—and biggest purse.

Olavo started jiu-jitsu when he was eighteen, with Carlson and Murilo, who was a black belt, and Zé Mario, who was a brown belt. Olavo echoed a familiar sentiment: "Everything out of Murilo," which meant that Murilo Bustamante was the innovator and genius behind Top Team.

Sitting companionably with our backs to the padded wall, sometimes forced to move as a squirming, twisting pair rolled into us (there is no stopping if you roll off the mats; everyone is too intense for that), Olavo and I watched Teta methodically obliterate somebody. Teta was Olavo's teaching partner, just twenty-three years old but a Liborio black belt and very, very gifted; he had great hips. (Liborio was another founder of Top Team, a jiu-jitsu great who started American Top Team in Florida.) In jiu-jitsu, you work for something and patiently set it up, and the technique can be almost inevitable—not fast, not a reflex, but a slow and steady outthinking of your opponent. (There is a cultural difference in the way the Brazilians go for submissions—slow, steady, inexorable—versus the Japanese style, which is more about catching your opponent off guard, snatching something.) Teta was young and handsome, dark-skinned with fine features, and his ears were undestroyed. He was a professional jiu-jitsu instructor and an avid surfer, and his ex-wife, Gabrielle, was also a fighter who had won Mundials (and was my best friend in Brazil). Olavo was not disgruntled by his young partner; he respected him. Teta was part of the new evolution in jiu-jitsu.

"In the past, twenty-three years old was always a blue belt," Olavo said, referring to Teta, "but he is a black belt. And a good one. Now you can learn from everybody. Now the kids can know everything. Now it's a big sport."

Jiu-jitsu is artistic; and it's as much an expression of style as your clothes. Your personal style of jiu-jitsu reflects not only your teacher and background but also your body type and personality type. Carlson Gracie's style was more about power and attacking, and he is the stylistic grandfather of Top Team. Gracie Barra, a different gym under Carlinhos Gracie and a deep and bitter rival, is a more technical jiu-jitsu school, more about playing from the half-guard, endless sleeve- and hand-control games, sweeping. Every school and instructor develops their own style. Olavo's personal style is very Top Team, very much about power, control, almost like wrestling; while Teta, who is younger, stronger, and more talented than Olavo, with better hips, has a more open game. He is willing to work from anywhere, more willing to lose and give up position because he trusts his superior skills and talent to find a way out, to come up on top. Some styles don't match up, of course—Margarida beats Teta because he is so powerful and so smart about his strength. And so on. Styles make fights.

Olavo muttered in my ear, "You have to learn from everybody, and stay open-minded, learn and watch carefully: Observation is critical. Watch how they grip. Guys who have been to a lot of different schools are very good because they learn so many different techniques. Now there is so much interchange that we have a lot of broad innovation and spreading ideas."

Being willing to lose is important, to take risks, to find new ways of doing things; I've heard this again and again from different fighters. Even back at Pat Miletich's place there was a guy who was great on the ground but too unwilling to give up position, content to sit in closed guard, and he was criticized for it; you're never going to learn anything that way. Maybe from one position you do it wrong, or you are too tired, but then you discover a new position. It's critical to remain open-minded, to let the new position come.

Olavo was also adamant about competition. "You can be good, but without fighting you cannot be a real fighter. You have to fight to learn—you have to feel the power in a tournament, when everyone is watching and the guy is trying to kill you."

I was starting to see things, to see what people were giving up, to see where a guy should go in a position, but I had no faith in my ability to remember without actually training. Toward the end of my stay, I did feel better, and I started to train a little bit, only to promptly reaggravate my poor, wussy shoulder. So I was back on the wall for good.

Olavo made an interesting point about jiu-jitsu players: "When they put on the *gi* and step onto the mat, the social differences disappear, and Rio is a land of great social differences. A judge and a street cleaner can be friends. . . . For me everybody is the same. Everybody has respect. Policeman, ex-criminal, everyone. One guy is rich, one guy is walking the street with no shoes; on the mat they are the same. The black guy over there was a thief—to me it's nothing. I don't care."

The best way to think about jiu-jitsu in Rio is to compare it to pickup basketball games in the United States, in the fanciest white-collar gyms or the most informal parking lots. Everyone, regardless of skill level, plays a little. You have bankers and lawyers alongside high school kids and blue-collar workers, and they all go after one another. Like street basketball, you go to the same gym and roll with the same guys for years. It's as much for the camaraderie as for the workout. There is tremendous respect; when you enter and leave the mats, you bow and shake hands with everyone there, even if it's thirty guys.

Of course, Top Team was something else entirely. Those guys didn't do anything but train and condition. It's like playing pickup basketball with the '95 Chicago Bulls.

Zé Mario Sperry was in the thick of it, his heavy, powerful body roiling and sweaty, upending and controlling his partner with devastating power. Sperry was thirty-eight years old, a founding member of Top Team, and a driving force behind its success. He trained and worked out obsessively, compulsively, almost manically. His suicidal work ethic was at odds with his conversational ease and laid-back manner. "Every day I have to go home and rest at night, take care of myself and rest, because tomorrow, I swear to God, I swear on the soul of my unborn baby, that I have to come to the gym and try to kill a lion," he said, and then broke into a laugh, mostly at himself.

Lion killing is a familiar theme; there is a basic choke called the *mate leão,* the lion killer, for its power and deadliness.

Zé (short for José) reminded me several times that he had a degree in economics, as did Murilo Bustamante. They could easily have been doing other things—they were connected and from good families in Rio—but there was nothing out there for them as rewarding as fighting. They both had been training full-time for at least twenty years. "After training for five months, and you are finally in the ring, facing a great opponent, you have been preparing and living for this moment . . . sometimes you can feel the presence of God. Your soul comes out. It's a very addictive feeling."

Zé's father was an officer in the air force, and he grew up in Leblon, one of the nicest areas in Rio. He started martial arts when he was ten years old, on a doctor's recommendation for his excess energy, and eventually became attached to Carlson Gracie's school. Murilo was already a blue belt, and they ended up being the prime movers on Carlson's famous *vale tudo* team, a team that was made up of legends.

Zé had always been a dominant fighter, right from the beginning, and he submitted most of his opponents in jiu-jitsu tournaments in the *gi,* instead of winning on points. He started fighting *vale tudo* when he was twenty-five, and his immense strength and berserk work ethic proved a winning combination, leading him to Japan in 2000. He had fought in

Pride several times since. Eventually, in the nineties, Carlson went to teach in the United States, and the team, left behind, began to go its own way, eventually leading to a complete split from the Gracie family. For a while, they were "Carlson Gracie's ex-students," until Murilo spontaneously came out with "Brazilian Top Team" at a Pride press conference; now there are copycat "Top Teams" all over the globe.

Murilo Bustamante is the other iconic figure at Top Team, the longest practicing and most thoughtful; he was also thirty-eight and had been a black belt since twenty-one. As one of the greatest technical jiu-jitsu players of all time and a yoga practitioner, he was truly a spiritual fighter and in great demand. He was nearly always on the road, to Sweden, Russia, Japan, and the United States, giving seminars and cornering fighters, so I didn't see him around the gym much.

One day at the gym, I got lucky, however, and we had a discussion about steroids and how they had changed the fight game. In Brazil, protein and creatine were expensive, while a cycle of steroids was easily available and cost maybe fifteen dollars U.S. Murilo lamented that it had changed not only the fighters but also the game itself; it was much more about power and aggression now, as the steroids affected the mind and temperament as much as the body. It was obvious who was using and who was not; the bulk and size of certain fighters were like flags flying in the wind—fighters who went from sixty-five kilos to more than a hundred in a few years. Just compare "all-natural" bodybuilders to those who aren't; your eyes are the best test for who is on steroids.

Murilo was a Carlson Gracie black belt who fought in the old *vale tudo* matches, and I imagine it had been hard for him to leave Carlson. He'd spent two years trying to heal the rift between Zé and Carlson and change Carlson's mind before he ended up following Zé to Top Team.

And then there was Rodrigo. Like the first time I saw Zé or Murilo, I was slightly starstruck when I met Rodrigo Nogueira, Top Team's biggest fighter, a hero in Japan and Brazil. I had watched his fights in Pride, and you can learn so much about a person by watching him fight that you feel you know him. Zé once told me, "It's why everyone is an expert; because you identify so strongly with the fighter. You think it's you up there." A. J. Liebling wrote about taking a friend to the fights who had never been, and within two bouts the friend was an expert, talking about what the loser should have done. That's an interesting side of masculinity, the way male fight fans and writers always know what a fighter should do, how he could win—expertise derived from watching fights on TV. Or a fan will say, "He's got no heart," about a fighter who has forty pro fights. I always think, What the fuck do you know about heart?

Rodrigo was twenty-eight years old and the youngest dominant fighter on Top Team. There was a triumvirate of him, Zé, and Murilo. Zé and Murilo were kind of the older brothers, the wise and experienced warriors, but Rodrigo was at the height of his powers. There were other famed BTT fighters, Ricardo Arona and Vitor Belfort, who trained elsewhere, in São Paolo or the United States.

After a morning training session, I rode with Rodrigo up to his house in a big, gleaming silver Land Rover with several other fighters and trainers, part of the champ's retinue. Rodrigo, coming up later than Zé and Murilo, had made big money. He was the fighter all the hungry young kids wanted to emulate. We bombed through the streets of Rio listening to the White Stripes and the Strokes.

Rodrigo's house was the nicest I came across in Rio, a giant place with high ceilings and dark wood interiors set on a massive cliff between São Conrado and Barra, right over the ocean. The day was an absolute sparkler, and I could see for thirty miles, the shipping coming into Rio, the little islands off the coast. Below us, the heavy swell surged on the rocks. Rodrigo leapt into his pool and called one of his dogs, a massive white mastiff, over to him, and then pulled the dog in, laughing.

Rodrigo was big at maybe 230 pounds and strong, but not muscle bound; indeed, for the Pride heavyweights, he was slender and normal-looking. His face was a handsome but battered mass, with a heavy square jaw, slightly uneven eyes, all angles and planes. He was famous for shaking off huge blows, weathering killer punches, but the evidence was on his face. He had become something of a sex symbol in Japan, ever since a top Japanese model said that she thought he was very handsome. And he was, in a rough-and-tumble way; he'd had his cheek and face broken several times by both Fedor Emelianenko and Bob Sapp. His ears were a mess, the left in particular a fleshy nub that looked like something out of *Star Wars*. Rodrigo was most appealing when he smiled or laughed, because his face was totally transformed. His smile was huge, and his eyes were squeezed to slits, and you could feel the good nature radiating off him like heat.

Rodrigo and his twin brother, Rogerio, who fought at around 205, were from a small town in the northeast, Vitória da Conquista, and their childhood sounds like a cross between García Marquez and Quentin Tarantino. Their father was an accountant and their mother a physical trainer, and they owned a coffee plantation as a kind of hobby, a place to go to out of the city. Rodrigo had a very active childhood. He would ride horses and bulls, and once he rode a horse all day long until the horse finally fainted dead away. You got the sense that Rodrigo's strength and stamina were on a slightly different plane from everyone else's.

The formative event of his young life happened when he was eleven. He was behind a truck on the farm when it suddenly backed over him. It ruptured internal organs and shattered ribs, and should have killed him. His brother tried to pull him out but couldn't; trapped beneath the truck, Rodrigo was sure he was going to die. Yet somehow he didn't; instead, he spent eleven months in a hospital bed and couldn't walk for about a year and a half. He had a lot of complications in the hospital—staph infections, lung infections. It's hard to know how the darkness affected him, the stillness, the endless hours of self-contemplation for a boy who wasn't self-contemplative. "I prayed a lot," he said simply. He came to know his body extremely well, and essentially he showed he was too tough to die. He wasn't a talker, especially about himself; he was a jock and a larger-than-life athlete, but I think that ordeal strengthened him, mentally—as I said, in jiu-jitsu a setback can be turned to an advantage.

His recovery was complete, however, and the wild boy didn't slow down much. The best Rodrigo story I heard happened when he was about sixteen. At a Halloween party, he and his brother stole a university skeleton that had been placed on the lawn as a joke. During the course of the night, the skeleton got lost, and neither brother could remember where. When an irate professor called the next day, demanding the return of his skeleton and threatening police involvement, Rodrigo begged for a little time, as he and his brother had had enough problems with the police already. At boarding school, Rodrigo had a maid whose boyfriend worked in a cemetery, and she said she could get him a skeleton.

Well, from one of the caves for the anonymous dead she got him a partially decomposed body, maggots and all, and Rodrigo took the body back home *on the bus*. The smell was so horrible the bus had all the windows down, even though it was winter. Somehow Rodrigo got the body home without being detected. From a doctor friend the brothers learned that they should leave the bones out, covered with chlorine, to bleach the skeleton; and so thinking they were finally in the clear, they placed the body on the roof of their family's house to bleach for a week while they returned to boarding school. Unfortunately, across the street was a police station. Curious about the decomposing body on the roof, the police stormed his father's house. Rodrigo got a call from his furious father and had to explain everything. Like I said, Marquez and Tarantino, and maybe a little Monty Python.

What made Rodrigo so dangerous in the ring was that he believed in jiu-jitsu; he trusted it. When a fighter goes for a submission and tries to win a fight, he often sacrifices superior position, because if the opponent is knowledgeable, then the submission fails and the fighter ends up on the bottom, or worse. Rodrigo attempted submissions all the time, and most of them failed; that's the way it is in modern MMA, where every fighter is highly skilled and schooled in submission fighting. Most fighters play it safe and work the ground only for position and to punch, without risking themselves. Rodrigo was a notable exception. He took huge risks and gave up position without a second thought because he believed in himself—in his jiu-jitsu—and it is precisely that belief that made him so dangerous. He *did* catch people all the time; fighters who had been avoiding submissions for fifteen years got caught by him.

Jiu-jitsu looks sort of simple, and there are only a certain number of submissions—arm-bar, rear naked choke, triangle, for example—that one can do, but there are infinite variations, because it is all about how you get those things done: whether you can set them up right, whether you can get them done against tough opponents who are strong. I can put a triangle on somebody who doesn't know what it is and get it to work, but it takes an extraordinary player, like Rodrigo, to sink one on a Mark Coleman, who has been pounding people at the top level for ten years. Submitting Mark Coleman is like acing Andre Agassi—it can be done, but it has to be so strong fundamentally and so well set up technically that it becomes unavoidable. Submitting someone like Fedor is even harder, as he is a sambo (a Russian derivative of judo, jiu-jitsu, and wrestling) specialist and an athlete at the apogee of the sport. It's like dunking on Shaq: You have to be extraordinary *and* having the best day of your life.

One night, after his muay Thai workout, I found Zé after the sun had long set and the red evening was darkening to monochrome. He unwrapped his hands, moving slowly, explaining to me some of his philosophy, the importance of the team.

Fighting is the most solitary form of competition; you are all alone out there. But what I hear again and again is how important the team is, and not just from the Brazilians, but from other MMA fighters as well. The team is what gets you there. Team members train and spar and cajole you, push you through the rigors and hellish boredom of training, and they support you and protect you from nerves in the days and hours leading up to a fight. Fighting is, strangely enough, a team sport. Zé said, "These guys, they are all studying jiu-jitsu ten years or more. They are strong, their bodies are very developed. Now we must develop their minds and spirits. The brotherhood protects you and makes you better; the most important thing is respect and honor and friendship. Union and respect and family sense are what are going to make you strong in the ring."

I ask: What's the most important aspect of the ground game? What's the key to ground fighting? What should I focus on? The answer, when it comes from Zé or Murilo, is enlightening: humility. Always assume that your opponent is better than you, that he knows more—you have to work harder in training and learn more. You know only 5 percent of what there is to know. Fight your own pride and ego and be open-minded and always learning new techniques, new things from anyone.

It was very revealing to me that these Brazilians, the greatest ground fighters in the world, should say that the most important thing, the biggest technical secret they can disclose, is for a fighter to remain humble.

As I walked home in the deepening dusk, I was convinced of one thing: that the ground game, in the *gi* and out, is almost infinitely deep. There are layers within layers—the places where Tony DeSouza and Teta and Margarida and other young innovators go, the levels of complexity, are deep and, to me, nearly unfathomable. One needs years and years to comprehend. That, however, is the pure ground game, pure grappling. MMA is a far looser, faster game; being able to punch and kick alters things radically, and many great ground fighters have been stymied by good strikers who could avoid their game. I wondered if this time Nogueira would be able to catch Fedor in something. Would he be able to lure Fedor into his realm? It was going to be the biggest fight of Nogueira's life, in Tokyo on New Year's Eve. I wanted to go. I pitched it to *Rolling Stone* as *Lost in Translation* but with Brazilian fighters instead of Scarlett Johansson, and they bought it.

* * *

I was ready for Tokyo to be cold, imposing, impersonal, and maddeningly foreign, but it was more complex and alive than that. I found it strangely friendly, despite the walls of neon. It was clean, cozy, and small. The streets were narrow, with alleys winding and twisting from any angle, and there were little coffee shops and bars and noodle shops tucked away in every cranny and corner.

Everywhere had about 30 percent more people than New York; there was a constant, somewhat uncomfortable press, all around, nearly all the time. The language barrier, while formidable, was not so isolating that I felt confined to my hotel. There was a wall of non-meaning in everything, every sign and every muttered conversation overheard, but as I was coming from Brazil, it didn't seem so strange. It was horrifically expensive, but that was avoidable: I used the subway, I ate in little noodle shops by choosing from pictures on the menu, and nobody seemed too put out by the tall *gaijin*.

Pride Fighting Championship was begun in 1997, aping the Ultimate Fighting Championship in the United States and for ostensibly the same reasons: to provide an "anything goes" format to decide which fighter and style are the strongest. The early Prides were a mess of mismatches and boring fights, as wrestlers fought boxers and savagery triumphed over all. There were some good fights, some diamonds in the rough, but also a lot of bad ones (and perhaps "worked" ones; in Japan, the barrier between pro wrestling and MMA is porous). Since then, Pride has evolved to the point where there are often many great fights on a single card. This is mostly because of money; Pride is far and away where fighters can earn the most. As Zé said, "If there is something else, tell me about it, because I'd love to know." Essentially, there isn't anything else with Pride money out there, except for a competing Japanese production, K-1, which started as a kickboxing event and has branched out into MMA. The UFC in the United States doesn't come close to matching Pride in terms of purse, at least not for the undercard. Fighters around the world, with the exception of the few top guys the UFC takes care of, go to Pride if they can.

After I arrived, I found Zé, Rodrigo, and Rogerio, along with the rest of the retinue (Amaury Bitetti; Rodrigo's two coaches; Danillo, the training partner; and Marco, the Italian), as they were blearily nodding over their noodles, just off the plane. I followed them up to their rooms.

I was a little nervous about the sleeping arrangements, but I managed to tag along and force my way into the gang, and Zé shuffled me off with the boxing coach, Luis Dórea, and the muay Thai coach, Luis Alvez. They had no idea who I was and seemed particularly nonplussed when I shouldered my way into their room with my bag and started camping out by the window, unrolling my sleeping bag and pulling a cushion off the chair for a pillow. I don't think they ever quite bought the idea that I was really a writer, but they didn't care too much—it was a Brazilian kind of scene; there's always somebody tagging along.

On their second day in Japan, we all woke early, jet-lagged and groggy, and went down to the gym to run and lift a little. Then I sat with Zé in the sauna, and we sweated and soaked and then showered off on the little stools in front of the mirrors, feeling a little like giants in playland.

We met up for the fabled breakfast at the Tokyo Hilton. It was the only good thing about this trip for most of the guys, who had already been to Japan eight or nine times that year. It was an elaborate, silver-service buffet affair with great food and attentive waiters, and it cost upward of thirty-five dollars per person. We had some complimentary passes and ate in relaxed splendor. The trick was to show the dining ticket but not get it taken away, so that you could use it again. Amaury, a friend and former fighter on Carlson's team who'd trained with Pat Miletich, was a jiu-jitsu instructor in Florida—and spoke no English. He ate like a hero, endless cups of good coffee, fresh-squeezed juice. Breakfast was the high point of the day, the only time besides training when we were all together, and we would sit there for hours, dawdling and chatting and snacking.

I would sit in the middle of the babble of Portuguese and, if I concentrated, understand the gist of what was being said; but often I would just relax, and it would fade into a comfortable mumble. They talked about fighting, of course. The boxing coach, Luis Dórea, had several good fighters in Los Angeles, as well as a half dozen Brazilian prospects, and both he and Luis Alvez had been to Japan many times that year for various fighters. Zé Mario had been there ten times, once staying for four days, flying back to Brazil for five days, and then turning around and flying back to Japan, a thirty-hour flight.

There was an evil hostess, the Dragon Lady, who became aware that we were trying to rip off the hotel, and she watched us like a hawk, confiscating all our tickets at every meal. It became obvious that we were going to play a game; we were engaged in a duel. I was going to try to wring everything from the hotel for free, and she would try to catch me. Everything fights, even the hostesses.

We would work out in the hotel in the mornings and train at night, slogging through the cold to a special room a few blocks from the hotel in a residential part of Shinjuku, wandering between skyscrapers like kayakers drifting amid icebergs. Zé would bravely lead the way, the stalwart soldier, and like ducklings, the Brazilians would fall in behind him, using him as a windbreak, wilting in the icy blast. Rodrigo and Rogerio always took a cab. The building we trained in, situated on a tiny one-lane street with quiet people bicycling past, seemed almost abandoned. Rodrigo would work out for maybe an hour: grapple, then spar, then work pads with Dórea and Alvez.

One night, the liaison woman from Pride came in with some urgent news: Sakuraba had gotten hurt. Sakuraba was a storied Japanese fighter who had crossed over from pro wrestling and become famous as the "Gracie Killer" when he beat Royce, Royler, Renzo, and Ryan Gracie, and he had fought some of the legendary fights of Pride. Wanderlei Silva, a Brazilian fighter who was undefeated in four years of Pride, had beaten the living shit out of Sakuraba three times, and they were going to fight a fourth time, but Sakuraba had busted a rib (I felt his pain) and was dropping out of the fight. The woman translator asked Zé half jokingly (but half seriously) if he or Rogerio would be able to step in and fight. Wanderlei was nicknamed the "Ax Murderer," with good reason. Zé shook his head strongly that neither was ready, and he was absolutely right. They weren't ready for Wanderlei; he ate fighters like them for breakfast (Wanderlei was at the height of his powers and seemed invincible). I think Zé could've fought Wanderlei and beaten him if he had been super prepared, in the best shape of his life. He would've needed a strategy and a plan and months and months to mentally prepare, because the Ax Murderer handled jiu-jitsu guys like they were tissue paper. Wanderlei was the principal fighter for a team called Chute-Box, which traced its roots to the old battles of *box Thailandes* and *luta livre* with the Gracie students. He was a stand-up fighter, a devastating striker with boundless animal ferocity.

Zé, Rodrigo, and Rogerio were whisked away to meet with a Yakuza boss who was a longtime fan and friend for dinner in secret, and I walked home in the dark with Amaury and Marco (another friend and trainer) and thought about the Yakuza guy I'd fought years ago, whether he was here and whether he ever thought of me.

* * *

The Brazilians came to Japan earlier than anyone else; we were still two weeks out from the fight. They came in order to have time to acclimate, to adjust to the cold and the time of a different hemisphere.

Rodrigo and I had plenty of time to chat in the idle hours, wandering the streets, dawdling on the way to and from meals, and I kept after him, pestering him about the past and the present.

When he first fought Fedor, he had had back trouble for a long time and two hernias from surfing that had never been properly dealt with. For a while, he had been barely able to walk, but through extensive rehab overseas he began to get better—and then he beat a Japanese fighter named Kikuta and returned to Rio. While he was in Rio, the Pride organization asked him to fight Bob Sapp. When Rodrigo told them his back was a mess and tried to decline the fight, Pride threatened to strip him of the heavyweight title. In desperation, he called his rehab doctor in Holland, who laughed and said, "Well, it's going to be a big test for you."

Rodrigo still had trouble walking and couldn't sit or stand for more than ten minutes or so without pain, and so had to keep alternating, which made flying interesting. Bob Sapp was the former NFL lineman who weighed 355 pounds. Zé assured Rodrigo that he could beat Sapp, that he had a strategy, and Rodrigo allowed himself to be convinced. Then, when he actually got in the ring with Sapp and looked up at the size of him, he couldn't believe that he'd taken the fight. His strategy went out the window, and he shot right away for Sapp's legs ("shooting for shoelaces," as a wrestler might say). Sapp grabbed him and bounced him on his head. Rodrigo came to with Bob Sapp on top of him, punching him in the face, breaking his cheek and eyebrow. That fight was one of the classic MMA fights of all time: Rodrigo hung on and found a way to submit Sapp.

Rodrigo's back still wasn't healed when it was time to fight Fedor. "For like two months I was not walking well. I was coming down in my shape, and he was in the best shape he's ever been in" was Rodrigo's take on their first fight. I'd seen the fight on DVD, and Rodrigo got pounded pretty thoroughly, and the camera kept showing pretty Japanese girls crying on the sidelines.

The second time they fought, Rodrigo's back was better, and he felt that Fedor was not in such good shape. The fight was stopped after a huge gash was opened on Fedor's head by a head butt ruled "accidental," and the fight was declared a "no contest."

In the months leading up to this next fight, Rodrigo trained twice a week with people at the gym who were supposed to act like Fedor, and Danillo supposedly fell into that category. As far as I could see, he didn't grapple like Fedor at all; he would pull guard. Murilo was more technical, his game was similar to Rodrigo's, and he was the calm spiritual *mestre*. Zé pushed Rodrigo hard and was always there, working and yelling. When they came to fight, Zé never relaxed.

As for my unwilling roommates, Luis Dórea and Luis Alvez: I watched Dórea work with Rod and he was good, a real pro, and Rod's boxing was smooth and hard. Rod said that Dórea was a good boxer; he just knew a lot about fighting, and was an excellent corner. He could manage the fight.

"And he always plays me up, makes me feel good, tells me about how I am better than my opponent all the time," Rodrigo said. Dórea had been brought in to raise Rodrigo's boxing, to build him up; and part of that is mental. Dórea had to convince Rodrigo that he was faster than Fedor.

Luis Alves was an old-school muay Thai trainer who didn't do much but seemed to be there because he'd been with Rodrigo for a long time. Rodrigo knew him and trusted him.

With a week to go, we entered a time of boredom. That was actually the hidden test of fighting: the deadly waiting. Everything, our common will and strength, was bent to the purpose of getting Rodrigo to the fight—in the purest, strongest, readiest state—and prepared to peak at ten forty-five p.m. on New Year's Eve. He had been training hard, and we were also focused on getting him rested, allowing his body to heal, allowing his stamina to recover while maintaining the knife's edge of strength.

W. C. Heinz wrote a classic novel about boxing called *The Professional,* and in it he describes the task of bringing a fighter to his apogee: "It is one of the most difficult of scientific endeavors, this struggle to bring an athlete up the mountains of his efforts to the peak of his performance at the precise moment when he must perform. That peak place is no bigger than the head of a pin, shrouded in the clouded mysteries of a living being, and so, although all try, most fail, for it requires not only the most diligent of climbers but the greatest of guides."

On Christmas Eve, determined not to lose to the Dragon Lady, I took one of the last of the free breakfast passes down the streets of Shinjuku to a Kinko's copy shop and made color copies on special, thick colored paper and meticulously cut them out—and kept everyone in breakfasts. The forgeries weren't perfect, but nobody was looking for them. I also had to carefully conceal my presence from the maids who cleaned the room or they'd start charging us for the extra person.

Luiz Alvez started calling me gringo *traquina,* for a TV commercial with a naughty kid who was always doing the wrong thing, and Zé liked it. They gave me grief, but took the passes when they needed them. They had accepted me as a member of the motley crew.

One day, for a break, we took a bunch of cabs to Meiji-jingu, the major Shinto shrine in Harajuku. Zé sat beside me in the cab, eyes bloodshot, grumbling and muttering. He wanted to be home in Rio, in the sun. He had an e-mail from a friend that said the surf was big. These guys didn't really want to be here; the magic was gone, and they were just here for one thing: to get Rodrigo through, to deliver him to that one day, that one moment, in as close to perfect shape and mental condition as possible. It is hard to miss the holidays, hard to be away from family.

We wandered down leafy boulevards beneath the shrine's massive gates, clowned a little, and took photos. As with any group of male professional athletes, there was a lot of farting and general hilarity.

It was cold, and the sun filtered weakly through the winter sky. Danillo made fun of the Japanese until Rodrigo gave him just a hint of a remonstrative look; and when we entered the shrine proper, Rodrigo quietly put a finger to his lips, enough to hush us all.

The shrine was extensive, and the grounds seemed to cover hundreds of acres; the architecture was classically Japanese: so utterly balanced that it calmed the soul.

The days crawled by, and then suddenly other fighters were glimpsed here and there, some old friends, some old rivals, as the big night approached. More and more fans stopped Rodrigo and Rogerio and Zé in the streets, asking for autographs. Fighters in Japan are revered. I would watch as salarymen in suits would get autographs and run off literally skipping with joy.

One morning, in the sauna, I asked Zé why he thought Rodrigo had had such success, and he ruminated in the heat for a few moments, sweat running in streams down his face. "He learns very, very fast. When he came to Top Team, he was okay but big and strong and fearless and he feels very little pain; and he got very good very fast." Rodrigo at one point even went to Cuba to train with its Olympic boxing team for three months. He learned like a sponge, soaking everything up. Zé, nostalgic for his own youth, wished he could have gone with him.

"Rodrigo is a good friend with a good heart," Zé told me, "and he's psychologically very strong because of that. Physically he's ready. now we just have to keep him believing in the strategy that we have been training. Move, box—Rod is faster—explode, get a good position, and let him make mistakes."

Zé paused, and shrugged elaborately. "I'm not arrogant," he said. "We could be wrong."

Rulon Gardner is an American wrestling legend. He won gold in Olympics past and bronze recently at heavyweight, and he famously retired by leaving his shoes on the mat. Somehow he was here to fight Yoshida, a Japanese Olympic legend in judo. The gimmick was gold medal in judo versus gold medal in wrestling. I'd seen Yoshida fight; he'd fought several times in Pride, and he was a tough guy. I couldn't help but wonder what the hell Rulon was doing, and if he was ready for the gi. Yoshida was one of only a few who still fought in a gi, and I was sensitive to the nightmare of the gi for the uninitiated.

I caught up with Rulon in the hotel and asked him, basically, why? And why start here, at Pride? Why not start a little smaller, in front of fewer people?

I found out that Rulon was here with Team Quest, an American MMA team with some terrific fighters who were extremely experienced at taking wrestlers and turning them into MMA fighters, as they were all former wrestlers. Dan Henderson, who was on the U.S. National Wrestling Team with Rulon, was a longtime Pride fighter who was on the same card as the Rulon-Yoshida fight; and Randy Couture, another member of Team Quest, was one of the most amazing stories in modern MMA, a man who had won and retained the UFC light heavyweight crown (205 pounds) at the age of forty-one. Couture was probably the smartest fighter I'd ever seen, and he made a habit of giant-slaying people who were supposed to cream him. When I realized that Rulon was here with those guys, I relaxed. They would have him ready. But the questioned remained: Why?

The answer was funny, when it finally came: Rulon was tired of being a victim. He had been wrestling all over the world for sixteen years, and he'd received numerous threats; people have wanted to fight him, hurt him, even kill him. "I wondered if I could defend myself.

. . . I knew I could wrestle, but I was apprehensive about the goal of hurting somebody." He looked me in the eye and said, "It's like women learning self-defense and becoming more confident in self-defense situations." Which is a little absurd; Rulon is 295 pounds of power and muscle, fueled by Olympic-caliber speed and skill. Yet here he was, telling me he was wondering whether he could physically defend himself.

The other interesting facet was his strategy. Rulon had a nice-guy image; he was not one of those angry wrestlers who wanted to punish people. "As a wrestler, it's about respect—you're not actually trying to hurt somebody. . . . I'm here for the test." Of course, this was at odds with the strategy he confided to me, a secret I could not divulge before the fight: Rulon was going to try to knock Yoshida out standing. He had been working on his hands for a few months and was confident. He was not going to play Yoshida's game on the ground and risk getting sucked into the *gi*. He had a beatific smile on his face when he told me, "Striking is your friend; if it's not your friend, you have no ally on your feet. I am going to hurt him a little bit."

There were still plenty of lulls, and I stayed in Rodrigo's ear. I wanted to know what he was thinking about Fedor.

"I can tell you right now, he's stronger, but I am technically superior. I have to move. When you fight at that level, anything can happen, but I can box him, and I want to play with him on the ground." Rodrigo actually sort of liked Fedor, and he knew that there was the need for a fighter to have big opponents. Ali had Liston, Frazier, Foreman; and Roy Jones Jr., in his prime, had nobody. A great opponent raises you up. "He pushes me—I'm much better than I was two years ago," Rodrigo said. "Before I had him, I felt like, I am going to train for what?"

Rodrigo had some theories about his strange popularity with the Japanese. First of all, there was the hype—they were excited about this fight. Second, Rodrigo thought it had to do with the purity of his technique; he's not a big muscle head, yet he beats the big guys. In a way, he'd brought technique back into style. The Japanese loved him because he was something of an everyman.

"I show how a small guy can win. I make good fights." He briefly digressed into the different kinds of fighters, those who are in it for money and those who are in it for the heart. Because MMA has so much more to it than boxing, fighters need to love martial arts from an early age. He pointed to Bob Sapp as an example, "Bob is just in it for money. He just picked up fighting and MMA recently—he will never be as good because his heart is not in it."

Girls approached shyly, heads bobbing, and asked for Rodrigo's autograph and to take pictures with him; he agreed, in return for phone numbers. He had sacrificed so much during his life to be a fighter—you give up your young adulthood, going out and drinking and having fun. He whispered to me, "I make a lot of sacrifice, but the only thing I cannot stop is girls." Then he burst out laughing.

Rodrigo genuinely enjoyed Japan, and not just for the adulation and the money. He appreciated the respect shown to fighters there. He told stories of an ancient woman who sold noodles accosting him to tell him how beautiful his jiu-jitsu was, how strong his *juji gatame* (arm-bar) was, and of a ninety-six-year-old man who told Rodrigo that he was samurai. They appreciated the purity of his technique. "In America and Brazil, they like you because you are on TV, or are making money, but here they respect your fighting spirit." He laughed, because his first MMA fights were in the United States, and people thought he was a Mexican and would scream, "Kill that Mexican!" to his opponents; in Japan they scream things like "Go forward!" and "Be brave!"

Modern Japanese culture seems strange to Westerners. On the plane I sat next to a Japanese woman who had published a book of short stories, and she told me that the trains were often late now, from the suicides leaping onto the tracks. There are suicide pacts, endemically forming on the Internet between strangers and adolescents. There is a word in Japanese, *otaku,* for rampant faddism, like the anime craze. Pride and MMA are part of this; they are popular in part simply because they are popular. As Hikari, a friend who was born in America but had spent the last six years in Tokyo, mentioned to me, there is the exoticism of the foreigners, the alien and extraordinary bodies of the fighters, from the freakishly big like Bob Sapp and Giant Silva to the bodybuilder-muscular like Kevin Randleman. There is a peculiar dynamic of envy and disgust, of avarice and disdain, that the Japanese feel toward foreigners, toward the Western body.

There were some old friends there to fight; Jens Pulver was there with Jeremy Horn, and also Monte Cox, the promoter who screwed me in Iowa. I don't hold a grudge—Monte's a promoter. I can't blame him for following his nature.

Jens has been fighting pro boxing (on ESPN2, no less) and winning. He was very confident coming into his fight with Gomi, who was considered one of the best in the world, as was Jens. For little guys, theirs was a marquee fight, coming near the end of the night. As Danillo remarked, Gomi was much bigger; he came down to 160 from 180, and Jens had come up; he'd been boxing at 142. Just the fact that he'd been boxing pro and had won his last four fights made me think that he was going to kill Gomi, whom I'd never seen do anything besides land a lucky knee in a few seconds to a shooting Ralph Gracie.

Fighting, especially in America, is always about heavyweights, and the money is a reflection of that. Lighter weights are usually better fights, because of the speed and the lightening of punching power. Heavyweights have to be so conservative, as any punch can be a KO, while the lightweight fighters can throw big punches without as much fear of instant obliteration. Even mediocre heavyweights get the big purses if properly hyped. This is true in boxing, and also true in MMA. People just want to see the biggest and baddest guys in the world.

Fight fans who can understand the technical aspects of the sport usually end up supporting the lighter fighters; in Thailand, where the crowds are very educated, the biggest fights of the night were under 120 pounds (although the Thais are, admittedly, smaller).

Jens, thirty years old and a five-time UFC champ at 155 pounds, had been dealing with the disparity his whole career. He ruminated that "for lighter guys, the money just isn't there. I left the dollar value behind. I used to look for the payday, but I don't anymore. I'm a little guy. Little guys have got to stay active and keep it entertaining—that's what little guys do.

"The first few times, the payday thing really got to me; my biggest fight had a payday of twenty grand, and some of these medium-talented heavyweights are getting paid three or four times that much just to show up—not even to win. Why not me? Twenty grand for eight months isn't that much."

Jens was one of my favorite fighters to watch at Miletich's place— he threw bombs and horribly heavy body shots. Like Bas Rutten, he was a devotee of the liver shot, a hard punch to the liver that can freeze a guy, and end the fight. I asked him about the switch to professional boxing.

"Boxing is just as tiring as MMA. It's a whole different world—so fast, so many combinations, you have to let your hands go otherwise you lose. . . . Even if you block everything and slip and move, you still lose the round." Jens was just trying to keep busy as a fighter and make a living, which in MMA is hard to do. The UFC, the only game in town for most Americans, had eliminated the 155-pound weight class. Jens had been boxing for eight hundred dollars a fight, but it kept the ring-rust off.

Jens was a short, slender man with a handsome, dark, batlike face and strikingly different-colored eyes. He had a Mohawk for this fight, and he was pale and vampiric. It was his "bad intentions" that gave him the sobriquet "Little Evil," however: He went into the fight to knock somebody out.

He was happy to be back at MMA but aware of the complications: There were so many ways to lose. "My first two losses were ankle and feet submissions—who would have thought I had to protect my feet?

"It's still small enough, it's like a get-together every time. You get to see all your old friends. Boxing isn't like that at all. There is no friendliness, you got cornermen trying to punk you out, all you got is your own people. With MMA it almost sucks to have an opponent because you don't get to talk to him until the fight's over."

Before this fight, Jens had been boxing at 142, which changed his whole body type because he had stopped lifting weights. He had two months to get up to weight, and he made 160, but Gomi had an advantage because he was coming down from 185. Jens respected Gomi, who had lost to B. J. Penn (whom Jens beat many years before and many think now is the best in the world), but Gomi had been on a tear since then. He was 4–0, and he used his size and strength to ground and pound. Jens was confident that if he could keep Gomi on his feet, however, he could make something happen.

Jens spoke freely, pausing every once and again to spit tobacco into a cup. "There is so much to know in MMA. You can't wait for your opponent. You have to ignore him and not preoccupy yourself with what he's going to do—if you think about all the things he's going to do, you'll freeze: You have to focus on what you are going to do to him. Worrying about his offense will hurt yours.

"I'll probably have to outwrestle Gomi, but if I can get him standing for two minutes, I have to capitalize on that."

Jens had coauthored a book on his own life that was published on a small scale, and in it he detailed a horrific home life with his abusive father. Jens was a little crazy. The joke at Miletich's place was

"Whenever you're sparring Jens, he thinks you're his father, and Jens *hates* his father."

But at thirty, in a hotel room in Tokyo, Jens sounded remarkably sane to me. "I don't need to be scared to death to fight hard; I just want to perform well. If a guy wants to fight me in the street, well, I got nothing for you." He shook his head.

"It's not aggression. Aggression will get you beat. Those guys who have to black out to fight, or who get nausea . . . I just want to know that my skills are better." This was Little Evil, so I wasn't sure whether I believed him. I had seen how emotional he could be when he won—he was crying when he first took the UFC lightweight title.

Jens thought Gomi was a momentum fighter. Momentum fighters get so broken when plan A fails that they can't get to plan B: "You can see a momentum fighter lose it. You can see it slip out of his eyes, until he's so beaten he can barely take a sip of water." I could remember in my MMA fight when I was too gassed to drink water.

Jens paused in his rambling monologue, thinking aloud. "Ten more seconds is all I ever ask. That's the good thing I learned about being KO'd twice. You don't see it coming—it's like death—you don't plan for it, so don't wait for it. So many people are afraid of getting KO'd that their hands stay home, but not me. I got to go out there and shoot the lights out and fall down."

Jens spat, and offered one more nugget as I stood up to leave.

"Rulon better be ready. That's the thing with wrestlers is that they don't like getting punched. He better be ready to trade punches and get hit."

When Fedor walked in at the prefight press conference, Rodrigo quickly turned to watch him—not nervous but curious. The appearance of the "Other," as Joyce Carol Oates might say. George Plimpton wrote in *Shadowbox,* "No sport existed in which one's attention was so directly focused on the opposition for such a long time—except perhaps chess—so that the matter of psychological pressures was certainly in effect."

Fedor was so relaxed that I felt sure it was an act, mere posturing. He and Rodrigo sat in front of banks of cameras, at high tables covered in microphones, like UN envoys. There were maybe two hundred journalists in the room, only two or three of whom weren't Japanese. Fedor and Rodrigo spoke through their translators, and the conversation went from Portuguese to Japanese, from Japanese to Russian, and then back. I could barely follow what was being said, but when a reporter asked Fedor about what he wanted to do after the fight, he said, "Visit Brazil," and that got a few delayed laughs. Rodrigo gave Fedor his big smile and said, "You should come down for Carnival." Fedor was in a tracksuit; Rodrigo wore Armani and Diesel.

Their fight had the potential to be a classic. Rodrigo was the technical submission specialist, renowned for his ability to take a punch and stage miraculous comebacks to submit his opponents. Fedor was the feared striker, the heavy-handed athlete who was so slippery, whose hips were so good, that he appeared unsubmittable. Styles made fights.

They both weighed in shirtless, and neither was large for a heavyweight, each around 230 pounds. They had both beaten much heavier fighters, guys who weighed fifty or even a hundred pounds more. Rodrigo was lean and muscular, while Fedor was slightly beefy, with the Russian heaviness that was so deceiving. Fedor laughed at his own chubby physique, but no one thought for a moment that he was out of shape.

The tightness of control at Pride was legendary. They didn't really know I was there, although the Pride office in Los Angeles did, and they couldn't have cared less. Pride existed for the Japanese, and although the overseas market was tremendous, there was little catering to foreign reporters.

Zé was instructed not to talk to reporters, and more than that, not to interact with *any* Japanese people. Picture taking and autographs were to stop. The reasoning behind that was never made clear, although Zé suspected it may have been about the ratings war on New Year's Eve with K-1, the other major fighting event in Japan. K-1 was having a slightly smaller show in Osaka the same night. It was a Japanese tradition on New Year's Eve to stay in and watch TV all night with the family, and the ratings wars were intense.

Late one night at Sizzler, Rodrigo was posing for pictures with fans, and someone from the Pride organization actually came over and made them stop.

Eventually, the day of the fight arrived. There was an ugly hum, a tenseness, a buzz that ran through all of us as we scrambled to make sure every last thing was ready.

It was cold and getting colder when we climbed into the bus, and the snow had been picking up all day. I'm not quite sure how snow can be Japanese, but this snow had a distinctly Japanese aesthetic, falling like a heavy, quiet haiku. The roads were slippery and slow with traffic and accidents; the bus fishtailed once and the Brazilians oohed. The windows fogged up and cocooned us in a white silence, strange buildings looming in the fog and vanishing.

When we arrived, there was a tangible excitement in everyone, and you realized that that was why these guys get addicted to this; not just the fighters, but everyone around them—it's a way to feel something. Inside the arena it was cold and concrete and brightly lit.

We found our room and began to soldier in for the long wait, running reconnaissance missions, wandering the halls—trying to stay calm. We arrived at around three in the afternoon, and we would be there all night. Rodrigo was not yet there; he was fighting last, so he planned on coming a few hours later.

We went up and found the ring, wandering like kids in a new playground. The ring seemed tiny in the cavernous stadium, and I watched Jens bounce and weave on it, his footsteps surprising both of us with their thuds. The floor had a little compression in it, and the canvas was fairly soft. Jens was out warming up in a baseball hat and overlarge T-shirt, and he slashed the air in the corner with his fists, fixed and flickering.

Another fighter (who shall remain nameless) was also warming up, and the steroids had thoroughly ravaged him—his face was like thick, rubbery leather. The chemicals, all that raging and fighting, had just worn him down like old shoes. He was still bullet-headed and enormous, absolutely exploding in all directions with muscle.

I was told that there was drug testing, and Rodrigo did piss into an open Dixie cup that a kid in a Pride staff shirt took away.

The show was about to start, and the Pride event staff needed Rodrigo to be up on the massive stage that was built for the introduction. Problem was, Rodrigo still wasn't there. Without a second thought, they got his twin brother, Rogerio, to do it. He did it with a little trepidation, his hat pulled down and his hood up, and I don't think anyone caught on. You see what you expect to see.

Rodrigo was having his own troubles. The snow had shut the highways down right after we had come through, and although he had tried to get on the road at three-thirty, it was impossible; by taxi on a normal road it was going to take three hours. So they went to the train station to catch the bullet train. But the bullet train wasn't running, because of the storm, so they went to catch the normal train, and that wasn't running either. Rod ended up spending two hours in a cold train station trying to get to the arena.

Danillo, Murilo, and I escorted Rogerio-pretending-to-be-Rodrigo out through the halls, with the cameras turning and twisting and snaking with us, a crew of three or four Japanese staff around us, scuttling and scurrying. I was trying not to laugh, trying to look fierce. Danillo was doing a better job, and of course Murilo was unflappable. He should really play poker.

After we dropped Rogerio off, Danillo and I walked around the main arena, out in the darkness and the presence of the crowd. The cheapest bleacher seat was $150, and everyone there was in a festive mood. Many of the women, especially around ringside, wore shimmery party gowns, ready to ring in the new year.

Danillo was leaping and shouting as the show began, a low hum of anticipatory music, and then bursts of Japanese narration. The drums began with Pride's signature *dum-dum-dumdum* repeated and growing, and a whole carefully orchestrated series of traditional drummers, drumming hard and theatrically, and a massive electronic display. The crowd was so excited, the tension filled the arena with a crackling electrical energy, and this translated to the fighters. When their time came to fight, they could barely control themselves.

The drummers kept moving and changing it up during the introductions, with the announcer Lenne Hardte shrieking and calling, her madwoman voice shimmering and wailing and playing the crowd, a different clarion call for each fighter. Danillo and I whistled and cheered as they called Rodrigo, laughing because it was Rogerio hiding under his hood and hat. It was completely electrifying,

Danillo and I stayed for the first fight, a quick finish of a good-looking Dutch kickboxer, Leko, by a tough Japanese fighter named Minowa (he won the "Quick" award, an extra ten grand for finishing the fastest). Minowa chased him around, rushed him, went after his legs, and caught him with a heel hook on the ground like wow. Danillo rolled back his sleeves to show me his goosebumps.

Anderson Silva, a fellow Brazilian who shared the locker room with us, lost his fight early on the card and had a smile of relief on in the ring—at least it was all over—and that gradually shifted to a thousand-yard stare in the dressing room watching the rest of the fights, a glazed wetness. We all studiously avoided eye contact. We had to focus on

Rodrigo anyway, to turn and give our energies to him, to pour our attention in the form of strength into his vessel.

A Pride staff member came by with a series of envelopes; fighters here are always paid directly in cash. I don't know how much Anderson stood to make, but Rodrigo would be carrying around two hundred grand in cash at the end of the night. In his early days, he used to get twenty-grand bonuses for submitting an opponent.

Rodrigo was sitting up watching the fights when we came in, but he quickly lay down on the tatami mats and rested his head on a muay Thai pad and covered his eyes with a rag, trying to get some rest. We all sat quietly and watched the fights, which became the constant background for the rest of the night, a TV going in every room and hallway.

Eventually, Rodrigo got up and started walking around, shaking out and rolling his shoulders for a few minutes in front of the mirror, then sitting back down. This is always the bad time, I think, the building slide of events. I was desperately glad it wasn't me—I could just relax and enjoy the show—but at the same time I was envious of that pure excitement Rodrigo was living in.

He would stand and blow out his nostrils, exhaling hard to clear them, and slap his legs and arms a little, and power stretch, bouncing. There was tension in everyone except Anderson. Anderson was calm, resigned, and depressed, but okay—he was still a pro. He was lost in his own world, in an endless replay of what had gone wrong, the grief of losing beginning to set in.

The Rulon Gardner fight started with the national anthems for both parties, full of unbridled nationalism, flags and gold medals on all the TV screens. Watching the fight was a little like watching a bullfight; there was a sense of the restrictions of both parties. The two Olympic ground fighters stood and struck because they were unwilling or unable to go to the ground, which made for a very awkward stand-up fight. Even a mediocre heavyweight boxer would have destroyed either of those guys; but if either of them had been fighting a straight boxer, they would have had him on his back in about two seconds and torn him to shreds. It was because they both were so good on the ground that they were forced into a standing fight, which was the weak spot for both of them; it just favored Rulon a little more than Yoshida.

It was interesting to watch Rulon learn as the fight went on—he realized what was happening, what he could and couldn't do. He relaxed, his confidence grew, his face got shinier with understanding. He had a straight hard jab that worked well on the smaller man. He won a decision by essentially taking Yoshida out of his game, and although it was in no way a demonstration of wrestling versus judo, Rulon did win the fight. It was a little slow, like watching soccer players play basketball.

The next fight was Pulver-Gomi, and it was a stand-up war, to my surprise; Gomi, looking much bigger, knocked Jens out in the second round. I had had no idea that Gomi could do something like that. I was flabbergasted, but Jens, true to his word, went down swinging.

The night progressed, slowly, ineluctably, and Rod got dressed. He got taped and they were putting his gloves on and no one had inspected the tape, and I was thinking to myself, *Jesus, no one looks at the tape? Are you kidding me?* You could turn your fists into casts, you could even add weight—but then two slim young Japanese employees in clean white polo shirts came in and pulled the gloves off and inspected the tape and signed it, so that was okay. In the room, just before we left, we all huddled tightly together, our arms around one another, and prayed "Our Father" in Portuguese.

Then it was time to get moving. Events were pulling us along now willy-nilly, a race for the end of the night, the approach of the new year, and the smiling, rotund, rubicon face of Fedor was waiting for us.

Energy was flowing and crackling off Rodrigo, and he would stop every few minutes and blast through a few hard combinations with Dórea. He was separate from us, the one going into the ring, isolated and alone, the guy he had the most in common with that night across the arena somewhere, preparing himself to step into the same ring. In the first dressing room, Rodrigo knelt in a deep prayer for a few long minutes, and Zé held the door closed with his foot.

As we kept walking from room to room, Rod stayed out in a big hallway and started running laps and shadowboxing. He was building the intensity. The Japanese guide wanted to keep moving but stood patiently waiting, as did all the Brazilians who had already started down the next corridor. There were a lot of people in this cold space that led outdoors, and the camera crew loved it. People were staring and taking pictures with their phones.

I realized what Rodrigo was doing; he had confessed to me that he was a slow starter. He was working himself up, building the pitch and pace so that he would have already started by the time he got into the ring. He was going to try to jump all over Fedor. He was taking control of the situation, this headlong flight through the bowels of Saitama Super Arena. There is an inherent danger in the fluctuating time of fights; a series of quick knockouts and your fighter could be in the ring before you've properly warmed him up; but if the preceding fights go the distance you may have warmed your man up too soon.

Finally, Rodrigo was ready to move on, and we did. Up in the last little room before the entrance, he continued to jog and shadow-box and hit mitts. He slowed a little as Wanderlei Silva and Mark Hunt went the distance, the crowd erupting in roars seconds before the crowd on the TV, about a two-second delay. I'd hear the roar rumble through the building and then glance at the TV and see the event that caused it, a takedown or a big punch.

Rodrigo was now just pacing, the need to conserve energy coupled with the need to keep moving. He was slapping his arms, his legs, his face, twisting and rubbing his ears—keying his body up. He is going to have to get off, I kept thinking to myself.

Dórea paced with him, his hands in the focus pads like lobster claws, both of them with their specialized hands that would sometimes leap into a dialogue that was only between the two of them; they were the only ones who understood and mattered in this world. They knew what they were talking about—they'd been talking about this for months and months—a tight, neat little conversation of hooks and jabs, *rat-tat-tat* on the mitts.

The decision came for Mark Hunt, who looked bemused, slightly surprised. He had been completely unintimidated by Wanderlei (and had outweighed him by seventy pounds). A K-1 heavyweight, he just wasn't scared by the whole stare-down routine. It was Wanderlei's first loss in Pride, and the crowd was in ecstasy.

Now it was time for Rodrigo, and we followed him again, and then he climbed through the scaffolding and stood alone on the platform that would lift him into the arena. He shadowboxed a little, and the whole thing shuddered under him. He spat into the depths of the darkness and waited, and the red light lit his craggy features and we all stared up at him and loved him, and shouted encouragement to him. It was time.

As he goes up to the screaming and shouting, we pile one after another up the stairs and suddenly everyone is racing down the catwalk behind Rodrigo, and I am last but I go too, storming down the aisle in a kind of frenzy. Down the walkway we go, above an ocean of upturned faces.

The three real seconds get through, but security meets the rest of us hard and fast when we step off the walkway and shoves us into the aisle with everyone else, to crouch down when the rounds start and sit up when the rounds end and the lights come up. Still, we are nearly ringside.

The bell dings, and they both rush out and touch gloves, moving like speeded-up movie clips, frenetic and exploding with anticipation.

They come out boxing, both trying to stay up, and at a furious pace. They search for range, throwing jabs and moving. Rodrigo jabs, and Fedor counterpunches with a bombing right that is laser straight and unbelievably quick. The crowd moans in shock as Rodrigo takes another big punch. In the ring, the truth will out, and it quickly becomes obvious that Fedor, standing, isn't worried about anything Rod can throw. He is much stronger—and faster. His rights are shattering Rodrigo's game plan.

They stand for almost the whole first round, and Rod chases, jabbing, although he is tentative in his footwork, especially after Fedor hits him a few times. When they do clinch, Fedor tosses Rod around like a rag doll. Fedor, with his hands down and low, strikes with blinding speed, a sound in the eerie silence like an ax splitting meat, and Rod staggers. I hear his nose break.

The crowd cheers at the beginning and end and when big moments happen, but other than that it is strangely silent during the working part of the fight; you can hear the fighters grunt and breathe in the silence. Sometimes someone screams, *"Nogueira,"* in a kind of Japanese rolling of the g's and r's, but that is it. Fedor is quicker than shit and hits harder than anything I had seen. He never stands still but is always drifting and moving.

With a minute left in the first round, Rod takes Fedor down and is on top, but the round ends before he can really get to work. Bebeo, an old top team member, joins me and is shaking his head. "This boxing thing isn't going to work, he needs to go to the *chão,* the floor." Bebeo yells this to Zé, who is up, and he nods and returns to his quick and quiet consultations with Rodrigo, whose back is to us. We know now that the guy is too much for him standing, Rodrigo wants to be on the ground with him, preferably on top. But there isn't much time left. The first round was ten minutes, and the second and third will only be five.

Things don't get any better. Rodrigo pursues, edging forward, all too aware of that fast, looping, heavy hand of Fedor's, and he does catch

Fedor a few times, but the difference in punching power is instantly apparent. Fedor doesn't even blink from Rodrigo's punches, and although Fedor never has Rod in trouble, it is obvious that he is hitting much, much harder. They go down sometimes, usually with Fedor on top, but instead of staying down, where even from the bottom Rodrigo might have a chance, Fedor quickly stands back up. And standing, he puts the hurt on.

All the coaching in the world cannot make someone a big puncher; a figher either is or isn't a heavy hitter. You can improve speed and boxing ability, but you can't make someone heavy handed. Fedor has changed his strategy and is more than ready to stand with Rodrigo.

We sit and stare quietly with sinking hearts. If things keep going this way, Rodrigo is going to lose. "He's got to put him on the floor," Bebeo says to me in the break heading into the third, shaking his head. The crowd is deadly quiet. Between rounds, Fedor stands and bounces, and Rodrigo is on his stool with his head down. They have been telling him all this time that he is faster, and he isn't.

It is not to be, although in the third Fedor seems to tire and Rodrigo keeps coming after him, punching and moving, and the round might go to Rodrigo, even though he's lost the first two, probably.

The bell dings insistently, repeatedly, and the inevitable sound closes the fight off and seals Rodrigo's doom. He tries to raise his arms like he felt the momentum shift, but he's kidding himself and he knows it. His face is running with blood. There isn't much doubt in the arena, and when the decision comes, it is unanimous for Fedor. Fedor never tried to decisively win the fight, but Rodrigo never threatened him, either. I feel like five more minutes might have been enough. As it is, through twenty hard minutes, Rodrigo's courage never flagged.

We all stand around feeling sick, wondering what the hell to do now.

The night wasn't quite over. All the fighters came out and entered the ring, and I was struck again by the fact that these men had so much in common with one another and so little in common with the fans: the endless hours of mat time and training, running and lifting and infinite punches and kicks into bags and pads.

Zé Mario had a flag draped around his shoulders like a cape, the Brazilian superhero. I could see Fedor, the Nogueira brothers, and Murilo discussing something, at ease and friendly, consummate professionals who understood one another. I would love to have heard what they were talking about. And then Fedor smiled and left, and they had their core group, safe and secure up there. They believe in themselves, they really do, they believe they can go out there and box and they do it. They believe they can submit the other guy, and sometimes they can.

The promoters had the crowd give self-congratulatory cheers as midnight approached. There was a brief countdown and a big cheer and we all (the Brazilians) found ourselves sheepishly looking at one another, depressed but willing to smile and exchange hugs; they included me even though I didn't deserve it. Rodrigo, with his face starting to swell, hugged me and gave me a kiss on the cheek, and I was filled with love for the guy. He just has a lot of love in his heart. It's what has made him.

Love has given him belief in himself. It's what makes a dog fight past forty-five minutes. Love is what makes us great, and this display of strength, heart, and love is what brings us all to the fights.

Two days later I left Japan. The Dragon Lady and the Tokyo Hilton never caught me, and the sun was shining brilliantly.

4

THE TAO OF THE PUNCH

The weakest things in the world can overmatch the strongest things in the world. Nothing in the world can be compared to water for its weak and yielding nature; yet in attacking the hard and the strong nothing is better.

—Lao-tzu, *Tao Te Ching*

New York City in January is never really a good thing—too cold, sheathed in black ice, silent and dark and gleaming. It was a far cry from Rio, but the doctors are the best in the world, I was told. I went to see a specialist for my shoulder, and he looked at the MRI and said it was an "umbral tear" (to part of the rotator cuff) and that I should just keep resting it, doing what I was doing, rehabbing it on my own. "Listen to your shoulder," he told me. For this ten-minute pep talk I paid $325.

For a while now, ever since Thailand, I'd been scheming to go to Myanmar, where the bare-fisted tradition is alive and well and they still allowed head butts. Brazil was inspiring, but I was a striker at heart; I wanted to stand and punch. If I was going to even think about fighting bare-fisted in Burma, however, I needed to be healthy and sharp as a tack. I couldn't throw myself to the wolves again like I had in Rio, just go in and hope for the best. I knew what I wanted: Virgil Hunter, Andre Ward's boxing trainer—his eye, his attention. I had spoken to him about the idea from Brazil, and he was willing to take me on for a while. But I had to get my shoulder healthy first.

It was while I was stuck in New York, doing the rehab, that I thought I would look at the internal side of martial arts, something I had never done in earnest. The internal arts had a strong historical precedent; they formed the bedrock of martial arts philosophy. I had always been intrigued but hadn't had the time. Now I had an excuse.

The martial arts are usually divided into two categories, for simplicity: hard and soft, or external and internal. The hard, or external, arts are the explosive ones, the punching, the kicking, karate, tae kwon do, boxing, jiu-jitsu—everything you've probably heard of. They rely on strength and training of muscle memory; they're about hitting and controlling with force or technique—force on force. Soft arts are more about redirecting the opponent's energy, flowing *with* him, and the focus is on the mental, on meditation, breathing, building up and controlling energy—called *chi*—internally. Tai chi is the main example, but arts such as aikido, pa-kua, iai-jutsu (sword drawing), and even jiu-jitsu could be considered "softer" than many hard arts (but the jiu-jitsu the Brazilians do has no real mental component, except what they add from yoga). These distinctions are just cheap, easy ways to differentiate the two; in reality, there is usually not a sharp line; this is the yin and the yang. As you get deeper into any hard art, you may move into the more mental stages and it becomes more about the soft. Even boxing.

One of the many myths about the division between hard and soft martial arts claims that in the birthplace of martial arts, the Shaolin temple in China, the monks all trained in a total program that took ten years to produce a perfect warrior. The teachings balanced the hard with the soft, the yin with the yang. With the attrition of wars and the need for new fighters, however, the training regime was shortened to two years and involved just the hard arts, which were quicker to learn and more immediately practicable.

When you start to read about and get into internal arts, you can't help but encounter a lot of mythology, a popular mysticism that was latched onto by the Western world for the last hundred years—Taoism, the magical healing abilities of tai chi, the archetype of the ancient Asian man who can perform miracles and is a fountain of Confucian, Taoist wisdom. The legends abound: Tai chi masters who can move people without touching them, or who can "root" into the ground and not be budged by seven men pushing on them with all their combined strength (kind of like yogis who levitate). Everyone is familiar with the ancient master who trains the young warrior in the kung-fu flick, a pervasive icon from *The Karate Kid* to *Kill Bill*.

I was willing to entertain these ideas—why not? It's kind of the fun side of martial arts, delving into mysteries. After all, most martial artists and MMA guys love kung-fu films; we all embraced spectacular martial arts heroism at an early age. And who wouldn't want to be invulnerable, or know the *tao* of the one-inch punch? The secret of *dim mok,* the death touch?

MMA, of course, has been the ultimate proving ground for all those guys who claimed to have techniques that were so deadly they could never even practice them—and they nearly always get stomped. Kung fu, with its strict stylization and emphasis on forms, is the biggest offender in this category. Team MFS has a T-shirt that says, "Team Miletich: Your kung fu is no good here."

And yet, there must be something to the myths, I reasoned. Tai chi and the soft arts come from medieval times in China, when life was cheap and dangerous and the monks were fighting all the time, for their lives, against robbers and bandits and invaders. There is no way that everything they did was horseshit; there had to be *something* to it. It is only in modern times that man has become so divorced from actual fighting that bogus systems can survive and flourish. I decided to try tai chi—I was injured and couldn't train hard, anyway— to see if there was anything in it I could learn, or take into my own study.

Robert Smith, who lived for years in the East and trained extensively in martial arts, what he called "Chinese boxing," transcribed the following, from Huang Li-chou's *Nanlei Anthology.* It is an inscription on a great tai chi teacher's tomb:

> The boxing prowess of the Shao-lin school is widely known throughout the world. Since it is essentially an offensive system, however, it is possible to counter its methods. There has arisen a certain school, the so-called Inner School, which controls the enemy's action by calmness. The founder of the Inner School was Chang San-feng . . . a Taoist living on Mount Wutang. Emperor Hui Chung summoned him but he could not go because of bandits. One night he dreamed of being taught a special kind of boxing by Emperor Hsuan Wu the Great. The next morning Chang killed over one hundred bandits by himself.

I didn't plan on killing a hundred men—but having that ability couldn't hurt.

I found the closest tai chi place to me, on Twenty-third Street, run by a practitioner named William C. C. Chen. (I always pick the closest spot for training, because otherwise I won't go.) He was exorbitantly expensive, around $230 for a month of classes, four classes a week. It is Manhattan, so I grudgingly paid him. I asked about private lessons, but that would've run $180 for a fifty-minute session.

Tai chi, as most people know it, is that "slow-motion, weird stuff" that old people do in parks. As they practice it, it doesn't even remotely resemble a fighting art. Or does it? Watching someone go through a tai chi form, you start to see fighting postures in there, but everything is so slow, calm, and balletic. They move gently from one pose to another, stepping and sliding, turning and kicking, all at a snail's pace.

Tai chi is based directly on the philosophy of Taoism, put forth by Lao-tzu. It is a mystical, natural way of thinking, and the *tao* is simply "the way." The world is in a constant state of flux, and the soft and yielding win out over the strong and hard. Tai chi is based on those ideas and the concept of yin and yang—that famous symbol is actually the symbol for tai chi, as well. The use and control of chi, which is energy or life force, is the primary focus of tai chi. In China, practitioners often do not study tai chi until they have had ten years of experience in other arts, but the "short form" (the shorter sequence of movements) has been shown to cause significant health benefits and has become probably the most popular martial art in the world because of this. The People's Republic of China did studies and found that tai chi was a very cheap form of health care, and they developed their own short form. I knew that I wouldn't have enough time to really get into it—that would take years of study—but I thought perhaps I could take something away.

In William C. C. Chen's studio there was an older crowd, nonathletes, maybe six or seven people. It could have been a dance studio, with its hardwood floors and wall of mirrors. Master Chen (it felt funny to call someone "Master," as in MMA you never hear that traditionalist stuff) came out and started teaching without much fanfare. He was a small, slender man, older and clean-cut in a WCCCTCC sweatshirt (William C. C. Chen Tai Chi Chuan—how's that for an acronym?). He looked to be in his sixties but was in fact a well-preserved seventy.

We began to move through the short form, and Master Chen was a pleasure to watch move. The form was a set of movements, fifty-some steps in all (there are many variations; some short forms are thirty or forty steps). There was a palpable tension about his body, an elegance of movement born of unimaginable repetition and study. He had been practicing tai chi for more than fifty years; how many hundreds of thousands of times had he been through this form, one that he himself designed?

That first day, I took his short book home to read: "During actual fighting, a master of Tai Chi Chuan could make his body soft as cotton, but at the instant of delivering a punch, suddenly become as hard as steel. One moment he was motionless as a mountain, the next as swift as ocean tides." Sounded good to me.

What became clear over the next month of studying with Master Chen was that he was an antimystic. He laughed about the farfetched claims of some tai chi masters, about moving people without touching them, throwing them over rivers. "I never seen it, maybe it's true," he would say, smiling and laughing in his passable English. He wasn't debunking anything; he was just sticking to what he had seen and felt himself.

He was also a minor celebrity in the martial arts world; he'd been on the cover of *Kung-Fu* magazine, he'd taken a Chuck Norris punch to the stomach to show "how to take the shots." I realized that Robert Smith had studied and written a book with Master Chen's teacher, Cheng Man-ch'ing. With Chen, I was studying with a piece of history, a direct descendant of great tradition. And all he wanted to talk about was fighting.

His two children, Max and Tiffany (both in their twenties), were rising stars in the san shou world. San shou is an emerging Chinese kickboxing style, similar to muay Thai, except that it allows takedowns, but no ground fighting after the takedown. Master Chen was often the tai chi representative at martial arts seminars, and he traveled nearly every weekend, around the country and throughout the world.

Seminars are a big part of the martial arts business; they are traveling classes, put on by famous masters and fighters. For three hundred dollars you might get two classes with a well-known master, four hours each. Everyone does them, from the guys at Top Team (that's why Murilo was traveling to Europe all the time) to tai chi and ninjutsu fighters. They are a way for professional martial artists to support themselves.

Seminars offer a valuable opportunity to see and learn from great fighters and martial artists, and Tony Fryklund, my friend from Pat's place, had essentially educated himself in MMA in his twenties by chasing seminars. "I was a seminar rat," he told me, meaning he would drive from Boston to New York or Maryland or wherever for a two- or three-day seminar by a fighter or instructor he wanted to learn from, and then come home and train on his own.

The seminar business is also full of hacks, martial artists who make money on gullibility and the myths that surround the field. Tony had a great story about a seminar he went to where the instructor was demonstrating a nerve strike. There they were, in a room of thirty people, and the guy called up a volunteer. The instructor talked about how he was going to hit the nerve in the neck and it would instantly KO his man. Then he had the volunteer stand next to him and cock his head away so that his neck was exposed and he couldn't see what was coming. The instructor hit the volunteer with a "nerve strike" with his thumb, full force to the side of the neck, and the man collapsed. Everyone applauded, but Tony was incensed. "Dude, the guy's just standing there and you blast him? Of course he's going down. You stand there and let me blast you with a hook and we'll see what happens." Tony was eventually kicked out of the seminar.

I quickly learned the short form and tried to focus on the precepts that Master Chen talked about extensively in every class.

Tai chi, like all martial arts, is an organic fighting process that is shaped by the temperament and experiences of the teacher. Master Chen had been a fighter in mainland China and Taiwan and had been training and thinking about fighting for fifty years. It showed; he had evolved several concepts into deep insights about how he saw striking.

Master Chen was all about body mechanics, the tiniest details in throwing a punch, the generation of power—what chi really is. In this context, tai chi's slowness suddenly made sense. People sometimes make fun of tai chi for its slowness: *"That can't be a fighting art."* But of course it is, and when you start to think about perfecting your mechanics, you need to move slower and slower, to really break down what your body is doing.

Master Chen's tai chi short form was all about "going to sleep" and "waking up"—he would keep harping on that. The body goes to sleep on the exhale and wakes up on the inhale, a coiling and uncoiling of the body around the hips; once again he was talking about generating power.

He spoke often about the "three nails," an important concept of his—in the big toe, on the ball of the foot, and on the inside edge of the heel. They are the places that your foot is rooted to the ground. It is as if your energy could drive nails into the floor to hold you; they are the basis from which you generate power.

Master Chen said, "When I start doing tai chi, I realize that power isn't in arms, it comes from the hips. And then, I start to think maybe ten years later and I realize it is coming from the legs. And then, after twenty years, I saw that it was actually coming from the toe." He reiterated this point continually: that you must feel power coming off the toe; driving energy down through your toes is what is sometimes referred to as "rooting," and it is what drives all your movements. F. X. Toole tells the story of a trainer who "taught her how to stay on the balls of her feet, how to generate momentum off her right toe; how to keep her weight over her left knee"—all things that could have been lifted from Master Chen's class.

What endeared Master Chen to me was his constant talk of fighters. He always used the reference of a fighter to illustrate his points, and when I told him I was a sometime fighter, he was delighted—I wasn't just there for the health benefits. I could understand a lot more of what he was talking about than most of the Manhattanites.

The common conception of throwing a punch is that the arm should be loose for speed but the hands strong in a fist. Master Chen described it as "hollow arms," meaning that the arms are empty except for the energy that activates them, and the hand should be open, curling into a fist as it hits. His hands were always in the shape of hands inside boxing gloves—never fists, the gloves won't allow it. You strike with two knuckles; Chen quoted Jack Dempsey about hitting with just those top two knuckles. In his book, Chen had detailed diagrams of bullets, showing how more powder and cartridge width increased velocity. He talked about generating speed from pressure changes and generating power from speed in a speech that made me think of Virgil Hunter. Chen was practical to the tips of his fingers. In the short form, one's movements should be led by the fingers (activated off the toe), and punches were the same. It's all about velocity, sinking down and rising—not up, but into a shape. And as all hard artists, like boxers and karate disciples, should study tai chi, so should tai chi practitioners study the hard arts, so that both supplement yang with yin.

Chen's most interesting concept was that of compression. He had this argument with many martial artists. When you're learning about strikes, you're taught to exhale on the strike. But it's not just exhalation; it's also compression. When a boxer hisses as he punches it's a form of compression. This is one of those obvious, head-slapping truths: An exhalation, an open-mouthed "whoo" of air, has no power. But when you control the air, when the karate guy shouts "*Kiai*" as he punches, that compression is what generates force. It's like a grunt when you pick up something heavy; you have to make an internal compression to generate power. Boxers hiss or grunt; the Thais yell.

"They say tai chi is about 'relax,' but really they mean 'relax with compression.' When you lying in bed, you are relaxed, but little compression. It's like a sick person in the hospital; they are walking around like a skeleton." Chen would demonstrate walking without compression, a perfect facsimile of a very old sick man, frail, scarcely moving. It was great because it wasn't acting; he was demonstrating a different way of being.

Chen continued, "When they say a boxer is 'out of gas,' they not mean tired, they mean cannot make compression," and I thought about my fight. He was dead right. It wasn't that radical an idea, but I had never heard it before.

"When you walk around with compression, you are thinking: How cool I am. The compression is filling you up."

Master Chen had an open-minded approach to his art, which gave him great strength. He was always thinking about it and refining ideas. I was extremely lucky to have walked into his studio. For him, tai chi wasn't about doing tai chi every day, running through the form (although that had to be done). You couldn't just run through the form blindly every day and think that in ten years you would get all the health benefits, become spiritual. It's work. Every time you went through it, it had to be done as close to perfect as possible. He tried to do tai chi as it was intended to be done, not necessarily as he had been taught it, or others had shown him.

He had other ideas he was working on, concepts he'd been pondering for the past five or ten years. Ideas about the hydraulics inside the body, ideas about why tai chi was good in the context of Western medicine—the internal organs are suspended and massaged, and circulation is vastly improved. His latest thoughts were about a punch: The impact is absorbed by the muscles; that is all the muscles are there for. Certainly, boxers have shown that big muscles don't equal heavy punches, although overall weight is a good indicator.

Chen said that great boxers learn to do all this naturally. I noticed right away that some of the postures in the short form looked very much like old-school boxing pictures of Joe Louis, coiled in on himself. I remembered Pat Miletich pointing to a picture he had on the wall of the gym and saying, "You see that picture? All the old-time boxers would pose that way, coiled up for an uppercut, because if you posed that way, it showed you knew what you were doing, you had been educated in the science."

Chen taught the short and long forms, and his attitude was that students should learn the short form all the way through, and *then* perfect it—instead of trying to get every posture perfect before moving on to the next. That way, you could start to derive the benefits of the form more quickly. Everything came from the short form; everything could be learned by learning the short form, although Chen laughed and said, "For fighting, you have to hit the bag and lift the weights, too."

When I talked to Master Chen's son, Max, who was preparing for the Golden Gloves, he said he just used the short form as a type of relaxation, of moving meditation. I was reminded of the *ram muay* and *wai khru,* the traditional, slow-moving dances that we had done before muay Thai fights. These had been moments of relaxation and could be considered moving meditation. But Max and his sister, Tiffany, didn't think that tai chi had given them a big advantage in boxing or san shou; they thought it was just "good for you." Master Chen said his own children didn't have the maturity to understand what he was talking about, but they would learn it. They were pretty good, tough kids, although I never got a chance to work with them. Tiffany loved boxing and was training at Gleason's, the most storied boxing gym in the world, while Max was more interested in the san shou and, someday, K-1.

On some nights, there was "form application," applying the moves of the short form to actual self-defense and fighting, and on those nights Master Chen had everybody put on boxing gloves and punch the wall, again focusing on mechanics, on slamming and retraction.

He did hit hard as hell, I have to admit. His hips and body coiled and uncoiled, and he had a kind of snarling yell, shockingly loud, as he punched the wall. It was all about mechanics, pivoting, winding up, punching through, and impact. I almost never got it quite right, but he smiled and laughed and showed everyone again the differences. They were subtle, but they existed, and they allowed the seventy-year-old man who weighed about 140 pounds to hit the wall like a much heavier person. The fingers activating, the toe, the compression, the sinking and exploding, all the myriad details flowed together.

In the end, the sum is greater than the whole. Tai chi is about the generation of power, hitting terribly hard and moving smoothly and uncoiling perfectly. But there is something more, something greater.

Master Chen had been a student of Cheng Man-ch'ing's, a man Robert Smith called the "Master of the Five Excellences" and one of the most legendary tai chi practitioners in history. According to Smith, Cheng had been dying of tuberculosis when he met Yang Cheng-fu, the greatest tai chi practitioner in the world. Tai chi reversed the tuberculosis and completely healed him. It's not quite levitation, but I wouldn't turn it down.

I was with Chen for only a few months, just long enough to learn the short form and get a sense of what it was about, but on the last day I had a minor breakthrough.

Master Chen was always repeating things, telling the same stories over and over, not because he was forgetful but because you needed to keep hearing them. You might have understood what he was saying, but you didn't quite *get* it. And then, one day, suddenly something would slot into place and you would understand what he had been talking about all that time.

Tai chi has an entire vocabulary in Chinese about varying forms of energy and *tantien,* the place below the belly where chi builds up. Master Chen almost never used those words, as they smacked of mysticism to him, and he avoided that. Instead, he would use the analogy of tires inflating with air.

On my last day, there were only a few people in class, and we were refining the form. Master Chen kept talking about shrinking and growing, sagging and waking up, and a certain tenseness in the *tantien.* Suddenly, I started waking up with the inhalation in my lower stomach; it would fill and tense, and a concept that had been eluding me fell into place. I could feel my *tantien.*

Master Chen smiled and shook my hand and I thanked him, and he said, "I think you have enough to work on your own now. It will help you."

5

A COLD GAME

Virgil Hunter and Andre Ward, Oakland, March 2005.

Kings Gym, Oakland

It takes constant effort to keep the slippery, naked, near-formless fact of hitting swaddled in layers of sense and form. Because hitting wants to shake off all encumbering import and just be hitting, because boxing incompletely frames elemental chaos, the capacity of the fights to mean is rivaled by their incapacity to mean anything at all.

—Carlo Rotella, *Cut Time*

I drove cross-country to Oakland in the spring. I was going to see Virgil Hunter and Andre Ward. Andre had won a gold medal at the Olympics in Athens and was 3–0 as a pro.

My shoulder was feeling better. The endless pulling on rubber bands seemed to have had some effect. I had talked Virgil into taking me on as a student. "Just imagine I'm a cruiserweight prospect," I said to him. He laughed. Virgil would never be able to pretend I was anything other than what I was. It's part of what made him a great trainer. I told him I wanted an amateur fight—having a fight focuses the training and clarifies the mind; it gives you a sense of urgency that helps you learn. I wanted a different kind of relationship with a teacher, more than I'd had in Rio or even Iowa. I wanted the one-on-one attention. If I was going to fight bare-fisted in Myanmar or MMA again anywhere, I better do it right. If my true love was hitting and getting hit, I figured I should have the best instruction available, at least for a while. And I was fascinated by Andre's story, the life of a red-hot young prospect with all the advantages, being groomed for greatness.

Finally, I thought it would be good for my understanding to take a look into the big-time world of professional boxing, from the inside.

The amount of literary material on boxing is staggering. World-class writers have fallen in love with "the sweet science," from Hemingway and Mailer to Joyce Carol Oates; far, far better writers than I have addressed the issue. In general, they fall into all kinds of hyperbole, all kinds of difficult and complicated constructions and emphatic descriptions, in attempts to describe the visceral. Boxing writing often veers from the sublime to the ridiculous.

So I was going to get some one-on-one attention with a world-class trainer and fight an amateur fight. It almost seemed a step backward, to fight an amateur fight at this point (four two-minute rounds, headgear—are you kidding me?), but the fight was just an excuse to train hard. And I wanted to see Andre in depth, close up. People didn't realize that although Andre had won gold at light-heavyweight, 175 pounds, he'd fought most of those fights weighing under 170 pounds. He beat a European champion and a huge (six-five) Russian world champion and gave up seven pounds. The critics were sniping at him for turning pro at middleweight ("*Didn't he have the power for light-heavy?*"), or 160—but he had never been a proper light-heavyweight.

I arrived in Oakland without a place to stay, and through a friend of a friend ended up crashing on the floor of an unfurnished apartment in East Oakland. The neighborhood was bad, in the process of gentrifying but not there yet. Rough open streets, old factories, and rundown buildings: the West Coast urban wasteland.

The next morning I was up to meet Virgil in the pearly gray dawn, and as I headed toward my car, I could see a rat's nest of papers and litter on the front seat. I walked slowly around the car in the warm morning light, with the ocean coloring the sky. One of the rear triangular windows had been neatly mashed in—the rock that had been used as a tool was still by the rear tire—all the doors had been unlocked, and the trunk had been popped. For some reason, I had thought things would be safe in the trunk. Of course, the trunk only keeps things safe from prying eyes; once you're in the car, you just pop the trunk with that little latch on the floor. All my sparring and workout gear, plus a backpack filled with street clothes, was gone. Ah, well, at least I'd brought my camera and laptop inside. Who needs street clothes anyway?

I drove through the morning calm to Coffee with a Beat, the coffee shop that Virgil called his office, on the park next to Lake Merritt in downtown Oakland. The sun came up warm, but it was cold in the shade, and through the trees I could see the glimmer of the lake. I walked up and saw Virgil, looking the same, regal and smiling. We shook hands warmly; he seemed genuinely happy to see me. He was instantly recognizable, tall, broad-shouldered, and lean, with his head shaved bald and a black mustache, an Everlast ball cap, and sunglasses. He dressed in trainer chic, crisp athletic gear that was clean and sharp. When his sunglasses were off, you could see his eyes were intense, probing; he wore the glasses almost like a poker player does, to help him conceal his thoughts and where his eyes were, so you couldn't read him.

We drank coffee and talked, moving one of the little outdoor tables into the sun. We caught up. I asked after Andre, and Virgil mentioned the cage-fighting article, which had been published in *Men's Journal* with maximum gore. "I hate to see you like that," he said lightly, and I laughed, because the editors had gone with pictures that made it look as bad as possible, despite my protestations and the photographer's wishes. I told him the whole story, about the weight mix-up and everything.

He shook his head. "You aren't fighting to take punishment," he said. "A true fighter learns how to say no if the fight is unfair. You don't have to fight; it's not a million-dollar title shot on the line."

He chuckled to himself quietly, mulling over his words. He looked at me through his sunglasses and said, smiling, "It's prizefighting, not pride-fighting."

We talked about what I wanted to accomplish, and what he was doing with Andre and Antonio Johnson, a fighter who had recently come to him. Antonio was another kid with a gigantic amateur background, and he could have made the Olympic team but didn't make weight— a sign that his discipline was a mess.

We made plans to meet up later at King's Boxing Gym, and as we stood up, Virgil said in his dry voice, "It's all about figuring out who *you* are." It's something you hear again and again in boxing: Boxing is about knowing your identity. If you are a boxer, someone with skill and technical virtuosity but perhaps without power, then box; use your science, move and hit and defend. If you are a puncher, with power to hurt with just one punch, then get yourself in a position to let your hands go and punch. "Let your hands go" is the refrain everywhere for "Start throwing punches." Your hands are trained to punch in combinations, just let them go and do what they want. Trainers and bystanders will implore fighters who seem oddly frozen, who could win the fight if they would only land a few combinations. Of course, everything is different for the man in the ring.

I drove back through Oakland, hot and dusty with those wide, hardscrabble streets. East Oakland was a picture of neglect and emptiness—though here and there old warehouses were being turned into fancy apartments because it was an easy commute to San Francisco, just a few blocks from the Bay Bridge. The sun beat down through a perfect blue sky, and the ocean was a presence I could feel and know, but not see or hear.

I remembered King's Boxing Gym from the last time I had been there, and it was essentially unchanged, sandwiched between the highway and the train tracks, between chop shops and massive concrete walls. A simple sign and a narrow metal door in an accordion garage door led the way inside.

King's was long and dark, sweaty and well worn, cavernous. I noticed some changes—some new equipment and more college-looking kids, a tiny bit of upscale. There was a refrigerator with protein drinks for sale. The price of membership was still right, thirty bucks a month to work out, fifty with a trainer. There were more hacks, more white guys with running shoes, and maybe fewer professionals. But it was still a serious place, a pure boxing gym, and the walls were covered in posters and flyers for fights, history peeling and aging on the walls everywhere you looked.

It was good to see Andre again—he smiled and we shook hands with genuine good feeling. I instantly noticed the subtle differences that age, maturity, and the crucible of the Olympics had brought him—he was a man now, and he knew it. In the year and a half since I'd seen him, his eyes had acquired a layered wisdom. The gym had pictures of him and a huge banner congratulating him on his Olympics win, and I muttered to him with a smile, "So this is your gym now?" and he grinned back and replied, "Something like that."

I met Antonio Johnson, a light-skinned black kid with a handsome, boyish face and a feathery mustache, almost Latino-looking. He had just turned pro at 140. He was as verbose as Andre was quiet, filling the air with a stream of street banter, discussing a fighter they knew on the TV show *The Contender,* a fighter Virgil had trained. "Babyface, he can crack a little bit though," Antonio said with finality. "He can crack" means he can punch hard, something every boxer lusts after, knockout power in each hand.

Andre said, "If they had me on that show, they would have to do it without my family." He was referring to the way the TV show always built up to the fights by having the fighter's wife and kids in the dressing room for tearful good-byes and good lucks, a sort of relentless, smarmy tear-jerking. Andre kept his wife and kids at a distance when he was fighting; he actually left the house and "went to camp" at Virgil's training house down the road weeks or months before the fight, to focus himself.

Andre had a fight coming up in just a few days, so I didn't talk to him, as I didn't want to mess with his focus. A critical element for a fighter is focus, something Virg started drumming into me on the first day. On the wall was a poster saying "The Three C's for Fighters: Conditioning, Coachability, and Concentration." More than any athletic ability, any natural speed or strength, those three C's make real professional fighters.

Virg looked at me with pursed lips and said, "I need to see what I got. Why don't you get up in the ring and shadowbox." I went through the ropes, feeling on display, and shadowboxed fast for a round or two, trying to look good. Sidelined by my shoulder, I hadn't really done anything since the Miletich camp, almost a year ago, and felt awkward and ungainly. But not too bad, I thought.

Virg stopped me after two rounds and climbed into the ring with me. "Now, real slow, I want you to step and jab, step across with a jab, then step back with a jab-right-jab," and he demonstrated for me, elegant and tall and graceful, almost balletic. I frowned and concentrated and tried to block out the watchful gaze of Antonio and Andre. I danced like Virgil had just shown me. I was very aware of how tight I was, everything seized up and bunched. Step, step, step back with the left-right.

At the end of the round, Virgil came off the ropes and told me, "Sam, your concentration was terrible. Twenty-six times you did that, and every time you ended on a straight right. Now, if I know you are throwing the right and then just standing there, I'm going to make you throw it and then come back on top of it."

"So never end on the right cross," I said dumbly. They call it "posing," or "taking a picture"—a fighter throws a punch and finishes frozen, contemplating the beauty of his last punch, there to be hit by a counterpunch. Keep moving, move your head and body after you punch.

"Come back with the jab, so that even if I'm countering, the jab is there to disrupt me. And jab as you move away."

I quickly came to understand one of Virgil's governing precepts, which is fight when it's good for you. Don't stand and fight when your opponent wants to. Move around—fight only when it's better for you. Muhammad Ali's first fight with Floyd Patterson is a perfect example. Ali just kept moving and moving and moving, and every now and again paused to hit Floyd, and then moved some more. Boxing critics hated him for it, the "cowardice" of it, but it was unbeatable. Floyd didn't have an answer.

I felt like a fool in the ring doing these slow, basic beginner moves, after I had been shadowboxing fast and well (in my mind, anyway). There were maybe four or five other complete beginners in the gym, just like me, college kids in running shoes with iPods, fat girls, a tiny Asian girl.

But I got over the embarrassment. I moved beyond those feelings—if what Virgil wanted me to do was slow and basic and endlessly repetitive, I reasoned, then I'd do it. I knew who I was—I was a writer trying to learn something. Virgil had told me that he was going to give me a straight right and a straight left, and with those two punches you could beat almost anybody in the amateurs, until you started getting along—and by then you would know how to improvise a hook, an uppercut. To be fair, I was somewhat discouraged—all this time and now I had to go back to the two most basic punches? But it's better to do a few things perfectly than a whole bunch of things badly in boxing. Championships have been won with great jabs. If I fought MMA again, having good straight punches would be a big help.

Afterward, as I was taking off my wraps, Virgil said, "Fundamentals, Sam, fundamentals. If you don't have them, you will run into somebody else's."

The next day, I went back to King's by myself, acutely self-conscious. Andre, Virg, and Antonio had all gone to Southern California to fight. I skipped rope for fifteen minutes, the bell dinging away like some kind of call to prayer. It divided the hours of the universe into three-minute rounds (with a green light) and one-minute rest periods (with red). For the last thirty seconds of the round, the light would go yellow and ding a certain tone, meaning "*Hurry up, the round is almost done, the end is in sight, give it everything you've got now."* I read all the signs fading on the walls as I jumped, and jumping rope was about the only thing I could do competently. I shadowboxed in front of the mirror for three rounds and then wrapped up and hit the heavy bag. My first thought was *Damn, that thing is hard,* as my hands and heart shuddered at the impact. The bag seemed like concrete, and by the end of each round I could barely keep my hands up. My punches would not have bruised a fly. My shoulders burned, and my left was shockingly weak. I had always prided myself on a decent jab, but right now it wasn't anything more than a love tap to the bag. I forced myself through four rounds.

Virgil had introduced me to Bobby, an older trainer who was a good friend of his, a big ancient black man with a beautiful, creased face, like a cartoon of the sun. Bobby was seventy-five and healthy and happy. He had a huge smile, and Virgil called him "Blackburn," after Joe Louis's legendary trainer. Bobby was old school to the highest degree and convinced that the Brown Bomber would have beaten Ali because (of course) Ali pulled straight back. I stood next to Bobby and chatted companionably as one of his fighters was shadowboxing. There were already a few women in the gym, but another good-looking woman poked her head in, and Bobby said, "Million-dollar baby," with a huge smile, and we laughed. He told me about boxing in the army and being stationed in Germany in the fifties and going on leave to Paris with cigarettes to trade on the black market. He is a living reminder of the decline of the sport.

Boxing has been in decline since the twenties, arguably, but still had massive popularity in the fifties and even seventies. It is an oddity, a curio of old Anglo-Saxon values that arose with the decline of the duel in Victorian England. Its popularity grew with the growth of all athletics in the wake of the Industrial Revolution. In his book *Manhood in America,* Michael Kimmel points at boxing's rise to prominence at the turn of the last century, along with the popularity of sports in general, as a counter to industrialization and the effeminacy of modern society. Boxing was about the return of the true craftsman, the "artisan." Kimmel talks about the artisanal vocabulary instantly adapted by boxing, which persists to this day. Boxing was a "profession," and boxers were "trained" in various "schools." Combatants "went to work" and "plied their trades" in the "manly art."

Before the rise of prizefighting you have to go back to ancient Greece and the early Olympics to find men fighting with fists or gloves for entertainment or defense (at least in the Western world; obviously, the East was different). Gladiators used weapons.

Prizefighting became popular alongside bull- and bearbaiting and their "dark sister," public hangings. Bare-fisted fighting favored the careful, conditioned man, as fights went on for hours with two to three punches thrown a minute. "The fancy" refers to the men who were fans and connoisseurs, of both dogfights and prizefighting, and as the fancy began to participate, the use of gloves evolved. Pressure from political antifight groups culminated in the London Prize Ring Rules in 1838, prohibiting striking below the belt, kicking, and butting. Later, the more famous 1867 Marquess of Queensberry rules solidified the use of gloves and the three-minute rounds with a one-minute rest, plus a ten count for a knockout. These rules in fact were a tremendous boon to prizefighting, legitimizing it, reducing the sky-high rate of fatalities, and bringing it into respectability.

Jack Johnson, the first black heavyweight champion, in 1910, chased the white champions all over the world before he got someone who would fight him for the title. His story is incredible. This was back when the heavyweight champion of the world was the be-all and end-all of manhood, the paragon of virtue, and the fact that a black man had the title was an almost impossible cross for white sportswriters to bear. Johnson didn't give a damn, either; he was doing Muhammad Ali in 1910. They pulled Jim Jeffries, the former unbeaten white champ, out of retirement, and Johnson beat the shit out of him, laughing all the time. The outcome sparked race riots and led to many deaths—mostly of black men, of course. Virgil's comment was, "Jeffries was exploited, man"—his sympathy lies with boxers, not color. And Virgil, although he was born in Berkeley, has roots in Texas; and the uncles who taught him to box had a direct stylistic link to Jack Johnson, who fought out of Galveston. Johnson was one of the first defensive fighters to be hugely successful, with a slippery, elusive style that confounded opponents. Virgil calls his own personal style, descended from what Jack Johnson did, "Texas slip 'n' slide." Over the decades, the game evolved from an Anglo-Saxon "stand-in-front-of-him-and-hit" brawl to the modern strategic and tactical masterpieces that were enacted throughout the twentieth century.

Just look at the numbers: In 1939, Sugar Ray Robinson won the Twelfth Annual Intercity (amateur) title, the Golden Gloves, at Chicago Stadium, in front of 20,000 people. You can't get 15,000 fans to come to a professional title fight these days. Dempsey-Tunney, in

Philadelphia in 1926, had a live gate of 126,000. Pay-per-view extends the live gate at forty bucks a pop but is perhaps promotionally short-sighted, as it limits the audience.

Television runs the show, and there has been much hue and cry about how it has killed boxing, with A. J. Liebling leading the charge in the thirties and forties. Local gyms and fighting venues dropped off precipitously—because you could see good fights on TV—and a strict boxing gym today has a sense of decay to it, the feeling that twenty years earlier there were three rings and two hundred guys in there working every day, but now there is one and it is empty. The bottom line is financial. Good athletes can make so much more money playing other sports without the risk and damage of boxing that it would be silly to fight. Football and other sports gained in popularity and took the best athletes at all levels; and the corruption of the "alphabet soup" organizations, and mandatory title defenses, muddied the waters.

I think the source of boxing's decline lies deeper in American society. Kids used to fight more; violence wasn't so frowned upon and didn't escalate as it does today with the prevalence of firearms. The penalties are severe today—getting in a few bar fights can lead to weeks or months in jail, heavy fines, and tremendous *hassle*. The cops will invariably arrive. Everybody in the early part of the century, through the Depression, would be in fistfights, especially as young kids. You would know who was the toughest kid on your block, and how you compared to him, and then you would know how he compared to the toughest fighter in the neighborhood, the city, the state; and you would see how the best fighter in the state got his clock cleaned by Sugar Ray Robinson or Jack Dempsey, and you would have a direct relation to and understanding of that controlled violence.

Even among fight fans boxing has been in decline—because of bad decisions and rampant corruption, fighters owned by the Mafia throwing fights, and scandals. Still, fight fans will pay to see big fights, and boxing remains big business, albeit for only a few top fighters. The huge purses of the eighties and nineties, riding on Tyson's mythic status, have likewise faded into legend. When Holyfield fought Tyson in the rematch in '97, they both made thirty million dollars.

Boxing is also filled with nostalgia, as Liebling noticed, and sometimes it's nostalgia for its own sake: He saw, even in his day, that everyone contended that boxing used to be better. The old fighters thought it was better back in the days when they were still fighting; and the writers thought it was better back in the old days when they first fell in love with the sport. Liebling calls the boxing writers (who last longer) "the most persistent howlers after antiquity."

Virgil, Andre, and Antonio returned, triumphant and easy, and Virgil gave the boys some time off. I met him often in the early mornings at Coffee with a Beat and got to know Nate, the owner, a little bit and even bought some T-shirts from him; he was a childhood friend of Virgil's. Virgil pretty much frequented only black-owned businesses. His mother had been politically active in the civil rights movement, and being in Oakland, near Berkeley, Virg retained some of that militant outlook, heavily seasoned with a street education.

We would sit and talk for hours, meeting people, carrying on conversations through multiple interruptions and digressions. Virgil had derived some of his philosophy from Miyamoto Musashi's *The Book of Five Rings*—a samurai treatise on fighting strategy—and when he saw that the Olympic symbol was five linked rings, he knew Andre was going to win gold: "His style, his philosophy is too much for anyone to get a handle on in four two-minute rounds." Virgil had intentionally kept Andre out of international competition, because that way it was harder for the much more experienced, older European fighters with eight years of amateur experience to get tape on Andre, to come up with a plan for him. They couldn't figure him out in the short sprints that make up amateur boxing. Virgil mentioned Bruce Lee and jeet kune do. "Bruce Lee nearly got his ass whupped by a man off the street, a big, strong, tough man, and only because of his conditioning was he able to win. So he changed his system. He realized he was too locked in place by tradition. In a fight, I'm free. If I'm locked in a system . . . Here's Andre in the Olympics, and the first fight he wins, the thing the other fighters are thinking about is his speed. Once I got speed on your mind, I got you thinking and halfway beat. So you're wondering if you can hit me, and then I keep you from hitting me for the first round, and now you're convinced you can't hit me.

"Like Tyson," he continued. "People would train to get away from the punch, and convince themselves that they couldn't handle the punch. They would do his work for him, and then Buster Douglas and Evander showed that you just had to have confidence in the fact you could *handle* his punch, and if you frustrate a puncher you got him beat—because he's used to people disappearing when he hits them. He's got no science to fall back on."

Boxing is full of great fights in which big punchers have been exposed. The most famous, classic example is the "Rumble in the Jungle," Ali-Foreman in Zaire. Foreman was thought to be an unbeatable force of nature, the greatest puncher of all time. Ali took a horrendous pounding, absorbed it lying on the ropes, and as Foreman tired, Ali came dancing back in the eighth round and knocked him out. He beat Foreman's mind as much as his body. Liebling had written, "Any fight in which one man can punch and the other must disarm him is exciting, like watching an attempt by a bomb squad to remove a fuse."

The Leonard-Duran fights are probably my favorite. In their first meeting, Leonard, the boxer, was a young, fresh kid out of the Olympics, and Duran (a shoeshine boy from Panama) was the most feared boxer-puncher in his weight class, maybe in history. Duran was called *Manos de Piedra,* "Hands of Stone." Leonard stood in and brawled with Duran, instead of boxing, and although Duran won, he was frustrated because Leonard had taken his best shot and kept fighting. The second time they met, Leonard stood in the middle of the ring when the bell rang, Duran's usual spot; and Leonard moved and danced and showboated and so confused and twisted Duran's mind that he quit, with the now infamous "*No más,*" to the howling outrage of the boxing community. Leonard took Duran's legend and wove it into his own. Making somebody quit—that's domination.

Virgil turned to me and said, "It's like this: When I was a kid in Oakland, we used to collect those big wolf spiders. We used to fight those spiders, the kids would, because they would tear each other up. Especially females. Now, I knew that in my basement there was a black widow spider. I had seen her many times, and I would go and check on it and find it in the same place. So I got the spider and cleaned up the whole neighborhood." That's Virgil's attitude: Think outside the problem, win with something overwhelming, leave nothing to chance.

I was curious as to how Andre's opponents were chosen. At this stage in a fighter's career, I knew from reading, it was important to bring him up slowly. Andre had what Teddy Atlas loved to call the "amateur pedigree," meaning he had more than 150 amateur fights, starting when he was ten years old, and he had the greatest amateur achievement—he won gold in the Olympics. Antonio had about 250 amateur fights, and some fighters will have more than that before they turn pro. It means that every week since they were ten or twelve years old they were jumping into the car, driving to a tournament, and fighting. Records aren't kept, as your win-loss ratio isn't so critical, but Andre hadn't lost an amateur fight since 1997 (and he claims that that was a judging error and wants to avenge the loss). Professional fighting is something totally different. It's scored differently, the rounds are longer and there's more of them, and of course there is no headgear. You're not looking to score points as much as to hurt the guy. To start a pro career, you might fight four or five four-rounders and then five or six six-rounders, then eights, and so on, depending on how you do. But the goal is title fights, and those are twelve rounds. As I heard T, one of Andre's managers, say, "They don't give away belts for nothing less than twelve-rounders." And title shots are the only goal as far as money is concerned.

There is a principle that Angelo Dundee (the legendary trainer of Ali and Leonard) referred to as "slow-teach," which is slowly exposing your fighter to bigger challenges. Just enough to stretch him, not so that he is seriously challenged or even lose, but more to just expose him to something he might not have seen, to force him to adapt and grow as a fighter. For Andre, the guys he had fought so far *knew* they couldn't come close to matching him in speed or skill, so they were forced to try to intimidate him, to rough him up and shake his confidence. It infuriated him. "They look at my baby face and say, 'Oh, you have to rough up Olympic champs,' and I'm like, '*What makes you think you can rough me up? Now that I won, I'm pampered?*' I went and took that medal from a bunch of tough guys."

In Andre's last fight, against a white kid from Louisiana, the kid had been hopelessly outclassed and had responded by fouling repeatedly, until he was disqualified. Andre smiled, his eyes soft, warm, pitiless brown pools. "He was looking for a way out. He knew he was going to be knocked out and didn't want to go like that, so he just kept hitting after the break."

I had seen Andre's fights so far, complete blowouts of much less talented individuals, nonthreats, called "opponents," boxing lingo for someone brought in to lose to your prospect. There are, of course, varying degrees of opponent; your fighter might be 4–0 and the opponent might be 2–6, and there are infamous opponents whose records might run 4–16, guys who are used to losing and are just out looking for a payday, record padding for young hungry contenders with money and intelligence backing them. A contender in today's world isn't taken seriously unless he is 20–0; remaining undefeated is incredibly important, and two or three losses can be the end of a career. MMA is different. There are so many ways to lose that guys at the top level can have six or eight losses. It depends more on who they fought.

In the gym, Virgil would have me shadowbox in front of the mirror, moving in super slow motion for five or six rounds, the slower the better. "Slow works the tendons, the sinews, and it hurts more; but it makes you stronger, gives you power. Speed will come when the mechanics are right." I thought about tai chi. My arms and shoulders would be screaming, and when I finally went to the heavy bag next to Antonio, it was a huge relief to be able to hit fast. Antonio was like a snake, in and out, his punches snapping the bag.

I had no idea that boxers did so much shadowboxing. Most days, Andre will do ten or twelve rounds of shadowboxing, working on his movement, sliding around the ring. Day in, day out, and you start to appreciate the extreme concentration needed to stay focused, the tremendous imagination required to envision an opponent in front of you for that long every day, to try out new things on him. Virgil said, and Bobby agreed, that shadowboxing was the biggest part of training, more than bag work or pad work. I had thought about shadowboxing as something like the *katas* that other martial artists do—rigid, structured, rehearsed movements done to train the body when no other training is available. And shadowboxing is like that, but it is kind of free-form *kata*, done endlessly (in front of the mirror at first). "You've got to fall in love with yourself in the mirror," said Virgil, and boxers do spend inordinate amounts of time looking in the mirror, critiquing everything about their stances, looking for flaws or holes, correcting bad habits. It leads to the effortless beauty and motion of great fighters, supreme athletes who have devoted their lives to moving well and with economy of speed and energy.

Virgil had me run the lake with Antonio at eight while he sat and had coffee. Andre was on vacation with his family. Antonio chattered a mile a minute, and we covered an immense range of topics. He was only twenty, from St. Paul, Minnesota, but he'd been fighting since he was eight or nine and had been one of the top amateurs in the country. He was filled with a supreme, unoffensive arrogance, a fully justified belief in his own powers, and was likeable. I managed to keep pace and conversation, but it took a lot more out of me than it did him. And then he took off, running at the proper speed, and left me gasping and pounding heavily along, deeper and deeper in his wake.

I caught up with him back at Coffee with a Beat, where he had finished his run and was stretching, and I stretched next to him in the cool sun. He immediately leapt back into the conversation. His gaze was rarely fixed on me at first; he watched me with his peripheral vision. He spoke of his God-given talent, and it made sense to me; Antonio and Andre were so gifted physically, so much faster and stronger than other men. Imagine that almost all your opponents are eight-, nine-, ten-year-old boys and you are a full-grown man, that's the kind of physical advantages they have. The best way to make sense of these tremendous advantages is to say that God gave you those gifts for a reason. It's a strategy to prevent arrogance and complacency, because in the end those gifts will not be enough. At the top level, in those title fights, you've got to have everything—now you're fighting grown men, too. Antonio had also wrestled in high school, and played football, and his own opinion of his prowess was epic; he didn't have to train or condition and he could make it to the nationals and take second, but of course that lack of discipline had kept him off the Olympic team. He knew that to take it to the next level, to win championships, his gifts wouldn't be enough—he needed everything. Andre had everything.

I sat down next to Virgil to eat some breakfast, and he looked at Antonio, who was still stretching, and said, "Antonio met Andre at camp and was really impressed by him, by his work ethic (Andre was the only kid consistently watching tape at night with the coaches in Olympic camp), and when he came to me, I saw a kid I could reach.

"Antonio has had a tough story, he's bounced from relative to relative, he's been in the streets without a role model. He's come so far since then, just in terms of self-discipline. I saw him just watching Dre, watching the way he carried himself, and he took it to heart." Andre does carry himself like a professional, totally dedicated and immersed, with the maturity of a thirty-year-old man at twenty-two.

Virgil changed the subject. "I watched your tape last night," he said, "and I enjoyed it." He was referring to the National Geographic tape of my muay Thai fight, five years earlier, in Thailand. I hemmed and hawed, always a little embarrassed in front of real fighters in case they should think I was putting myself in their category. I said, "Well, you can see how bad I was," and laughed, and Virgil looked at me and quietly admonished me: "Sam, you got to stop telling yourself and the world that you are a bad fighter," meaning not that I was a good fighter, but for my confidence's sake, I needed to start thinking positive.

We talked about muay Thai for a while, and Virgil said, "You said that when a boxer fights a muay Thai fighter, the Thai fighter will put the boxer in the hospital, and I disagree. I've seen the system and I know I can beat it.

"Now, listen, of course I am going to think boxing is superior, but here's the truth. I watched those fights and there isn't any lateral movement, any circling or feinting; they just come forward at each other. We use our feet, too—but not to kick, to move. And all that knees and elbows on the inside is open to being hit through."

In my MMA fight, I had gotten a good muay Thai clinch on my opponent, and he had bombed me down the stretch with uppercuts. On the tape you could see my head snap back with the impact, so I had to agree.

Virgil continued about my Thailand fight. I had rattled the guy with that good right hand. That had hurt him, that was a boxing punch. Then I kneed him, into the bone under the heart. "There's a narrow little bone, about an inch wide, running underneath the heart," he said. "We don't know what they call it but we know it's there, and it is a great target. When he's bending a little, with his weight coming forward, it can be decisive." It's where my knee had caught him.

We sat in silence, sipping and musing, and I thought that no one had ever talked to me about that fight with analysis.

"I could beat it," Virgil said, "with the right athlete. I would get them setting up, because you have to set to kick. They can't hit while backing up, or moving, and we can. Also, their punching power isn't there; they punch with the elbows behind the fist, similar to how they throw elbows, and we punch with the elbow and shoulder behind the fist."

He hit on a good point, one that most people don't get, and that is how *hard* boxers can punch when they get to the pro level. MMA fighters and fans pooh-pooh boxers because they don't realize how heavy some of those punches are, the result of ten years of constant training, endless repetition. Boxers are grown men who have spent their lives honing that punch, building its speed and power, and the difference between a boxer's punch and a normal man's punch is the difference between a baseball bat and a whiffle-ball bat. One punch can change your life: "One hit'll quit 'em." An uncle of Virgil's was in a high school fight when a teacher laid hands on him, and he hit the teacher and knocked him out with one shot. World-altering power—the uncle went to jail, and the teacher was never the same again, had to quit teaching in a year. There is also the difference of being able to *handle* a punch—fighters get hit all the time, even amateurs—and knowing how to take a shot can be critical. Sometimes regular guys in bars can't handle a punch and get hurt; one of Pat Miletich's great fears was that one of his guys would hit somebody in a bar, someone who had never been hit before in his life, and the sheer shock would kill him.

One of the things Virgil had me working on was pivoting my hips and shoulders when I punched, getting my whole body into the blow. You've got to be able to hit someone hard enough to make him respect you.

I found a new place to stay. I rented out the top floor of a house on Picardy Drive in West Oakland, just a few blocks from the hood and a five-minute drive from Virgil's house. The owners were actually next-door neighbors to a friend of Virgil's, and I could hear him on the phone, describing me, "Yeah, he's a writer, a white kid."

Sheila Glenn and Kevin Thomason were a white married couple in their late thirties with two pit bulls, Amos and Stitch, both rescued from the pound. I learned a lot about pits from being around those two. Sheila and Kevin were both great and helpful and friendly, and although the dogs were a handful, they were a tremendous comfort. I missed being around dogs.

I moved in with my reduced wardrobe and then went to Virgil's house to train.

Virgil's house, the "training house," was a typical big Oakland house perched on a steep hill, and looked out over West Oakland all the way to the far-off shimmer of San Francisco. The air in Oakland was clean and much better than in L.A.—the clarity of long views was remarkable. Even the tap water in Oakland was clean, the cleanest water in the state. Nobody bought water in Oakland—I actually got harassed when I bought it in the supermarket.

I joined Antonio and Virgil in the garage, with the door open and the brilliant sun streaming in, a sense of peace high above the hood, above the hustle and bustle. Antonio was on the treadmill with his wool hat on, and the radio was blaring into a feeling of clean air and space. I rode the exercise bike for ten minutes to warm up, stretched, wrapped up, and started to shadowbox, still working on those three steps Virgil had shown me. Then he had me start in on the heavy bag, in and out in a straight line. He was adamant and unwavering on the basic fundamentals, on twisting the jab all the way over. But his chief concern was telegraphing, giving a little visual cue before you punch or move.

"You drop that left off your chin every time. I'm gonna see that—either keep it pinned or let it free, but don't drop it when you are going to punch."

If you telegraph your punches, you add to your opponent's reaction time, giving him more time to see the punch and slip or block it. He sees the punch before you throw it. The key to hitting is being totally unpredictable. If he can't get any kind of read on you, you are putting him on the defensive. Virgil is the real deal; he doesn't teach the same combinations that everyone knows and just go over them on the mitts again and again. He teaches *fighting*. Andre's shadowboxing never looks like other boxers'; it doesn't fall into that overly comfortable rehearsed sameness. It's almost awkward at times, because real fighting is often awkward.

Virgil was on the phone when Antonio finished his run on the treadmill and came over next to me and started talking about the jab, showing me what I was doing wrong, and Virgil instantly squawked at him, "Yo, T, we're not teaching Sam how to be *you*, we're teaching Sam how to be *him*!" and Antonio got it. He laughed and said, "You right, you right," and smiled and vanished upstairs.

"Now shadowbox this next round, doing what we worked on. I want to check your concentration," said Virgil. I shadowboxed carefully for the round, shuffling shoes, scraping the mats.

"Now, Sam, you're critiquing yourself, you're thinking too much. You can't worry so much what it looks like, you've got to just let it feel right."

I went another round, worrying less about Virgil's concerned eye and trying to enjoy myself more, and got a tight-lipped nod. "Better. Now I want you to shadowbox the whole round and pick up your feet; I don't want to hear them." He demonstrated in his brilliant white shoes, gliding, dancing his elegant waltz, his feet hushed. "Focus on your feet." And so another round went by, stepping and moving, listening to the tap and scrape.

"When I hear your feet so loud, pounding, it tells me that you are too stiff, too rigid," he said, and then we did dance. I put my jab out straight, and Virgil led me by that outstretched arm, pushing and pulling, with me stepping quietly one-two behind him, trying to keep the tension to a minimum and feel where he was going, trying to keep his feet split with my lead foot. By the end of the round, I felt a little better.

"Just feel where I am going," he said. He would turn easily and smoothly, and I began to understand what he wanted, waltzing around the garage.

The worst was to come. We went to the mitts, and Virgil would touch me and have me jab, and then come back when I left the jab out there and *whap* me on the head. After a few times of this, he said, "Sam, I can see you tense when I come to hit, and I can see you get embarrassed and flush, I can read the lines on your forehead. Any one of those things is too much. I can make you do what I want to do." *Wham,* he hit me again. I was red-faced with indignation. I hadn't been hit in a long time, even just training, and felt awkward and out of joint, lumbering and tight. My left shoulder, of Brazil fame, was burning. Virgil shook his head.

Around we went. Virgil didn't tell me to stop bouncing, but he did say between rounds, "Sam, bouncing is something that happens when you're young. If you're a fighter and you've been in the game since eleven, twelve years old, then when you're eighteen or nineteen, you can bounce and move, like Andre. And when he gets older, he won't bounce like that, but he'll be able to call it up when he needs it. For a thirty-year-old man, bouncing is a waste of energy, just bouncing up and down."

Whap, he'd tap me, but I began to read him a little and retract my hands fast enough, despite the pain in both shoulders, still overexcited and off, and Virgil would laugh when I threw a wrong punch—he just couldn't help himself. When I would stumble or get ahead, we would circle, giggling.

"Don't let me rush you. Wait for things to be right, be deliberate. You don't want to be flying down the freeway so fast you can't see the scenery, because you'll miss your exit. I'll try and hurry you up, but don't let me, stay within yourself, within what you want to do, and wait for the opening."

We finally called it quits, and Virgil, if not happy, was at least content with my progress and understanding for the day, and he helped me take off my gloves and wraps, something no one had ever done before.

"I was thinking about what you said, you know, show me how you want to be?" I said to Virgil, glowing from the exercise. "The fighter I want to be like is Sugar Ray Leonard, with his hands like this," and I showed him how Leonard would stand with his arms across his chest, a pocket fighter who could out-quick everyone. I was kidding. I knew what kind of fighter I could be: the tall white guy with decent punches who blocks and takes everything. Not a bob-and-weave wonder—that's for athletic black guys. But I wanted to hear what Virgil would say. Could I be a pocket-fighter like Sugar Ray?

"Well, you've got to have the reflexes to dodge and slip if you want to fight out of the pocket like that, but it's possible. What you've got to remember is you are seeing Ray Leonard after three hundred amateur fights and twenty professional. He didn't start out like that. You got to fight like *you,* who *you* are. If I got a guy who can moonwalk and throw a bolo punch and land it every time, then I'll have him throw it. That's who he is."

That afternoon, I spoke to Pat Miletich on the phone, and he said, "You're going to fight a pro fight, right?" Pat has always had a slightly exaggerated take on my abilities; if I could stay in one place and train full-time for a year, maybe. Virgil eventually warned me that if I really got into a gym and stayed there, somebody would try to take me pro.

Over the next few days, I got a handle on what Virgil wanted to try to do with me. Self-expression, slowness, fundamentals. He wanted me to be able to punch with balance by the time I left, and then I could develop on my own from there. "We're not going to spar you until the end. I want to get you right," he said.

Back in front of the mirror at King's, I was going slower and slower, just two punches for five straight rounds. Virgil sat right on top of me, making me slow down. I could have been embarrassed, but there was no point. Just try to learn, see if you can get it right. There were a lot more beginners in the gym that day anyway, a lot more college-looking kids. Virgil said it was because of Andre and the exposure he'd given the place. Slower and slower, to the point where I was punching at tai chi speed.

V was in my ear, about balance and that rear foot being like a shark's tail, streaming out behind the body, where power comes from. "If you get the feet right, everything else will fall in place, that's where speed and power come from," he said. And I could hear the echo of Pat Miletich saying, "If you want your hands to move faster, you have to move your feet faster," and William C. C. Chen saying, "Everything from the toe."

* * *

173

Every morning, I would get a call from Virgil around seven or eight o'clock with the plan for the day. We would meet for coffee, or run the lake, and after a few days he called with a different plan.

"Sam, I want you to meet me over in Hayward, at Joe's place. We are going to work with Heather—I'm going to work you together."

Heather Hartman was a woman whom Virgil and Andre had known for years. They would see and talk to her around the gym all the time, as she was working with the same strength coach, Mike Benz. She was a professional soccer goalie, but the women's pro league had folded; she was still playing but not making any money. She was twenty-four years old, and she and Virgil had discussed it for months before they decided to train her. "Virgil kept saying I had long arms," she said.

Joe's Karate Gym, in Hayward, a town just south of Oakland, was where Andre and Virgil had first met, many years ago. Virgil had just finished his workout (he was still fighting), and a nine-year-old boy was hitting the bag, and peeking at him. Virgil saw something in him, and gave him an approving nod, and the boy went back to hitting the bag. Joe and Virgil had maintained their relationship, and the boxing ring was open for Virgil to use in the mornings, and so Heather, Virgil, and I often met there.

Heather was a tall, strong blond woman, powerful through the shoulders and legs and sporty in a way that reminded me of the New England girls I had grown up with. She was very serious and dedicated, and one of the reasons she was sick of soccer was that she was tired of being the most serious player on the field.

We shadowboxed in front of the mirrors, hit some pads with Virgil, and then sparred. Heather would come after me with everything, and I had to work on my defense and keep her from hitting me, sometimes touching her with my gloves if she was too open or standing still where I could hit her. She was deadly serious and came out swinging, looking to take my head off; I was surprised by her genuine aggression. She was tenacious, and I had to move and block and be careful, because she *wanted* to hit me.

Virgil was deeply satisfied, because I needed the defensive work and she needed to start the process of getting comfortable in the ring. Not that I was comfortable—it was the first time I had been in the ring in more than a year. We went five rounds that first day, but in the days that followed we would go eight or even ten rounds, Heather usually charging, and me dropping back, and as she got better I had to work harder to avoid getting cracked. I came to see Virgil's wisdom in training us together, because it was good for both of us.

"There's a method to my madness," he said. "I am using you and Heather because you can complement each other. I want to work on Heather's natural strength and aggression, because she'll be able to overwhelm these other girls. You need to work on your defense, especially against amateurs, who are going to be charging. You need to touch and move, instinctively—you've got to outthink them. It's a thinking man's game."

Virgil and I once discussed Heather while we walked around the lake.

"You know, I got the women's finals for the nationals at home on DVD and I've been watching them, and I can see from the way they hook that they've been trained to fight like men, instead of doing what comes naturally," he said. "You got to look at what you got; their hips are different in the way they move. The mechanics of how they throw a hook is going to be different. The first thing I'd be drumming out of a woman fighter is that this is a man's sport."

Heather's real strength lies in her aggression and determination. "She has the fuel," said Virgil. "Every fighter needs to have fuel, and she's got it. Fighters feel helpless. They have been victims, and then they start victimizing others and then themselves, and real fighters learn to use it, to harness that aggression. I never thought I would train a girl. We were talking and she said, 'God would work it out,' and I realized that God had put us together for a reason."

Heather's mom had been in and out of mental hospitals her whole life, diagnosed as schizophrenic when she was really manic-depressive. She tried to kill herself numerous times. Heather had a twin sister and an older brother, and they had to deal with her mother going through spurts of health and sickness. "You could see it coming, her bad days," Heather said, very matter-of-factly. I could imagine what that must have looked like to a young child, seeing your mom sink into a funk and knowing that she might really kill herself this time. Heather's father died in 2001 from some sort of infection. After Heather told me these things, her constant relentless aggression in the ring made total sense, and Virgil knew he had something. Heather had the fuel; I had to wonder if I had it.

* * *

The days began to develop a rhythm, running in the morning, training at King's in the afternoon, sometimes at Joe's with Heather, sometimes at the house.

Antonio and I would run the lake easily, chatting about girls and movies, and then he would blast off and run five stairs before I could run two. He said to me as we finished up once, "I don't like fighting but I love it, you feel me?" and I did, I felt him. What he meant was that he doesn't start fights, doesn't want them to happen, but he loves it when he's in it, the flush and rage, the joys of hitting and being hit.

Virgil said that Antonio was "uncoachable" until he reached him. Virgil, with all his experience at the juvenile hall with troubled kids, is a master at reaching them, because he speaks and understands street language and credibility. He commands respect—that's how he can reach tough street kids, because he was one of them and understands their mentality, and he is interested. His attentiveness and ability to listen are intense, and his ability to see into a person profound.

Later that day I worked with Virgil down in his garage; the door was up with a cool breeze coming off the ocean, and the sun was blasting down on Oakland below us. We listened to up-tempo jazz and Cuban drums, complicated rhythms. Boxing is all about rhythms; Sonny Liston would only work out to "Night Train" on an endless loop.

"Sam, you go through changes in your career, even you. You have to be objective and look at yourself honestly, and the situation—this goes back to knowing who you are. You change. There are different phases of fighting, and right now you are thirty years old—you're not thinking about being a young fighter, you're thinking about being the toughest thirty-five-year-old man on the planet. Better than you ever were in your twenties."

V had me throwing the straight right into the bag and then coming back with the hook. He wanted me to stand still when I did it, but as I threw it, over the course of the round, I crept to my left. He said, "Look where you are now. That's what happened without you even thinking; it means you want to punch moving left."

I already knew this about myself, and I thought it was inevitable for an orthodox fighter. An orthodox fighter is right-handed and leads with his left, keeping his stronger hand in reserve for the power punches. As you move with each punch, you are always taking tiny steps with your left foot, and it means most orthodox fighters drift to their left as they fight. I had noticed this even back at Harvard, in sparring; I told a friend that anybody who could move right would kill everyone.

Virgil brought me back to the present. "Now concentrate on staying in the same place," he said. "As soon as you start moving, you become predictable. I'll see what you do, and in the later rounds I'll have you moving into my right. I'll set you up."

In between rounds, in the one-minute rest period, Virgil would elaborate. "It's like mountain climbers reading a mountain, when you start reading a fighter. You study, you look for different routes; ways up and ways down, things you would do if you were hurt, if the light changed. But you study just like a subject in school—you go back to it and check it. I give you a double jab and see what you do, and then I give it to you again, and then later I come back to it—'Yeah, you're still doing it'—and then I find the right moment."

We hit mitts and my left arm began to burn, and Virgil whapped away at me, slapping my head and going to the body, forcing me to cover and have defense and then throw the quick four, jab-right-left-right, *bapbapbapbap*—and he kept saying, "You're killing it, don't try and kill it, just relax, relax your face, just deadpan your face and it will relax your whole body," and I instantly felt how my face had frozen into a rictus. I relaxed it and let it slump expressionless, and finally my whole body started to relax, my shoulders eased, and I just tapped the mitts and Virgil was happy. "Relaxed, you can go on and on."

He told me, "The more relaxed you are, the more economy you'll have in your motion. The first time Holmes fought Norton, he threw maybe seventy punches and landed thirty-five—and when he fought him three years later, he threw fifty punches but still landed the same amount."

That night in my room, I heard gunshots, not too far away, the loud flat cracks, closer than expected. I waited for sirens, and it was much later when I finally heard them and saw the chopper, strangely quiet out the window. The choppers here must have had some kind of noise-reduction system, because they seemed so much quieter than the ones I used to ride firefighting. They would flutter over at night like in some kind of science-fiction film, robot hunters from the future.

I woke early, at five or six, and there was a particularly vocal bird outside my window in the deserted predawn, singing a song that sounded familiar. Eventually, I realized it was the car-alarm progression, the one that everyone knows, the varying beeps and blares of a standard car alarm. The bird had picked it up and built on it, but the underlying theme was recognizable.

I climbed into my car and rode down to King's through the hood, my daily ritual. What made a poor neighborhood in Oakland was the same as what makes a poor neighborhood anywhere; it's the numbers of people loitering, with nothing to do but hang out and watch the street go by. I drove through the wide streets without looking too hard, only peripherally noticing the windows and doors guarded by wood and iron, the out-of-business shops and restaurants, old cars, things that could never be on the street in Massachusetts, sometimes with brilliant spinning chrome rims, music thumping, in front of and behind me.

One morning, I met Andre and Virg down at Coffee with a Beat and sat chatting with Virgil while Andre did a local TV interview. The Emile Griffith documentary, *Ring of Fire,* had just been on TV and we ended up discussing it at length. Emile Griffith was a very tough fighter in the sixties, who had won something like six world titles, and who also preferred to relax at gay bars. Benny "the Kid" Paret had insulted him at the weigh-in, called him a *maricón* ("faggot" in Spanish), and in his anger Griffith killed Paret in the ring. At least, that's how the story goes, that's the one-sentence Hollywood pitch. The documentary was excellent, with an emotional meeting between Griffith and Paret's son. Griffith begged for forgiveness, and got it.

Virgil mused that it was the smaller guys who were usually getting killed in the ring, often taking bad beatings, walking out on their own power, and lapsing into comas and dying. Pat Miletich said that boxing averaged ten deaths a year worldwide. The American Medical Association puts the figure at .13 per 1,000, whatever that means, and I've read anywhere from five hundred deaths since 1884 to nine hundred since 1920.

The lighter-weight fighters are often the ones "drying out," cutting weight to make the fight. Fighters will cut ten or fifteen pounds to make weight, and that dehydration makes them more prone to severe injury. It seems that it's not the one big punch that proves fatal; it's the accumulation of damage in a long fight that is so dangerous. It's actually safer to get knocked out than to stay in there and take repeated beatings. There is a key difference between MMA and boxing, which in fact makes boxing *more* dangerous. It has to do with "stoppage," when a referee stops a fight. In boxing, there is the standing eight count if you are stunned (rarely used these days) and the ten count if you are knocked down. This means you have eight or ten seconds to clear your head of the effects of a blow. It's from the old rules, to give a man a "sporting" chance, so that some lucky punch wouldn't decide a fight. In MMA, because the game continues on the ground, and a stunned fighter is in danger of getting hit unprotected, the referee stops the fight more quickly if one fighter cannot "intelligently" defend himself. So if you get caught stunned, just a little bit, just for a second—something that might get you a standing eight in boxing—the fight is over in MMA.

I asked Virgil, "Shouldn't the cornermen have thrown in the towel?" and he nodded judiciously. "But remember, the corner works for the fighter; the fighter pays his salary. Now, as for me, if I don't see a way to win, then we'll be back to fight another day. But Paret's trainer knew he could take shots. He'd taken beatings and come back to knock people out—maybe he was playing possum. But here's where his trainer is going wrong—that's no game plan. His trainer should have been working to fix that problem, not to accept it as part of the plan."

Paret had indeed been famous for the legendary amount of punishment he could absorb, and many feel that the referee, who has been criticized for the slowness with which he stopped the fight, was waiting for him to stage another comeback. Griffith had Paret in trouble, and the referee seemed sluggishly frozen as Griffith laid into Paret as he slumped in the corner.

Virgil places the blame on Paret's manager, a man who knew little about boxing and who exploited the illiterate Cuban for one last fight. Three months earlier, Paret had fought Gene Fullmer and lost a particularly brutal match. Fullmer was equally famous for the amount of punishment he could deliver, and he himself said he'd never hurt anyone as bad as he had Paret. The documentary showed a brief clip of that fight, and the shelling Paret was catching made me cringe. "Man," said Virg, "Fullmer used to come up here to Oakland to get sparring, and his partners would have to wear baseball catcher's gear to keep their ribs from getting torn up. He was perfect for what he did, which was get in and hurt you." Paret's damage from that earlier fight had contributed directly to his death.

Andre finished up his interview and came and sat with us. He told me how former world champion and all-time great Roy Jones Jr., one of his promoters, had said that Andre still fights like an amateur. In the amateurs, you are just worried about scoring points in the brief time you have, while in the pros you're more concerned about hitting harder, pacing yourself, and doing damage. An interviewer asked Andre about what Roy had said, and he just laughed and replied, "Well, I've had a hundred and fifty amateur fights and three professional, so what do you expect? Ten years of my life I've been an amateur, so it's going to take time . . . but that works for me, because I can use that for leverage when they want me to fight somebody I'm not ready for, if they try to push me too fast. I'm on a four-year plan for a title, and right now I don't care if there's two people in the audience—as long as I am getting the right fights.

"I respect Roy, he's the fighter I'd want to emulate—he didn't have a Hagler, a Hearns, a Leonard in his era. He didn't fight bums, but he made them look that way. He's out of boxing, unscathed, plenty of money, brains and family intact—that's a great fighter." Roy bucked the system and started his own promotional company, another thing Andre admires.

We sat away from Virgil and just talked. Andre sipped his green tea, and I sipped my fourth cup of coffee. Andre was slender and strong, with broad shoulders and a dense torso, a rocky, solid core. He has big brown eyes that are almost soft, and I could see why they call him baby-faced, why his opponents hope that he's just a pretty boy who has been boxing clean in the amateurs and whom they can rough up. His look is polite and church-going, with a wispy young man's mustache and beard. But there is a slight droop, a downward tug at the edges of his face, a look of sadness and knowledge. He has suffered; he knows his identity in the world, and despite his apparent youth, no one will rough him up and shake him from his game.

We chatted about his two kids, Andre Jr. and Malachi, and their mother, Tiffany, and how they met. Andre's brother had been going to school up in Olympia, and Andre was visiting him when he met her. "My brother was boxing until he was fifteen or sixteen, and then he got tired of it. He had the talent of the two of us," Andre says demurely, "but he pursued other interests. He didn't love boxing, he just liked it; and to do what I do, you have to love it, that's the bottom line."

I asked Andre if he ever struggled with the commitment, and he replied instantly: "All the time, all the time. I didn't understand what was possible, but my father did, and Virgil did. My brother and I, we went to school and then went to the gym every day; other kids got to play at each other's houses, or get jobs. I didn't understand it then, but looking back, I'm glad we sacrificed so much. It hit me recently, I'd say about eighteen or nineteen, when I had Andre Jr., my first child. I realized the best way to make an income was to go out and win the men's U.S. National Championship. I set goals for that at seventeen and won it in the under-nineteen bracket, and got fifteen hundred a month as a stipend. There are so many camps and competitions abroad. That's when boxing started getting real to me. There was a time even before my father died that I just wasn't in it. I knew how to come into the gym and make it look like I was working, but I was just going through the motions."

He sipped his tea and continued. "It was in 2002, my last under-nineteen fight. I was up at the Worlds, and my father was working, so he wasn't there. One of my rivals, Curtis Stevens, was there, and the brackets came in the first night, and he was my first fight. So I called my dad and said, 'You gotta be here.' He grabbed his wife and jumped in his CRX and came down. That's how he was—he would tell his boss, 'Sorry, my son's fighting,' and come, there was no missing it. I've got that same spirit. He came, I won, I looked good; and I won the next night, and that was the last time my father saw me fight. He looked great. I thanked him and told him I loved him.

"The day after we got back, we were supposed to run this hill at five a.m., but he called me at four-thirty and said he wasn't feeling well—and my dad doesn't do that; he's always there for training. That was the last time I talked to him. The next day, I was just back from a run with Virgil and was still wet when I answered the phone, and my cousin Debbie was crying. 'What's wrong?' I asked her, and she said, 'Lemme talk to Virg,' and I said, 'What's wrong?' and she said, 'Your father—' and I said, 'My father what?' She didn't want to tell me, but now I was going crazy, and she broke down and said, 'He's dead.' I just threw the phone. It didn't make sense to me."

We paused on the sunny morning. I was very quiet, just listening, careful not to break his thoughts. He was very intentionally telling me this story; it was a part of him that he wanted me to know.

Andre continued: "I went upstairs to Virg and I kept saying, 'It's over man, it's over,' and he broke down and was crying. It was a crazy time. At my father's funeral, I made a vow. I told him, over his casket, 'Papa, I'm going to bring the gold back.' But it was hard, I was depressed for six months, a year even. I didn't want to box. I just wanted to be depressed. I couldn't pray, couldn't read my Bible. God slowly but surely put the right people around me. My mother, Bishop Calloway, and my whole family, even though they were hurt, too. Slowly I just kept coming back, I started getting that itch to be in the gym. My first fight back I looked great, I knocked him out. That's how we are in my father's family—we take a loss, we come back hard. It's not that we're big and bad, it's just in us, in the blood.

"Plus, there's the spirit of God in me—people take that lightly. It's like the new fad to profess Christ. But this is real. Reporters made comments like 'Andre Ward found God on the way to the Olympics,' like it's some new thing, like once I got success I started talking about God—but it's real. I get revelations that are hard to explain, but you just know, nobody sustained you or delivered you but God. You just know.

"I know God is real, and I really believe that I have a bigger task than just boxing. I mean, I have an idea of what it is, to share the gospel, to get it out, to tell people the good news about Christ—but I'm not sure what form it will take. Boxing is a platform, a pedestal to get eyes on me, to get the word out."

Though sometimes in his postfight interviews Andre sounded fanatical, the more time I spent around him, the more his ardent faith felt real and sane. I hadn't spent a lot of time around people who had really taken God into their hearts, although my older sister had recently been "saved." But as I got used to the language and the constant references, the quoting of scripture, it came to feel more normal to me.

Andre was a much needed shot in the arm for Oakland's boxing community and a source of great pride to all kinds of people throughout the city. When I wore an "Andre Ward S.O.G." (Son of God) T-shirt, guys stopped me at the taco stand down in the hood and in the mall in Emeryville, and once a little old white lady stopped Virgil at Lake Temescal to say how impressed she was with Andre. I went with him to throw out the first pitch at an A's game, and beforehand we joked around that he was going to bring some heat. When he got out there, he lobbed the pitch in to home, and I asked him, "What happened?" and he laughed and said, "It's a little different out there with everyone watching—I just had to get it over the plate." We walked as a group, Virgil and Antonio and a few friends and I, and everywhere we had to wait patiently for Andre to sign autographs and pose for pictures, something he did tirelessly. He would linger and chat and pose for as long as people wanted him to, and he wouldn't be rushed.

Andre would sometimes go to Vegas or elsewhere to watch big fights—part of building a name for himself was to be seen at ringside, and his promoter would arrange for it. ESPN's *Friday Night Fights* was coming to San Jose, just forty-five minutes south of Oakland. San Jose had a larger Hispanic population and was more of a boxing town. Boxing in the United States has always resided with the poor, with the immigrants. It was Jewish and Italian and Irish, and then black, and now it's Hispanic.

The way television was working those days, they would broadcast mid-level bouts on cable, but the big title fights would still be pay-per-view. So ESPN had fights on Tuesday and Friday, and Showtime and FSN had fights, but not the best quality, as boxing was still hamstrung by its greed. Instead of pushing the sport onto free TV—like the Super Bowl—and increasing the long-range popularity, boxing promoters were still stuck on the short-term profit. If the Super Bowl or World Series had been pay-per-view all these years, would they be the cash cows they are today?

On the night of the fight, Andre was outside the training house talking on his BlackBerry, resplendent in a silk suit, with cuff links and alligator shoes, hair cut neatly and mustache trimmed and chocolate skin smooth and glowing with health. He was all smiles. He had just found out that I had gone to Harvard, and he said, "You keep a lot under your hat." Virgil had talked to me about the way fighters dress, and Andre had echoed it. Other fighters often dressed with sideways ball caps and bling, all street—looking like rappers or street thugs—but Andre and Virg were trying to "take the game over." Bob Arum and Don King, the dominant promoters, were aging and wouldn't last forever, and Andre was "punching to make money without punching. It's business; you got to look respectable to get respect. You got to give yourself the best chance to make the most money with the least risk, because one bad fight can do it."

Andre knew that if he wanted to be taken seriously as a businessman, not just as a fighter, he had to dress the part. Of course, the really beautiful thing about fighting is that nothing matters unless you win. In the ring, the truth will out.

I went inside, as he was deep in conversation and Virgil was showering, and leafed through a press pamphlet from his latest fight. The interviewer had asked him to pick one word to describe himself, and he said, "Chameleon."

I sat there and thought about that, and about what Norman Mailer had written: "Of course, trying to learn from boxers was a quintessentially comic quest. Boxers were liars. Once you knew what they thought, you could hit them. So their personalities became masterpieces of concealment."

There is something about great fighters that is hidden in plain sight; in one sense, they are the most open people in the world, willing to tell you everything; but in another, they mislead, or allow you to mislead yourself. They stand up in the ring exposed, practically naked; and yet their strategy, their reality, is a secret. Fighting professionally is about illusion, deception, and it becomes woven into the fighters' lives. When I first started talking to professional fighters, like Tony in Iowa, I thought he was open and forthcoming, but now I realized much had to be hidden. Look strong when you are weak, Virgil would counsel. Catch your breath but look like you are about to attack, so that he doesn't realize you are catching your breath. Force him backward while you recover.

Virgil emerged in a brilliant vintage Everlast Sugar Ray Leonard sweat suit, and Bobby showed up, and we piled into two cars. I rode with Don and Will, Don's son. Don was a short and slender, dark black man with long tight braids and glasses, wearing a batik shirt. He was in his late forties or early fifties, but his hair was still dark and his arms dense with muscle; he gave the impression of wiry power. He dressed and carried himself like a jazz musician. He was a trainer and a novice cut man and had known Virgil for a long time and was his assistant trainer, wrapping Andre's hands, and developing as a professional cut man. The cut man is in the corner to look after the fighter's bruises and cuts so that they don't become a reason the fight gets stopped. If a fighter gets cut from a punch or, more likely, a head butt on the eyebrow, and the blood is interfering with his vision, the referee or doctor will stop the fight. If there are millions of dollars on the line, a cut man who can stop that bleeding in thirty seconds (or keep a bruise from swelling an eye shut) between rounds becomes a valuable asset. "I could always do shit with my hands," Don said, "and I never been afraid of pressure. I don't have no stage fright and I'm not afraid to work cuts, even though I don't have a lot of experience."

We arrived in San Jose, parked, and walked to the venue, Andre in his shimmering suit and everyone else dressed well. Bobby was with us, and he had just had eye surgery, so he was wearing thick massive black glasses and looked like Ray Charles in his white Kangol hat.

I got my media pass, and we went in and sat ringside. The preliminary bouts were under way, and the ESPN TV crew was running around setting up; they would only televise a few fights. Nonito Donaire was fighting Paulino Villalobos, and Nonito (or Nito) was an old-time friend of Virgil's and Andre's—he trained out of Joe's in Hayward. Villalobos had lost his last six fights and was an opponent, and he came straight after Nito, tough and moving forward. Nito could do what he wanted—he moved, took potshots, and stayed elusive—and suddenly Virgil was galvanized and began yelling to him in a clear voice that I could tell Nito could hear, "Use your jab, Nito, it's working, use your jab, and then go underneath—there you go, there you *go!*" Virgil was tense and committed. ESPN was a big deal to these up-and-comers, they had to make an impression, they had to look good. If you are fighting on TV, you have to look good, make an exciting fight, because that's where it all starts. A ringside official whom Virgil knew turned around and said, "He can't hear you," and Virgil responded with a short laugh. "I bet he do. Uppercut to the body, Nito!"

I heard a woman in the crowd behind me scream, "He's dropping his left!" but none of this really made much difference. Nito looked terrific and was having his way with the guy. His opponent suddenly seemed old, a working-class Mexican in his late thirties, chasing a payday. Mexican fighters are the current face of boxing, looking for a way out, a combination of the economics of their country and machismo; as a friend of mine said: "The Romantic period came late to Spain." The Mexican fan base is huge and loyal, like the U.S. fans of fifty years ago.

This was my first live boxing match, and I was ringside with a media pass and instantly struck by how different it was from boxing on TV. Boxing on TV is clean, detached, almost sterile and two dimensional compared to boxing from ringside. There's a reason ringside seats are so expensive—you can understand the punching and the meat intuitively, you can feel the weight and power, things that TV conceals.

Often the judges at ringside will score the match differently from people at home watching on TV, which generates controversy, but it is easy to understand, because the fight feels so different, so much more savage and desperate, from ringside. At the fights, I realized boxing is *more* brutal than MMA. Its arcane rules force the combatants to stand and fight. No matter how much they might want to do other things— like clinch and wrestle, or fight without trading blows—they have to trade. Boxing gloves, those grotesque lobster claws, keep you from getting cut, and they certainly protect your hands so you can punch, but they don't dissipate the force with which you get hit. The concussive blow is still there, despite the padding, rattling your brains around in your skull. You just don't cut.

Andre was being gracious and working—this was part of his job—tirelessly shaking hands, posing, and signing photos that I was carrying in my satchel. He'd brought a thick stack of hundreds of photos, and they were all signed and given out by the end of the night. Little kids flocked to and followed him, play-acted for him, and I thought, *They're always drawn to great boxers, aren't they?* There's something of a Pied Piper in certain boxers. Bundini Brown, Muhammad Ali's manager, companion, and the man who coined "Float like a butterfly, sting like a bee," once said of Ali, "He turned around and cared for other people, like little babies and poor people and drunks and dope addicts, and was interested in riding subways and walking in the slums—I had to stop and wonder why is he doing this?" There is a connection between fighters and those outside of society's rules, like children and drunks and the homeless, who need a protector and a source of ultimate strength and safety. Fighters step in and out of society; society's rules (don't cut in line, don't punch people in bars) have a looser hold, because society asks them to cast those rules away on certain strict occasions.

The next fight was José "the Punisher" Perez against some absolute opponent, a kid without any semblance of ability who didn't belong in the ring at all—and José could box, he had some science. It was sickening. I watched him trying to break this kid down, to dominate him, to physically ruin him, and I felt disgusted with myself, and with fighting. How have I been able to watch this and be involved in this without really getting what it is about, which is destroying someone? It's about killing someone without killing him. You are supposed to try to kill someone up until the point when the referee and the rules step in to save his life, at which point you must instantly revert to a normal human being.

Maybe it was the crowd, screaming for a knockout, that bugged me. The kid was so outclassed, so terrible with his flailing jab. He kept fighting, he was game, and somewhere in his mind he thought he had a chance. There was none. He thought he was being brave, but he was just taking a beating. The crowd wanted clean hits and a KO, and suddenly I was casting around for something positive about this whole scene. The Punisher couldn't put his man away, and the kid took his bow at the end, but the whole thing looked absurd. Sure, he was courageous, but he never even had a chance. In boxing, all men are not created equal.

Virgil muttered, "His corner should be arrested," for letting the kid fight. José not being able to knock him out looked bad for him, because the opponent was so god awful, and José's father was promoting him as the number one featherweight prospect in the country. We could hear a group of Mexicans behind us complaining that José wasn't what they thought he was.

The main event was next, with local favorite José Celaya, from Salinas, against James "Spider" Webb. Celaya was about 26–2 and had been knocked out, and Webb was 17–0, but Webb was here to lose to Celaya. That was the plan; Celaya was the heavy favorite and rising superstar, while Webb was a decent but surmountable opponent. Of course, no one had told Webb that.

Webb looked like a tattooed redneck from Tennessee, and he came out and danced around in camouflage in his corner, a shorter, muscle-bound bodybuilder. Celaya was smaller but had the crowd behind him, cheering like mad for anything he did. As the fight started, Celaya was the better boxer, but Webb was much bigger and stronger, and he kept coming, punching straight, firing and firing. He was in shape. I looked over at Bobby and said, "Whaddya think?" and he snorted. "If I said 'grape,' you would know what I mean," he said. I laughed. Bobby meant neither one could punch hard enough to bust a grape. He was disgusted by almost all modern boxing. You could almost hear him start in with "Man, what Sugar Ray Robinson would have done to either of these cats . . ."

Webb was flat-footed, and Virgil said that was because he was taught hands before feet—"The feet will never catch up . . . you got to teach feet first." But Celaya was outgunned, he wasn't strong enough to hurt Webb. Celaya bobbed and weaved, ran backward and had superior hand speed, but he couldn't hurt the much bigger, better-conditioned Webb. In the fourth, right at the end, Celaya was knocked down. In the later rounds, it turned into a war, both fighters bleeding from head butts, and though Celaya rallied, he wasn't hitting hard enough to take it to Webb, who ate his shots on his arms and played possum. "He's beating on him, but he ain't really hurting him," said Virgil in my ear. Celaya went down twice in the eighth and that was it.

The promoter Don Clark walked by us, cursing and swearing through the roar in a good-natured way, and Bobby and Virgil burst out laughing, because Celaya was Don's big draw and "ain't nobody going to pay to see him now—he's through."

Don yelled over the thundering crowd that he had picked Webb up from the airport and he had said to him, "I throw a hundred punches a round—I hope your boy is ready for that."

Bobby said, "He knows who he is, and there are two people in the ring, anything can happen."

"It's a cold game," said Virgil. "Celaya just got retired in front of his home crowd." As we walked out of the arena, Andre was on the phone to Diego Corrales, who had just won a knock-down, drag-out war of a fight against Luis Castillo in a giant pay-per-view title fight. It had been the fight of the year, maybe the fight of the decade, with Corrales coming back from getting knocked down twice to win by knockout. Diego had been the better boxer (at least Virgil thought so) but had gone to war, had been sucked into trading with Castillo—and it had made for an electrifying fight. Virgil wasn't impressed, as he felt that Diego could have won without getting all beat up, but the fight had shaken up the boxing world. I could hear Andre telling Diego, "You are getting these guys knocked out," meaning that Celaya had seen the fight and tried to do the same thing, win a crowd-pleasing war instead of outboxing and outthinking his opponent.

Carlo Rotella wrote in *Cut Time*:

> The warrior syndrome: . . . the tendency of some dead-game fighters with sound boxing skills to abandon technique, shape-shifting lycanthropically into brawlers who win exciting fights and inspire the fans' love by accepting several doozies on the kisser in order to deliver one of their own. In the long run, those fighters lose more then they gain: . . . they begin to lose bouts that they could have won by boxing rather than slug-ging; they suffer extended beatings, cheered on by crowds expecting their pulp-faced hero to pull out one more one-punch comeback; they survive in the business too long on guts and will; they get punchy.

The fighter loses sight of his own identity; he wants to show he's just as tough as his opponent, so he brawls. Andre's opinion on the Corrales fight was similar, even though that fight was grabbing boxing headlines. He murmured: "It was a great fight, no doubt. Promoters, managers, fans—jumping up and down, it's a big party. But at some point that night, both those fighters go to their rooms and look at them-selves in the mirror; they both are going to have to lay on that bed and look at the ceiling. You don't know what kind of damage you may have taken in that fight. After all the hoopla and cameras and lights, and everyone has gone home, the fighter is sitting there by himself, and eventually he's going to have to look his kids in the eye. And if something's not right with the man, then nobody's going to be there with him."

After the fight, we fell back into the routine of training, and the days flowed together. This is what boxers do, they work. Road work, bag work, plain "work" (sparring), an endless compilation of hours of training. It's a journey that never ends. A forty-year-old fighter works as hard on his skills as a ten-year-old does. I could see fighters progress. I saw Heather come along, and also a young amateur named Karim, whom Virgil had been working with at King's. But Karim's commitment was often questioned, and to his face.

"Did you run today, Karim?" Virg would drawl, and Karim would reply with an emphatic yes. Karim was short, muscular, and leonine, a coiled spring of power, an awkward fighter but tremendously quick and strong, something that had intrigued Virgil into training him. Virgil saw the potential. But Karim had a wife and kids, and a job, and sometimes his commitment wasn't there. That's the other thing pro boxers need, the commitment. It is easy to become enthusiastic and fall in love with fighting for six months, or a year; but to stay in love, to force yourself into the engine of pain every day for three years, then five—that's where the pros separate themselves.

Karim walked off and Virgil muttered, "A fighter will break his own heart, and then the trainer's heart." What he meant was that a fighter will put in the time, the work, for years—and then suddenly become derailed, allow himself to be derailed, by a woman, or a situation, and will lose the ability to focus in the gym. He breaks his own heart, and of course the heart of the trainer, who has invested so much of his life and his future with the fighter. The trainer and the fighter have as deep a codependency as there is in sports, totally reliant on and tied to each other. The trainer has nothing without the talent and will of the fighter. He literally has nothing—he makes money only from the fighter. A trainer is defined by his fighters. He pours a tremendous amount of time, money, and emotion into the vessel of the fighter. Virgil has always had his job with the county and so has been able to train patiently and not rush his fighters for a payday. But he did mutter to me about Andre, "This kid is taking me places I would never have got to." There is always the danger of the fighter leaving the trainer, going to another trainer, and in fact there are rules in the gym (along with "No spitting on the floor") that prevent a trainer from talking to another trainer's fighter. Stealing fighters is universally despised but an ever-present threat, especially when a fighter starts making money.

I kept working, with Virgil and on my own, trying to concentrate, trying to stay focused. Virg worked me with the mitts, telling me not to raise up as I jabbed. I was coming up onto the tips of my toes, floating. "Don't raise up," he said, nearly every time. He finally put one mitt on top of my head and held me down. "Don't raise up, because you'll get hit." It was frustrating because my body wanted to do it a certain way, and I was fighting it. I kept raising up, just a little.

We stopped. "It's not about getting it right or wrong," Virgil said. "There is no right or wrong. It's about not getting hit. We know getting hit is bad for you, so we avoid it. That's what we're working on here, not getting something 'right.' Don't critique yourself." I was reminded of a skipper I'd worked for on a yacht, who'd told me, "Nobody laughs if it works," when we tried doing things in unorthodox ways.

Then he had me throwing rights, the right cross, anchored on the front foot and pivoting on the rear, for power, and he stood on my left foot to pin it in place, stood on it hard. It was a little embarrassing to be a grown man and be treated like a child, but Virgil was trying to get me right, trying to get me to punch with balance, something that should have been done when I was eleven years old.

I was hitting the heavy bag later, and between rounds Virg said, "Sam, you're always in a hurry. I'm starting to realize the kind of guy you are. I got to slow you down, make you deliberate. Nothing ever got to a hundred miles an hour without going through twenty."

Andre was preparing for his next fight, in Memphis. He would be fighting on the Johnson-Tarver II undercard, which refers to the way the promoters put together a night of fighting. You have to have a draw, a main event, with names that people recognize and want to see. Promoting is about establishing a narrative. In this day and age, it is nearly always going to be a title fight, meaning for a world title, a belt. I won't even get into the "alphabet soup" of ranking organizations because I don't understand it and not many do. It comes down to this: There is no federal governing body in boxing, just state commissions, and pretty much anybody who wants to have a big fight and call it "for the whatever-weight championship of the world" can. There are three or four organizations that have some real meaning, and quite a few that don't. When a fighter wins all the titles in his weight class, he "unifies" the belt, which means he really is the world champion—now it means something.

On the same card, or schedule, will be six to ten lesser bouts with up-and-coming fighters. Andre would be on the undercard, as this was going to be only his fifth professional fight. After he has fifteen or twenty fights, he'll be the main event, contending for a title. How fast he gets there depends entirely on him, how strong he looks fighting these second- or third-tier guys, how many knockouts he gets, how popular he becomes. The boxing community has opinions about him, and they are waiting to see what happens. He won gold, a major achievement, and that means he can box. But is he strong enough? And can he take a punch? Andre was rocked early in his second fight but survived smoothly and came back and knocked the guy out. Was geting rocked indicative of growing pains—or was it a sign that he's not powerful enough for the pros? The fight fans and writers, the boxing community, are always the smartest guys in the room. They are instant experts, and they form opinions based on misunderstandings and hearsay and "facts" heard from other writers and commentators. The truth is that they are easily swayed and misled by hype and flashiness, and the real core people who understand boxing are few and far between.

There is no better illustration of this than the example of Mike Tyson, Iron Mike. Most boxing fans you talk to still love Mike and would pay to see him fight, which is absurd when you think how long it's been since he's had a meaningful fight, ten years or more. Tyson has been a C-level fighter since he left prison, years and years ago, but for his rematch with Kevin McBride that ended so fittingly, there was more international press and pay-per-view than there was for a somewhat meaningful fight between Miguel Cotto and Mohamad Abdulaev that same night.

Boxing fans are still victims of the myth of Tyson's invulnerability, his fearlessness, his monstrous power and rage. Tyson won the heavyweight title and unified the belt at nineteen, the youngest fighter in history to do so, and he obliterated everyone in one or two rounds, millions of dollars a fight for a minute's work. Some people still consider him the greatest heavyweight of all time—because they *want* him to be, they want to believe in that mythical creature that no one can withstand.

Once Buster Douglas managed to survive six rounds and show that it could be done, Mike was doomed. Holyfield completed the revelation, and that's why Mike bit Holyfield's ear off—he wanted a way out. I love Mike Tyson, not so much for his youthful invulnerability but for his intelligence. He can be beautifully eloquent (and horrifically crass) when he speaks about himself, and his tragedy is our tragedy, because your heavyweight champ speaks to your generation. The heavyweight championship is not so much a title as a morality play, it's been said. Look at Jack Johnson, or Muhammad Ali—look at what the world does to the heavyweight champ.

Tyson is no exception, and his mournful tale is about America at the end of the twentieth century and the beginning of the twenty-first: money and corruption (in the corrosive sense), and Tyson's inability to escape from his own nature despite his fervent desire to do so. He has tattoos of Arthur Ashe, Che Guevara, and Mao Tse-tung—he has always wanted to change.

Virgil was incensed by Tyson's last fight, against the towering six-foot-six, 271-pound McBride. "People aren't paying to see Mike Tyson fight," he said angrily. "They are paying to see Mike Tyson destroy somebody. Don't put a big man in there with him—he's always had trouble with real tall guys. I saw that fight, and Tyson hit him with some good shots and he didn't go nowhere. People want to see Mike destroy. You give them that, he gets four or five fights over the next two years against guys who can't handle his punch and then a title shot and he's through, but he's made another thirty million."

After the fight, Mike said that his ferocity was all gone, he couldn't even kill the bugs in his house. He had completely lost the killer instinct in the sixth round. "At one point, I thought life was about acquiring things," he said. "Life is totally about losing everything."

I would meet Andre and Virgil for early morning runs at Lake Temescal, a small lake in a narrow fissure of the hills above Oakland. We would run, and then do sprints and shadowbox in the sand, and then jumping exercises and weighted skip rope and medicine ball work. Virgil's disdain for weights was total, and he and Andre trained for explosiveness and flexibility and speed—Pilates and Acceleration and core strength. Virgil's refrain to me was "Get strong doing what you're doing," meaning the way to get strong boxing is to box. You get strong fighting, hitting the heavy bag, not lifting weights. It's all about functional strength, strength you can use. What matters is being strong in the fight, and hitting hard, with technique. Another favorite saying of Virgil's is "Give me a two-hundred-pound man in condition and you've got some-thing." What he was saying was that any man that size is a danger if he's in shape and has been taught how to punch. If he can crack a little bit, "You've got something." I had high hopes for my right, as Virgil and Tommy Rawson both said it might be something. I would've loved to be "heavy-handed," but I wasn't. I started to think about accuracy, about hitting right on the button on the chin, the magic KO spot, like the spot on a dog's belly that makes his legs spasm when you scratch it. If you hit a guy perfectly on the point of the chin, it snaps his head, which shuts off his brain. That's the knockout.

Virgil took Andre to Texas, to Houston, to train there for the last week before his fight. James Prince, Andre's manager, had a huge facility and several pros there. They wanted to get Andre used to the heat and humidity, get him in the same time zone.

James Prince had come out of Houston with the Rap-a-Lot crew, and he had made his money in music, as one of the founders of gang-ster rap. He and his guys were the real deal. They had come from the baddest part of Houston and were not kidding when they said they were gangsters. His group was called the Geto Boys, and I could remember listening to them in seventh grade and being stunned. Prince had a combination of business intelligence, street smarts, and street cred. You didn't fuck around with James Prince.

I stayed behind in Oakland and worked. It was hard sometimes to know how my training was going; it's a little like getting fatter or skinnier—you don't see it, because you look in the mirror every day. You don't always see yourself improving in boxing, but with hard work and, above all, concentration, you do.

Bobby had agreed to keep an eye on me. Virgil had said, "Now, learn from Bobby, but don't let him change you." Bobby was a tremen-dously charismatic guy, and just to be hanging out with him felt like a privilege. I enjoyed the way he talked, the cadence in his voice. He'd had a barbecue sauce business once and on his old business card it said, "Where the Sauce Is the Boss." He was always laughing, smiling, and then scowling when things got serious.

"Sam, what's a jab supposed to do?" he asked me.

"Set everything up, feel him out, open him up, keep him off you. Everything," I answered.

"Yeah, well, a jab is supposed to push his nose through his face. Start with that. Then work on those other things."

Classic fighter parlance speaks of a punch like a living thing—an *educated* jab, a jab with science. A fighter with an educated jab can do all kinds of things with that one punch—he can paw at you, disrupt your balance, he can crack it like a whip, thrust it like a spear, blast it to the body. Max Schmeling beat Joe Louis in their first meeting with his educated right hand, a punch that he said threw itself when the time was right.

So Bobby had me on one end of the double-end bag, just working that jab, just trying to build up power. My shoulder would still fatigue quickly, and after a few rounds my jab wouldn't have busted a grape.

Bobby had me moving, bouncing in circles, and he differed from Virgil on the right cross. Bobby didn't want the pivot off the rear foot; he wanted just the hips to move. It was interesting how they both wanted almost totally perpendicular stances; you stand with your body on edge to your opponent, whereas before I had been a little more squared up. Muay Thai, with the kicks and knees, is more frontal, and with boxing you want to minimize the target. Bobby wanted me to learn to move, to flow, to bounce. "They won't even recognize you when they get back," he laughed. He showed me how to bounce and move in tight circles, a seventy-five-year-old man, still strong.

Later, we would sit and watch the gym, an endless pastime. The gym was like that. It was open from noon until late at night, and often you would go for three or four hours, two of which would be spent working out and the rest of the time spent bullshitting and watching. Bobby was often critical of certain trainers.

"It's dangerous, because a trainer holds a fighter's mind in his hands. The fighter depends on him for the truth, and if the trainer don't got it, the fighter is going to get hurt."

A week later, I flew to Memphis to meet Virgil, Andre, and company. I took a bus to the hotel, which was about a thirty-second ride. The good hotel in town was full, and we were all staying at the Airport Ramada, the shittiest expensive hotel I'd ever been in; I had roaches in my room on the second floor. But the staff was all sweet black ladies who whispered softly and courteously, southern and polite, and in the end they took such special care of Andre and all of us that we were happy to be there, even with the runway about five hundred feet away and planes landing all night.

That night we worked out briefly, just to get a good sweat on Andre. Virgil knew Andre's body as well as Andre did, and knew that if Andre had to make 160 at the weigh-in, he could be 162 the night before and the night's sleep and the nerves in the morning would take those pounds off him. We often walked at night, after dinner, on the brilliant grass under the epic southern sky with planes and pink and red clouds in the twilight, to keep the weight off.

Andre was promoted by a company called Goossen Tutor, run by two experienced brothers who had been in the training and promoting business for some twenty years and were eyeing the coming gap provided by the decline of Bob Arum and Don King. Dan Goossen was the promoter and Joe Goossen was the trainer, and they had some big names and some titles, most recently James Toney. In this particular fight they had Glencoffe Johnson.

Glen Johnson and Antonio Tarver were light-heavyweights, 175 pounds, who had both knocked out the seemingly invincible Roy Jones Jr. Antonio Tarver was an Olympic bronze medalist who was considered to be a very talented boxer, while Glen Johnson was always described as a journeyman. A journeyman fighter is a professional, perhaps without the great physical gifts necessary to win titles, but who has the skills and heart and determination to make it to title fights time and again—only to lose to more gifted fighters. Glen had lost a bunch of tough decisions— some of them considered unfair, "robberies"—and was admired more for his grit, drive, and resilience than for his skill. He was skilled but didn't have the natural speed or athleticism that Tarver had. A journeyman is supposed to lose to a great fighter. But when Tarver and Johnson fought for the first time, Glen won a split decision by banging to the body and coming after Tarver and pushing him all over the ring. This fight in Memphis was going to be their rematch. Since Goossen had the guy with the belt, the top draw, he could put all his people on the undercard, and Andre, with his Olympic gold and reputation as a future champ, was starting to be a draw of his own.

I had spoken briefly on the phone to Dan Goossen about Andre. He was friendly and voluble, and willing to chat even though he was not quite convinced that I was for real. Goossen was big time, not as big as Don King or Bob Arum, but pretty big.

"Andre wants to be one of the greatest fighters of all time," he said. "That's not a reputation you receive by winning a gold medal or even becoming champ. He's a special athlete. I compare him to Lebron James, a young man way beyond his years, tremendous maturity.

"We've been challenging him since his first pro fight, and sometimes it's hard for young fighters to understand, he sees his friends fight guys that you tap on the chin and they're knocked out, or guys that start bleeding during the national anthem. But until you've had a few tough fights, the jury's always out. When Lebron went pro at eighteen they put him in hard, in the starting five, and look at him now. With Andre, we want to give him that competition—a little bit less, so he's always got an edge—but always someone who is helping prepare him for his future fighting the stars of the industry. We'll put him in with left-handers, tall guys, punchers, runners, holders, every style you can think of. His greatness will be measured in the fights he has down the road, not the ten or twenty fights he needs to get there."

While Glen and Goossen were in the good hotel in downtown Memphis, in the Airport Ramada with us were the rest of the Goossen team: a strikingly good-looking British woman named Rachel Charles with her pretty seventeen-year-old daughter, a photographer, and Gabriel Ruelas, a three-time world champion who now worked for Goossen. When I first met them, I was impressed by Rachel's good looks and flashing charm, but I almost didn't notice Gabriel. He was so slight and quiet, a slender Mexican man with glasses and a crew cut and a mustache. His face was unmarked, with a slight thickening around the brows and nose, but he didn't look like a fighter. When Virg murmured to me that Gabe was a three-time world champ, I did a double take. His body was rail thin under a short-sleeved collared shirt and shorts. The only hint, the only ostentation, was a giant gold WBC ring with diamonds dripping off it. He had killed a man in a title fight in 1995.

Andre's whole week had been planned out, like a politician's, and the next morning we were scheduled for St. Jude's Hospital to meet children with leukemia and other forms of cancer. It was a boiling hot morning, and as we loaded up a van, Rachel rather imperiously ordered Gabe around. I saw Virg out of the corner of my eye ever so slightly shake his head, bemused.

We drove through the flat jungle of Memphis, AC blasting, crowded freeways and construction everywhere. St. Jude's was not a hospital; it was a complex, a massive campus with a $1.5-million-a-day budget, run entirely on donations. Everything was clean, groomed, manicured, big gates and stone sculptures; it felt like a law school. We pulled up at one of the front entrances and waited for half an hour, since Glen Johnson was on his way, and chatted to the St. Jude's media crew. They had thirty-five full-time employees in the media crew, with their own cameraman and photographers. We stood around chatting in sunglasses, looking cool, Rachel and her daughter in designer clothes with lovely, movie-star ankles, while Gabe and I carried boxes of T-shirts and pictures for Andre to sign and give away. The T-shirts were plain white with the Goossen Tutor emblem across the front.

There were children all around, under the eyes of very, very long-suffering adults. The adults were suffering through the normal trials of children with warm, weary indulgence, because somewhere they had acknowledged the death of their own child. Yet they were finding themselves enjoying life and a semblance of normality.

Inside it felt more like a hospital, but very relaxed and warm and friendly, with large bright murals and colors and statues and gift shops. There was an easiness of passage, a casualness with which the kids—bald and stick-thin and pale, sometimes with strange discolorations or bandages—roamed with their friends.

Andre was guided by the hospital media people, and we all followed in a kind of constellation, Virgil and Don, Rachel and her daughter, and the Goossen photographer and Gabe and myself. One of the media guys laughed at the size of the entourage. "It's always boxers who have the biggest crews." There was local TV there, and St. Jude's own TV, and three or four photographers. I tried to stay out of the way.

Andre sat down with some small children around a fake fire to read a few stories. Some of the kids seemed normal; some were in trouble, bald and blue-veined with soft eyes staring from their skulls. It was a circus, with seven or eight people standing around watching Andre be a nice guy, and Virg and myself in the deep background, watching the whole choreographed situation.

The iconic image for me that day was a tiny little girl, maybe five, walking past us with her little sneakers that had the flashing lights in them, wearing a pink shirt that said "Hope," bald from the treatments. She had huge, anonymous blue eyes behind a white mask that covered her face. She was followed by her mother and attached to an IV machine on rollers that she pulled herself, trailing it with one firm, determined hand. The little girl was just wandering, pushing her way between us, and her mother—patient, overweight, loving, tired, resigned, wise, and proud—said smiling, "She's a big girl," like any of a million moms might say.

Glen Johnson arrived, with his wife and his strength coach, a white guy with bullet-hole eyes and corded forearms and braids who looked like a pro wrestler. Glen and Andre made the rounds, greeting children in beds, signing photos and T-shirts. People didn't really know who they were, because nobody followed boxing anymore, but the kids were happy to be touched by celebrity and attention, to have the monotony broken, to feel something different. Glen's manager, a white guy in a green shirt, walked alongside Glen for a few minutes and said to a kid, "You want to see his muscles?" while tugging on Glen's shirt, like Glen was a prize dog that he was showing off. The manager quickly went outside and sat with his trainer and their respective wives, all in sunglasses and looking hungover, and I heard him say convincingly, "Well, that was very moving" when he left.

In contrast to all of this were Andre and the kids, who were graceful. So what if it was free advertising and branding for Goossen Tutor? It was making these kids happy, and they needed it. Andre just enjoyed the kids, a big brother and a father. He wasn't thrown by the cameras, he wasn't thrown by the fact that many of these kids were dying. He made the best of their time together and the kids responded. The kids don't want to know that they're dying either. Andre calls himself "Son of God" and even has SOG on his fight shorts, but it's not a messianic complex, it's a loving, grateful thing: We are all sons and daughters of God, he's reminding himself and others. He's toeing the line, he's staying right with God.

Somehow Andre and I lost everybody, and he sat in the front lobby on some seats with kids who just kept coming and coming, patiently lining up. He was clearly enjoying himself, and they were enjoying his company. And then the press corps found us, and the cameras.

We left the hospital later in the afternoon, hours after Glen and his entourage had left. Andre said as we sauntered out, "I don't let anyone rush me. They'll say, 'No more signing,' but if there is anyone left who wants an autograph, I'll stay and sign it." I thought of Rodrigo in Japan, signing away despite the Pride executives watching, who finally sent a lackey over to make him stop.

Virgil said to me quietly, "I learned a lot today."

There was a public workout in downtown Memphis that afternoon, and we headed over around five. It was hot and sweet that evening, the sun slanting redly over the buildings through the lazy, summery weekend air, even though it was a weeknight. The workout was at an outdoor stage called the Pepsi Pavilion, right next door to the stadium where the fights would be held a few nights later. It wasn't crowded, but there were a few hundred people milling around, drinking beers, with a band on the side, and an armada of black bicycle cops in blue shirts. Up on the stage was a boxing ring, and the fighters and corners with all their friends and entourages were hanging around on the stage.

It was hot and hazy, almost dreamy, and the crowd seemed bemused and befuddled, drinking beer from plastic cups and listening to the rock-jazz jam music over the loudspeakers. Dan Goossen (a large, red-haired man with an Irish complexion) was perched on the lip of the ring apron, doing his promoter thing in designer clothes and lightly tinted sunglasses, like all promoters acutely fashion conscious, since part of what they do is promote themselves.

Ann Wolfe was just starting her workout. She was a black woman, maybe five foot nine but heavy, with slab-sided muscle, powerful shoulders and arms. Her face was beautiful but hard and worn and so sad, the history of the world on it. "Ann Wolfe had a hard life," said Virgil, and he knew her trainer, Pops, well. Pops had found Ann sleeping in cars and on the street with her baby in her arms, and she had come to boxing late, in her late twenties. Now she was a seven-time world champion, but her face was still etched with sadness. I had seen her on TV once when she fought a very tall, strong white woman, and Ann had nearly killed her with a wrecking-ball right hand that put the woman down with her eyes crossed and open and her legs jackknifed beneath her.

Andre worked out next, and he and Virgil had discussed what they were going to do. Rachel had said, "It's just for show, do whatever, dance around a little," but Virg said, "Let's get a good workout in while we're at it, and give them what they want to see." We were three days out from the fight, and some fighters wouldn't do much, but Andre was so young and full of energy that he needed to go hard and brief.

Andre was in a different category, even from Antonio Tarver, the main event. His movement was quick and powerful as he shadowboxed, his speed deceptive. He was graceful; there was a sublime quickness, his body daring and shifting, his feet drifting and touching, slips and slides and feinting with his whole body. Of course he was fast, but speed comes from many places. Andre was as still as stone and then he moved in unexpected ways—and he didn't telegraph, which made him that much faster. His control over his body, his link between body and mind, was the most complete thing I had ever witnessed; his feints were with his whole body, not just his head or hands, and this made them irresistible. Whatever his mind could imagine, his body could do, flowing and skipping, bounding and bouncing.

There is a tendency, which I succumb to, for "normal" men who encounter good professional fighters whom they like to wax poetic, and fall gracelessly into silly hyperbole. Mailer wrote about Ali as if he were the second coming of Christ, and other writers went even further regarding the Greatest. Andre Ward, to me, a regular guy with regular reflexes, was an incredible, sensational fighter—but at the top level there are a lot of guys who are incredible and sensational and more. Andre had a shot at being up there—but he hadn't proved himself yet, not in the professional world.

Virgil joined him for pad work and was working almost as hard as Andre, pushing him around, walking quick in steep, dizzying circles, Virgil's eyes intense and boiling. It was a performance, but the genius of Virgil was knowing that it was good for Andre to perform like this. He was young and needed a hard workout with only three days before the fight. Over the loudspeakers, there was a long drum solo on the jazz jam and Andre and Virgil slipped into the rhythm, probably without even noticing.

To cool down, Andre stripped off his shirt and skipped rope, which energized the female attention in the crowd. He skipped effortlessly in the blazing heat, muscled and sleek. He wasn't bothered by the crowd—his gracefulness extends in that direction. He plays to it without uneasiness or ego. He stayed onstage until he was ready to leave and said a few words into the microphone without faltering, just that Memphis had given him the key to the city and now Memphis was his second home. He existed in a state of grace.

Antonio Tarver was doing his workout when we left, and Buddy McGirt, a three-time world champion and now a great trainer, was holding pads for him with his flip-flops on, barely moving around the ring at all. Compared to the frenetic dance that Virgil had led Andre in, it seemed strangely static.

We talked about this in the van on the drive home, Virgil holding forth on why Andre was different, why he was, as Roy Jones had said, a throwback to the golden age of boxing: because Andre had the killer work ethic. It was why Ali and Frazier were still going at it hammer and tongs in the thirteenth and fourteenth rounds of the Thrilla, and why current fighters like Tarver and Johnson (in their first fight) were both exhausted in the ninth and stood in front of each other and didn't even punch. Neither Tarver nor Johnson would even be near the level of Holyfield if he were still around as the light heavyweight champion. He would have been too talented for Johnson and too hardworking for Tarver. "Tommy Hearns was only a slightly above average fighter, but he would put himself through such a hellish camp that he could put *things* on you," said Virgil, talking to Andre. That may have been true, but Hearns seemed to me to have been pretty talented, with his big right hand.

"They can't do what you do," Virgil said, encompassing all current fighters, and Andre listened impassively, staring out the window. Part of what a trainer does is manage his fighter's mind—more than any other sport, the trainer controls his athlete's perception of the world and of himself.

We bought an electronic scale. Andre planned on having a "flush" later that night; he would fill the tub with ice water to flush the lactic acid out of his system, and then get a rubdown. It was a trick he'd learned in the Olympic camp.

We ate a little at the hotel and then walked in the turgid night, bugs swarming in the pools of light and everywhere the thrum of the freeway and hum of wires and planes and technology.

The next morning, I sat down with Gabriel Ruelas for an interview. Don Clark wanted to tag along; he had seen the fight where Jimmy García died and wanted to hear what Gabe would say. Gabe was eager to talk to me, he wanted to talk. He knew that despite all his world championships and great fights, what everyone always wanted to know about was Jimmy García.

"There's an article you should read," he said, "'Dream of Life, Dream of Death,'" by Gary Smith for *Sports Illustrated* in '95. I have a lot written about me, but this one is very different. The best thing about me, it gave me chills. He really touched me." I have since read it, and it is a great piece of boxing writing, and an excellent look into the kind of man that Gabriel Ruelas is.

The short version is that Gabriel Ruelas, the WBC super-featherweight champion, fought Jimmy García, the Colombian champ, in 1995, and after the fight García went into a coma and died three weeks later. Ruelas was the heavy favorite going in and outclassed García for the whole fight but never managed to put him away, and García's corner—his father and brother—kept sending him in for more punishment. If we look at boxing deaths the way we look at firefighting deaths, where we look for common denominators of "tragedy" fires, one of the common factors of "tragedy" boxing matches is the father as cornerman—strange, frightening, but true. Also, García had taken a bad beating six months earlier, from Genaro Hernandez.

There was a certain amount of inevitability to the conversation. Gabe had made telling the story a part of his life—it was part of his identity now, thrust upon him by the circumstances of the world. He and Jimmy were tied together forever; he would never be free from the onus. He knew that everyone knew, that they were thinking about it when they looked at him, and they had questions, even though some were too polite to ask. They came like me and Don, under the guise of being journalists. Gabe explained it this way: "In order for me to move on, I had to make it part of my life—I thought maybe I could get away and put it behind me, but I can't. So I say to people, 'Don't worry about it, it's okay,' when I see them bump their friends to tell them not to talk. . . . Sometimes people are rude, they ask, 'Are you the one who killed that guy?' and if they are very uneducated, they say to me, 'How does it feel to kill a man?' But they are just uneducated, you can't get mad."

It was an interesting choice of words, as Ruelas was from a part of Mexico in the mountains near Guadalajara where there was nothing, no stores, no roads—"If you ate it, you either caught it or grew it"—and Gabe grew up uneducated in a way that few in the world still do. There were no clocks; he used the sun to tell time. "We didn't know any better, so it was great, we were beautiful. I learned to appreciate everything. We were illegals, crossing the border without green cards, and a guard stopped me, but he had just seen me fight and asked for my autograph. . . . We made something of ourselves, my brother and me." He and his brother both had excellent careers with the Goossens. They had been dirt-poor boys selling candy before they found boxing, and they were called the "Candy Kids."

Gabe looked at me across the table, his eyes soft and large behind his glasses, his voice quiet. Boxing writers never want to write about someone being punchy. Listen to Joe Frazier talk, to Thomas Hearns talk. Young fighters whisper it. Andre muttered it to me about Gabriel: "He ain't right." It's a scientific fact but one that everyone in the game wants to avoid thinking about: the price of fighting. The slurred speech, called cotton mouth, the slow encroachment of dementia pugilistica. Writers avoid it when talking about their heroes. (I smoothed out Gabe's dialogue here, granted him an eloquence and clarity that perhaps he didn't have.) It can happen from one fight, from one concussion, maybe from just one punch. Professional soccer players are getting it from heading the ball. Gabe's speech was ever so slightly slurred; he was a tiny bit slow and stuttered. When given the time to speak uninterrupted, he was eloquent. But when he had to drive us to the workout, dealing with conflicting directions in an unfamiliar city, he got lost and flustered. Virgil took over and said to him lightly, "Relax, champ, you don't need to be doing this," and there was a sense that fighters have given so much to us, they have sacrificed everything for us, and that they should never have to give again, everything should be given to them. Gabriel is still paying the price of all those wars he fought in the ring. Andre has seen it and knows about it. It's what he was talking about when he said the winner still has to go home and look in the mirror, to look his kids in the eye and wonder if he's still right.

"The reason I'm still in boxing is because I want to stay as close as I can," Gabe said, and he meant literally. "I sit where the judges sit, so I am very close, but it's a two-edged sword, because I'm around what I love, but I can't really do it. I'm right there but I'm not. It's rare that I'll watch a whole fight. I sit there and wish I could be in there, and it's not the money, forget about the money, it's love." His brother is unable to even go to boxing matches. It's too painful for him, he misses it too much.

Gabe's voice was soft and high and reedy, and I wondered if he were better and smoother in Spanish—probably. He smiled, and he seemed like the gentlest soul in the world.

"I see older fighters making comebacks, older than me, and it is very tempting. Small promoters are always coming to me with offers, some of my greatness might rub off on them. I do think about it. I've even tried it a few times, but you get older and can't do the job as well as you used to. It's very frustrating." I can imagine how addictive that feeling must be, to be the champion in a title fight—to be the center of the universe for a night, bigger than a movie star.

Gabriel, of course, had not known how badly he'd hurt Jimmy, or even that Jimmy was in real trouble until much later that night. He hadn't meant to kill Jimmy—except of course, that he had, within the constraints of the ring, been trying to kill Jimmy.

"After Jimmy died, my killer instinct was gone; I would get a guy in trouble and back off him—I thought nobody could see it. I thought I was fooling them, but my wife and corner could see it. The instinct every fighter must have—your life is at stake—I never got back. My biggest loss was that win. I lost boxing."

There was an easy familiarity to Gabe's speech. This was a speech he had given a thousand times and one he would continue to give for the rest of his life, in some form or other. When he began to warm to a topic or train of thought, his speech cleared and flowed.

"The next year I fought Arturo Gatti, and I had him out on his feet. I was putting the final touch on him, and I couldn't close the deal. That was it. I was trying to force myself to get it back, and either you have it or you don't. This sport isn't for everyone." I heard the echo of Pat Miletich.

"You have it or you don't in this business, it's serious. People don't realize how serious," Gabe said.

Don said quietly, "I saw you dominating at the end of every round, and you were hurting him at the end of every round, but his corner wouldn't stop the fight. Do you blame them?"

Gabe was quick to shake his head. "As a fighter, you want someone like that, who will get the best out of you, and let you fight. But blame . . . at first, of course I blamed myself, but then I realized, if I had to point the finger, I could point it at so many of us—you are watching, you want to see us trading punches and knockouts, and we'll give you what you want. This is not a game. I blamed myself, and then you, because without fans we wouldn't be here. But did Jimmy train like he was supposed to? This is not a game. Your trainer has to do his job and get you ready for war."

Gabe looked at Don carefully, meaningfully. "You haven't been in deep waters yet," he said. He knew Don was Andre's corner. "The further Andre advances, the more costly mistakes become. You never want to think fatal, but this is the only sport where you can take a man's life and walk free." He broke off, and then muttered, "I never want to say that, I feel bad when I say that. You never know enough. You never know which way the fight is going to go until you are there. A learning experience can be very costly."

I asked about Jimmy cutting weight and being dehydrated, as I had heard that dehydration plays a role in ring deaths. Gabe was dismissive.

"Yeah, he cut weight, but I used to cut twenty-five to thirty pounds over a month, twenty pounds in two weeks, and like Gatti come in twenty pounds over. Did Jimmy do it right?"

Gabe looked at us, from one to the other, and said, "How safe can you make a sport that's about hurting other people?"

Jimmy lingered for three weeks in a coma, and then he died. He had been a national hero in Colombia and the country plunged into

mourning. The media was outside Gabe's house every day with reporters knocking on his door at all hours. Gabe talked to everyone and did
hundreds of interviews. There were death threats against his father and
brother, who had cornered Jimmy, and Gabriel went on the radio and
begged for the family to be left alone.

"I'm a mama's boy, I'm proud to say it. I take her to the fights
with me in Vegas, and she plays the slots. I met Jimmy's mom, and
the worst thing I ever saw was her face. I could see my mom there,
and that was what did it—she killed me. I think I could have kept on
fighting if I had never met his mom. . . . I wanted to hug her, and she
pulled back. She said, 'I can't, I'm sorry.' She bowed her head down.
She was looking at my hands, and I wished I had no hands. She said,
'I cannot touch the hands that killed my son.' The way she was looking at my hands—that killed me, because my ma had made everything possible."

Gabe was shaking his head and nearly laughing in a sad, dry way.
"She killed me. Had she known what that was going to do to me, she
might not have done that. She would never have done it. She didn't
know what she did. She took my life away from me."

He paused for a while, and we all sipped our coffee.

"Once you get in the ring, you have to make that change that
everyone is supposed to, you go in there to take care of business. I
couldn't do it. I kept trying to make it happen, but you can't make it
happen. You either have it or you don't."

"I couldn't turn that switch. Even second- or third-rate fighters
can have it. A lot of opponents have it, and they fight their asses off.
They have the heart of a fighter. They're going to go down punching,
that's a fighter's heart; it's not about being a world champion, it's about
having a fighter's heart."

Gabe hadn't made money like De La Hoya had (who has?), and
he still worked. When he was training kids and back in the gym, being
around boxing made him want to come back. He told Joe and Dan
Goossen that he wanted to fight again, and they said, "If we see it in
you, if we see it in your eyes, and we think you can do it, then we'll be
happy to have you back." Gabe fought a guy he should have destroyed
and had a hard time winning. The Goossens said they didn't want to
be part of the comeback, that they were looking out for him. "I respect
them so much for saying that," he said. "I fought a little more and my
wife, my boss, said, 'Forget it. You look like your old self, but once
you get in the ring it's not you anymore.'

"I wish I was back up there before, with the killer instinct. I know that it's okay to miss it. Dan said to me, 'You can't make boxing come out of you—you got to have it in you.'"

The week rolled onward to the fight. There was a big press conference, where all the promoters made endless speeches about the "great city of Memphis" and the quality of their boxers and the entertainment that would be had on the big night. The Rap-a-Lot crew and James Prince were all there. They were big men (although Prince himself was small) and from the hood, with money. They dressed in immaculate Polo and Hilfiger and wore platinum and diamond watches and had platinum teeth. Prince had always loved boxing—he had wanted to be a promoter like Don King before he'd even gotten into music. He told me that he found out that Arum and people like him were taking as much as 25 percent of a fighter's purse, and he thought he could fix that. He said in his soft voice that he wanted to "protect young fighters from promoters, who will try and exploit them and use them up." Prince and his crew formed Andre's legion of protectors, tough black ex-street men with plenty of money now, ghetto fabulous, but still with the hard eyes, the watchfulness. I don't think you could ask for a better guardian angel than James Prince.

Andre was a little concerned about weight. He was fighting at middleweight, which is 160, and because he was still filling out as a man, middleweight was getting harder to get to, and he was hungry. That afternoon, I jumped rope in the little conference room with the crappy swirly carpets, the room silent except for my skips and Andre's grunts as he shadowboxed, his little cries, *ut,ut,ut*. Don and Virg sat as still and silent as statues, for fifteen minutes. I stretched and then Andre did some rope work and calisthenics. There was an old balloon from some forgotten party and Virg held it up for Andre to hit, and Andre muttered, "You are one of a kind, my friend."

Back at the hotel, Virgil and I went to get a big tub of ice for Dre's bath. Virgil started goofing with the three girls who worked at the restaurant, just talking complete and utter nonsense but so serious that they had no choice but to believe him. He'd been married seven times—he was engaged right now—and they were all wide-eyed and trying not to giggle. Virgil was a big fan of something the English call the "wind-up." You play someone very seriously with something you know will make them crazy, just to get them to lose composure. I've seen him do it to little boys who come into the gym. "Oh, I heard about you, you were the one crying when that Korean kid stole your bike," and the little boy will be raging, "That wasn't me!" Virgil used to do that at the juvenile hall with young toughs in front of their friends.

The girls were all sweet Tennessee girls, soft, big, buxom, black, and braided, incredibly polite and almost absurdly demure.

The next day was the weigh-in, the real one private and underneath the stadium, while a public one would be held later back at the Pepsi Pavilion. Back again through the twisting concrete tunnels underneath the stadium, and it felt just like the UFC, just like Pride had felt, the same kind of concrete and hallways. Andre made 160 and his opponent, Ben Aragon, came in at 159.

Andre had his Endurox shake for right after the weigh-in and some PowerBars and things like that, and immediately his mood began to improve, the gloom that had settled on him lifted, and his natural good humor reasserted itself. The public weigh-in, some hours later, was just for show—everyone could go eat after the official weigh-in. By the time the public weigh-in happened, every fighter had probably put on three or four pounds, just by rehydrating.

That night, back at the airport, we went for our after-dinner stroll underneath that open, pink, burnished Tennessee sky, with the sun slanting and the whole empty landscape swirling around us, and I fell into deep conversation with Andre. The late sunset was becoming early twilight, with the cold deepening gloom of night behind the clouds, and we saw a giant shooting star, a real burner with a smokey trail. Dre and I spoke of the way we both had been blessed, and our responsibilities to that blessing. It is something I feel strongly, a sense of duty to experience life. Dre felt a combination of an opportunity and a mandate from the blessings of his physical and mental gifts. I silently wondered at the hype that was starting to surround him; he was being groomed as the next Roy Jones—it was going to be very hard to live up to the standard he was setting for himself. Was one world title going to be enough? Three? Five? I thought, *It is lucky he is so young that he doesn't quite feel the enormity of the burden that they are placing on him,* the way everyone was so convinced of his eventual greatness.

Later we walked with Virgil and spoke a little about God, and Virgil was serious but not preachy, a very deft touch. He made it clear that you have to think for yourself; don't fall under the persuasion of an eloquent preacher with his own agenda. Find it for yourself by reading John and Proverbs.

We had all done a careful dance around faith, Virgil careful not to ask me directly how I felt, and I careful not to say—because my feelings are complicated, and I don't express them well. But here Virgil said, almost in passing, "You should learn more about God, Sam," and Dre paid me the best compliment I'd ever heard: "God could use a man like you."

Fight day arrived, and the tension started building early in the morning during breakfast. There was talk about the different types of gloves— a puncher's glove (like Everlast) versus a boxer's glove—and how a puncher's glove with less padding can jack up your hands. At this level, every little advantage is exploited, every opening seized, reflective not so much of an actual advantage but rather a viewpoint, a method of thinking. Virgil and T (of Prince's entourage) sat and talked to Dre and me, and T told a story of an opponent who came on and won a fight, and ended with, "You got to take these bums serious." He wasn't lecturing Dre but just speaking a thought that was hanging in the ether—there was no danger of Dre taking his opponent lightly. He said, "I don't care if I'm fighting a guy who's 0–12, I'm still going to bed early—nothing changes."

Then T and Virg got up and I sat with Dre to keep him company while he finished his oatmeal and fruit. He was in a chatty mood and talked for a while about his dad, his white father, who had been superman to Dre—he could do anything. He would take no shit from big men. "Every year some big black dude in the neighborhood would give him some shit about his two black kids, and he would never back down." He would get mad and protective. Dre felt the same way, ferociously protective of his children.

He spoke about his dad's sudden death again, and how it had left him searching for answers. "I still am looking for answers, even though I know God has his purpose. He's still with me—I am him and he is me. We will meet again, I believe that." Dre looked at me with those sad eyes.

The day wore on interminably, and now I could feel the tension coming off Dre, not nervous about fighting but just wanting to get started. After a light lunch, Dre, Virg, and I walked across the steaming hot parking lot, under the brilliant sun, and talked about politics, oil, and the vast conspiracy that we all can just barely sense under the surface, that conspiracy theory being something I share with the African American community.

Finally, we left the hotel, with bags and gear and nice clothes. On the way out, a cleaning lady called to Dre, "Y'all come back victorious." Dre smiled and said, "I got no choice."

Underneath the FedEx Forum there was the same clean, impersonal corporate athletic feel that all these stadiums had. Dre's dressing room was pretty small, and Virg took one look at it and told me it was too small for me to be in there watching, so I went and found my seat. I understood Virgil's desire to keep the dressing room pure—I can appreciate the mind-set that refuses my entry, the maintenance of professionalism. Rachel and Dan Goossen had gotten me an excellent seat, out with the other reporters and journalists. I had my big laminated ringside media pass around my neck, warding off security with it like a cross against vampires. And I was just in time to witness the first of several executions.

The undercard held the worst mismatches I had ever seen anywhere. No one else was too amazed; it must be a pretty common occurrence. There was a spate of quick stoppages, and Virgil joined me to watch, as Dre didn't need to be ready for a while yet. A trainer who knew Virgil, and whose fighter had just KO'd some slob, muttered as he went by, "I wish he'd put up a fight."

The worst case was that of Anthony Peterson (maybe 14–0), a muscular black kid in against a short, hairy-backed, white balding dude without skills or grace, a guy from Arizona who was supposedly 3–0. It looked like a complete mismatch, and it was. In the first round Anthony moved around him and then caught him with his first punch, a deep swinging hook to the chin and the guy went down and flipped over like a sack of rice. There was a lot of razzing and catcalls, and he took a long time to get up, with the paramedics helping him out, but finally he did stand, smile shakily, and wave. Fans were taunting him, but Virgil called, "You awright, man" as the guy walked in front of us, and I looked at V and saw him purse his lips and shake his head.

Ann Wolfe was fighting a Canadian named Marsha Valley, whom she'd fought a few times before, and Ann was clobbering her, but Marsha was pretty game. Marsha was no threat to Ann; she was nearly part of Ann's retinue (Pops, Ann's trainer, had clapped for Marsha when she came out).

A famous promoter was sitting behind me, and I heard him say loudly, "If I put on this mismatch with men, the commission would have me in a lot of trouble," and I thought, *Did you see the earlier fights?*

Marsha couldn't fight a lick and had no idea how to punch, but she moved around and had plenty of spirit and made Ann work and stalk her for six rounds in a contained, workmanlike fashion. Ann fought like a man and hit like a man; she started digging monster shots to the body and put Marsha down in the sixth. When Marsha got up, Ann came after her with another body shot in the exact same place and that ended it. Ann made seventy-five grand and Marsha made six. None of these undercard executions were on TV, and most people never get to see this stuff.

The crowd would mutter and chat, and the place wasn't even close to full yet. The cheers would come when big shots landed, for displays of animosity or rage, and for showboating. I suddenly realized, *The crowd cheers the punch, not the fighter*. For the most part, they don't really know who the guy is, or the narrative drive behind each and every fighter. They don't care, but when they see a big punch, a great shot, there is a collective yell that escapes everyone's lips. It's the visceral thrill of impact—you *know* that one hurt—that charges the audience. It's why pro wrestling is popular, it's the spectacle of the big hit, the massive pile driver off the top ropes. A big punch does something to the crowd. It connects the crowd and turns it briefly into a single animal, reveling in awe and rejoicing in the physical power.

Eight o'clock and finally it is Andre's fight. The ring announcer, Bruce Buffer, calls out "Ann-draayyy Ess-Oh-Gee Waaard," and Andre enters to gospel music by Kirk Franklin.

There is tension out there for us in his entourage—anything can happen, this is a fight. We all know that Aragon shouldn't be a challenege for Andre, but everyone also knows that he better not have any trouble, he better not screw up. The fights only get bigger from here out.

Andre is the bigger man at 160 and obviously enjoying it. Aragon is hopelessly outclassed from the opening bell. Andre is tight and under control—he doesn't come out looking to kill, he just moves and pops crisp jabs through Aragon's guard, knocking his head back each time. Tap. Tap. By the second round, it is obvious that Andre is in no danger; his control of the distance is complete, and Aragon has no way of addressing the issue, no tool that might allow him to mix things up.

Andre takes his time, and Aragon stops punching and starts trying to survive. Early in the third, Andre switches briefly, he steps into southpaw and catches Aragon moving with a straight left that rattles him, and the ref, looking for an excuse, jumps in and stops the fight. Aragon reveals how hurt he is when he takes a huge stumble and wobble on drunkard's legs. It feels a little anticlimactic, but Aragon has nowhere to go, no chance of anything.

Andre took a few bows and thanked Aragon, and there was a sense of relief among us all at ringside: Andre had performed; he was on track and still anchored to his destiny.

Among the retinue backstage, the release from prefight tension had people talking nonstop. Virgil was going on about Andre's need to be ruthless, though my sense of the fight was that Andre was so unchallenged that he had not been feeling too aggressive—he was so safe and secure that he could take his time and get the other guy out when he wanted. There was a very professional, old-school feel to what Dre had done; he had felt his opponent out, allowed him his two rounds, and then pressured him just slightly, just enough to get him to crack. It was beautiful in its restraint and control, the safety of his fight. Andre could have gone ten more rounds, just like that. The caliber of opponent that will bring out his best is going to be world class. He won't come out guns blazing, swinging at trees and knocking down walls; it's not his style. He had said to me, "I'm not fighting for nobody but God, my family, and myself. I hear people talk about me—oh, he can't do this, he can't hit, however it is—I know how to win. I've been winning a long time. If I can get out of a fight unscathed, without getting hit, and that displeases you, then so be it. I ain't fighting for you. The brain wasn't made to get hit."

He'll come out fast and tight and under complete control, and destroy you with speed and poise. "Not a superstar but a guy who consistently beats superstars—a shining star," Virgil said.

Right after the fight, I stood with Andre in the hallway while he waited to take his piss test. He mentioned how, during the Olympics, he had been nervous about it because he had been taking multivitamins.

We all stood in a circle and held hands and prayed, thankful, and for the safety of Aragon and everyone else in the ring that night. Dre was still wired, praying, "Praise God for this team, and protect this team, vindicate yourself and us, make believers out of these commentators and not just in me but in you, oh Lord, love to all and thank you."

While waiting, Andre could barely contain himself, leaping and pacing about, the Vaseline still gleaming on his face. He talked about how he could hear the ring commentators, Jim Lampley and Larry Merchant, clearly throughout the fight and how their disparaging comments (they thought he was matched too easy) had motivated him. I asked about the fight.

"He was on queer street," Andre said. "I'm glad they stopped it because I was coming with another big left. I don't believe that God's blessings will take me anywhere that his grace won't sustain me. You got to be ready for anything in this business, it's an ice-cold business." He laughed. "I'm telling you it is."

The main event had packed the place to the rafters and charged the air. Virgil muttered to me that he thought Tarver might knock old Glencoffe out. Both fighters were versions of the truth, they both had their own stories—but only one version would survive the meeting.

"Tarver looks more *composed* than last time," said Virgil. The fight started off going Tarver's way and stayed there. Tarver had made the adjustment; he had the better game plan. He went high and low, he made Glen pay, he changed up the rhythms and threw Glen off. By round four, Virgil raised his eyebrows at me and said, "Tarver's fighting a real smart fight."

Tarver would step back and counter, even potshotting and having fun sometimes, tip-tap-*boom!* But Glen had a great chin, and he kept coming with his quick steps and his face shining with determination. His face gleamed like a ship at sea, and he was throwing big body shots that Tarver was rolling with. Glen was very hardheaded—he had a real set of whiskers, a steel chin—but that wasn't going to be enough. Tarver outfought him, especially early—he confused him and kept him off balance with a series of pitty-pat punches and then a hard one in there, pit-pat-pit-pat-*bam*. He kept Glen out of his rhythm. Tarver tired, and in the last few rounds he did barely enough to survive and win, and Glen was still coming hard, but it was too late. Tarver won a unanimous decision, but I had the feeling that if the fight had been fifteen rounds, Glen would have had his lunch.

Memphis was done, and we all packed up and filtered out, back to Oakland. Just a day later, and I was back at King's, hitting the heavy bag like we had never left, and Virgil was watching me with a mildly disgusted look on his face. He shook his head.

"We're going to have to throw that right hand a lot, because that jab isn't enough to keep him off, that pat-pat double jab ain't nothing.

I know it's your shoulder and it hasn't come on like it should have, but you are going to have to make him respect the right hand." I tried to make that double jab stick and flung myself at the bag with everything, but the jab was still weak, a mincing love tap.

"I'll be honest with you," Virgil said. "If you were still hitting like this after a year, then boxing ain't for you. For three months, you are doing good."

After the workout, Virgil looked weary and said to me, "We have to focus on your fight now. Straight punches, keep everything in front of you. We're going to utilize what we've got, and I've seen that right hand, so that's going to be the main weapon. Make him respect the right, let him know that you can hurt him with that hand, and then win the fight from there. Three things. One: straight punches. Two: good defense, hands up and under control. Three: conditioning. And we'll beat him."

We fell back into our seamless, timeless routine, training and running. I would meet with Heather and work on my defense, and I would meet Virgil for coffee and walk or run the lake.

One typical sunny afternoon, Virgil and I were walking the lake, stepping carefully around goose shit and talking. I asked him about his family, his brothers, and how he was led into fighting. "When I was six or seven, I was the best slap-fighter in elementary school," he said, and I thought back to my childhood memories of slap-fighting with my dad, his face serious (not that the blows were) and his hands as big as my head, knifing through the air. No one at my school would slap-fight with me. Virgil told stories of his uncles and their street-fighting days. How his grandfather had such fearsome hands that he used to keep them in his back pockets, to show peaceful intentions.

"The closer we get to your fight," he said, "the narrower our focus becomes. Training gets easier. We try to do just a few things right, and if you show you can do them, we'll advance a segment for your next fight, until you string ten or twelve segments together, and you get to be complete, and then we start volume two."

I finally got to start sparring again, and it was as if I had been asleep. I had forgotten how much *fun* it is. It's the point of everything. I sparred a couple of guys at Joe's who were smaller than me, and not very good, but I had a great time.

Back at Virgil's house, Andre had come to work out a little bit. He couldn't stay away; he just had too much youth in him to rest for more than a few days. He and I went downstairs and opened up the garage door on a dry, cool, sunny Oakland day, the city stretching away below us, down the steep driveway to the sea. We started stretching and warming up, and then Andre said, "You want to hear something that will really fire you up?" and he dashed upstairs like a kid. He came back with a CD and threw it in, and he looked at me and said, "Here's the white boy in me," and he played his favorite song. It was the *Rocky IV* soundtrack, and the song was "No Easy Way Out," which is maybe the silliest, cheesiest song ever recorded. He blasted it as we shadowboxed, and Antonio stuck his head down and looked disgusted and left. The clear blue sky was shimmering outside, and the sun was warm, and the shade was cool.

I shadowboxed while Andre worked the heavy bag, and I focused on not telegraphing, being ready with the right. Andre worked his conventional and southpaw stances. We played through "Eye of the Tiger" twice, and as that guitar started, that nearly funk hard crunch, Dre yelled, "Here we go!"

Virgil popped his head in once, looked around, and withdrew. The sun and wind through the open door felt good.

We put some reggae on and stretched and talked quietly. Andre was developing a theme that he thought about often, how boxing is perceived.

"There's a stigma attached to boxing, some of which is warranted and some isn't. The other day, I shook this guy's hand, and he asked me how my day was, and I said, 'I woke up this morning, so it's a good day.' And then he said, joking around, 'You didn't have to use those hands this morning, did you?' Implying that I didn't have to beat nobody up." Dre gave me a look that said, *C'mon, man.*

"I understand that they don't understand. Slowly, we'll change all that, with what comes out of my mouth, how I carry myself, and what happens outside the ring. We're going to change the game, and by 'we' I mean myself and Antonio and my little brother, Shimone, and whoever else God puts in our circle, they're going to change the game." He gave me a little look—God had put me in his circle, however briefly, and he was aware of me as a writer and how I could help him change the game.

"Why do team sports hold all the attention today? In boxing, you have a man putting his life on the line, and in basketball you can ride the bench and still make millions. It's up to the fighters, too, though—

why should I be on TV if everything that comes out of my mouth is 'm-f' this and 'f' that? We're role models, like it or not. In the public eye, you got to carry yourself a certain way. A lot of guys don't know better. If they knew better, they'd do better."

We went upstairs, where Virgil had cooked eggs and veal and Antonio was already chowing down. I ate a plateful too, and afterward talked to Virgil a little bit, just the two of us. He was a little disappointed that Antonio hadn't gone downstairs to work with us.

"I knew you guys were good down there—you were better just working out with Dre. You don't need me every workout yelling at you; sometimes you just got to work on the things I yelled at you for last time." He was absolutely right; sometimes you need to be left alone as a fighter to focus on your interior world, to let your concentration become total and to live in that imaginary fight and try those things again and again that you need to get right.

We talked about getting older, how being a fighter is not something that happens in a few months—it means years of study and toil, mindless conditioning and mindful practice. It is never finished. As soon as you let it slide, you are not a fighter but an ex-fighter, still dangerous but inhabiting a different plane, the regular-person plane.

Virgil said, musing, "When you retire from fighting, you become the best fighter you could have been," and he meant that your understanding of the game reaches its deepest level.

I had one more day of sparring at King's before I would start resting for my fight. There was a trainer at the gym who disliked Virgil, who envied his success and always wanted to fight any of his guys with anybody he could find. The trainers' egos came out and dueled each other through their fighters. Virgil sort of ignored the guy, as Virgil had much bigger fish to fry; but the other trainer would go around the gym looking for people my size. He wanted to spar with us. He had a kid, a tall, thin, light-skinned black kid, who could hit a little, especially if you stood in front of him—I'd seen him do it. He hit hard. The kid was only nineteen and 175 pounds, but he could hit if you let him get set. He was athletic, confident, with smooth, shelling punches like artillery. He was better than me and had a few years in the gym, and his trainer badly wanted me to spar him, because he thought he could beat me up. I had thought I could spar with him when I watched him earlier, if I kept moving.

Virgil surprised me when he asked me if I wanted to spar the kid, as a few weeks earlier the trainer had suggested it, and Virg had quickly said, "But Sam doesn't have any fights and your boy has fights." The trainer had said, "C'mon, my guy's only nineteen. Sam is thirty—he has man-strength. He's a man." Virg had replied, "But in the gym, we measure age in boxing time, and Sam only has a couple of months in the gym," and so on. Virgil had obviously liked what he saw in my last sparring session, and he wanted me to work with the kid.

I had run that morning and done hill sprints the day before, so my legs weren't fresh, but I thought that I could get through three rounds. The kid and his trainer were in back, and I knew that the trainer was telling him to kick my ass, to light me up.

Virgil was talking quietly to me. "Just use that jab, and move, move in and out, don't stop. His trainer is telling him all sorts of stuff, but you just move and use your jab."

The first round went pretty well. I moved constantly and hit him and even caught him once with the right. He caught me but not bad at all. His punches to the head were nothing, and I found myself scrambling all over the ring, but it was working beautifully. I even had him bleeding a little, although he wasn't hurt.

But for some reason, I wasn't breathing right through my mouth-piece, because when the round ended, I was way out of breath. This had happened when I sparred those kids in Hayward, too; I just wasn't breathing right or was moving too much and I got winded.

The second round, he came out leaping, on the attack, and he started to hit me a little bit, but the head shots were fine, nothing at all. He didn't even give me a bloody nose. I felt a little cowardly always moving away from him, letting him chase me all over the ring, and I started to slow down. I wasn't moving as fast or as crisply, and he leapt in and dug a good right hand to the body.

Do you even need to hear what happened next? The shot landed right on that same sweet spot on the crest of my left rib cage—the same spot I had busted at Pat's, and it felt like lightning came out of his punch, like he was driving a boiling-hot dagger through me. I cried out and almost doubled up, and from then on he clubbed me around. My mind cried out against the injustice of it all as I recognized the fact of what had happened, the shooting pains all through my body from that spot. He even went back to the body a couple of times, but nothing like that first one. Then Virgil said between rounds, "Go back to what you were doing. You got to trust in your conditioning—you were beating him."

Virgil was confused. None of the kid's shots had been that good—why was I suddenly struggling? I tried in the third round, but the kid knew he had me. I heard his corner saying, "Go back to the body," and I waved it over. I said *no más*. If I took another good body shot on the same spot, I would probably have died.

He made me quit. That's the worst thing that can happen, for someone to make you quit. It's a domination that is so total it becomes mental as well as physical. I felt ashamed, but far worse, I had felt that rib go, and I knew in my heart it was broken, it was worse than it had ever been. Virgil shook his head and said, "You were kicking his ass that first round." The punch that had killed me hadn't been a big shot. Virgil hadn't seen it, but it had been right in the worst place.

I climbed out of the ring and felt miserable. Not only had I let Virgil down, but I had quit in front of these guys who didn't know and didn't care about my rib or my story. They just didn't like me. I walked over and said thanks to both of them afterward, and they barely acknowledged me. I wanted to explain to them about my ribs, how this had first happened in Antarctica, I'm not a pussy—but they didn't care. I really felt the difference from MMA. There is a cold dislike in boxing for everyone else, which blossoms into a savage hatred in the ring, carefully cultivated by everyone involved. Nobody's really friends, although there is family in boxing.

Henry, another wizened black trainer who'd been around for years, came over and said, "You did pretty good until you got tired." I said, "It's gotta be broken again," to Virgil, and he said he didn't think he'd hit me that hard.

I walked out with Virg, and I was convinced, down in my heart, that I was fucked again. No question. The pain was worse than when I broke it the first time. I couldn't believe that this was happening, but in a sense it also felt inevitable. I knew it was going to happen. I knew without any more doubts how terribly, terribly vulnerable I was. I was like a video game character with one ridiculous weakness. I absolutely *cannot* take a punch on the point of my left rib cage. At the end, he'd teed off on me, hitting me a bunch of times to the head, and they hadn't bothered me at all. Please hit me in the head.

I could feel a funny notch on the ribs—some crepitus, I thought—so I went to an emergency room and got an X-ray. I didn't even want to know how much it cost. But when the results came, I was so surprised I had them double check it. Not broken? But it hurt worse than when it *had* been broken. How could that be? I showed the young doctor the spot. I had him feel the big notch, but he looked unconvinced and went back to the X-ray and said, "No, it's not broken, although you might want to get it X-rayed again in a few days."

I had trouble sleeping for a few days and couldn't breathe or twist or flex. I would take more Advil in the middle of the night and lie there taking shallow, gasping breaths.

Virgil and Andre were concerned, and both of them wanted me to get my ribs thoroughly checked out, as I hadn't been hit hard enough to do the damage I had sustained. I was so depressed from the pain and from the shame of being made to quit, in front of Virgil, after all he had done for me, that I didn't even want to eat. I had made plans to return to Thailand a month earlier, and was still going, but I was so heartsick that everything seemed impossible.

My reasons for going back were still valid, however. I was curious about the dogfights and there were some active dog men in Thailand I had become aware of, so I thought I would finally get a chance to see a real dogfight. Perhaps the dogfights would shed some light on the entertainment of violence, and the entire picture of human fighting. I had to see it.

Apidej had always meditated, and I felt as if I should try to figure out what he was doing. The old martial arts traditions all had meditation as a part of them, a sharpening of focus. The tai chi had given me a little taste of the internal, and Virgil talked about the concentration that was so important for boxing. I was curious to see whether meditation would help.

And finally, if I was really going to fight in Myanmar, fight *lethwei* (bare-fisted with head butts), then I could tune up for a while at Fairtex, get my conditioning back—and *then* go train in Myanmar. Myanmar (formerly Burma) borders Thailand, and was under a totalitarian military dictatorship. They still had slavery in Myanmar, and parts of the country were under rebel control. It was a whole different story from Thailand, a universe away. I wasn't feeling too confident about being able to get a fight there; the three or four contacts I had for Myanmar were all silent. The fights there were seasonal, and I was out of season. I sent out e-mails, but no one responded.

I had laid these plans, but now I doubted I would ever fight again, because how could I fight if I couldn't spar? Even days later, the pain hadn't diminished, and I was just so *tired* of being hurt. The most chilling part of it was that it just didn't get any better, day after day.

Virgil and I had coffee one last time at Coffee with a Beat, out in the sun. Virgil smiled at me. "Sam, you look like your dog died or something," he said with a laugh. He told me he was proud of me, how far I'd come, and how much farther I could take it on my own. "You've got an understanding now. You can develop yourself." He was a little surprised I was leaving. "You've been building bridges out here," he said.

He told me the story of Corinthians, and of the Apostle Paul, who had this terrible thorn in his side. Paul asked God to remove it three times, and God didn't remove it, because he wanted to show Paul that his own strength was greater than his weakness. Virgil repeated that, and we both sat silently contemplating that line. A woman walked by, and Virgil talked about the sound of her footsteps. "I listen to people walk," he said. "That can tell you a lot."

Virgil went on. "Did Dre ever tell you the story about the Olympics? After he fought the Russian, his second fight, he was totally drained. Spent, he was finished. He went to get on the bus and was thinking to himself, *What am I going to do?* when a woman he never met before stopped him and said to him, 'God is with you, giving you strength.' And his strength came back."

As we parted for the last time, for the first time in days my black mood lifted. I was back in control, back in my own story. You're always going to be hurt; you'll never be a hundred percent healthy. This is fighting. But my strength is greater than my weakness.

6

THE SLIGHT RETURN

Sam and Meditation Master Ajan Suthep,
Wat Thaton, Thailand, August 2005.

I arrived in Thailand in the middle of the day, and as I stepped off the plane the smell of frying food hit me with the shock of recognition; the heat was familiar, but the smell was utterly unique. When I caught a cab from the airport, the taxi driver surprised me by knowing where the Fairtex camp was. He just nodded and started driving, although I was ready (from the old days) to explain the directions in my mangled Thai. The surprises were to continue.

In the five years since I had been in Thailand, Fairtex had undergone a total transformation; it was now a spa as much as a training center. The whole grounds had been shifted and covered in a beautiful massive wooden structure, and everywhere was dark paneled wood. A cool blue swimming pool shimmered idly, flanked by several workout studios with gleaming mirrors, carpeted floors, and the fanciest in equipment: stainless-steel dumbbells, ceiling-to-floor mirrors, the same expensive Hammer Strength machines as in new gyms in the United States. The grounds were cultivated; trees and bamboo sheltered every path. I walked into the front office and dropped my bag, reeling from the changes; the room was now an Internet café and restaurant. There was staff in clean white polo shirts and other foreigners casually eating. My jaw hung open.

I checked in with a man I didn't know, then wandered around, stupefied by memory. I was surprised at how emotional I felt. I had forgotten the epic quality and depth of feelings I had gone through here. I walked by newly planted gardens and fountains and a cage in which two baby monkeys clutched at each other in terror. Philip, the owner, had added some giant toucans to his menagerie, and they preened their massive, horned selves while their eyes glared balefully and their scaled talons hooked the balustrade. I passed colossal fish tanks with long, silvery carp and then stumbled into a boardroom, where I found Philip, looking the same: tall, broad, and Chinese. He waved me in, beaming, and introduced me to the room.

Bart Van Der Molen was a massive, hulking man with a dour face. He was Australian and shook my hand politely, but his expression was black and vicious. (I later got to know Bart, and he was a great guy, very friendly—but unfortunately for him, his default expression, his regular, normal look, appears to be furious.) His hands were like bricks, and I wondered what he was—an ex-fighter, some kind of gangster? And what was he so pissed off about? Under his immaculate suit, he was obviously built like a truck.

They were all discussing Steve, a slender English fighter in shorts and a T-shirt who was sitting next to me. Steve was young, quiet, but keen to fight. They were talking about whether Steve could get down to 72 kilos by the next day, for the S-1 Tournament that was to take place on the queen's birthday in the center of Bangkok, on the fairgrounds in front of the old palace. Bart said with total confidence, "With about fifteen hours, I can take it off him." Steve was at 77 kilos, just under 170 pounds, at that moment, so that meant about a pound an hour. It was decided that Steve would fight—there was a possible prize of forty thousand baht (about a grand U.S.)—and the meeting broke up.

I moved into my room and met my roommate, Hamid. He was a professional fighter from New Zealand, of Moroccan descent, with a pleasant smile and black curly hair. About twenty-eight years old, he was sponsored by Fairtex and getting ready for a big fight in Australia. I watched him train, and he went to the body well, with ripping body shots that made me shudder. He had the kickboxer's bulging trunk and core, with skinny arms and legs, and he was going to tell me his whole story but decided against it. "If I start telling it, I might end up out at a bar drinking for a few days."

I found Apidej, and it was wonderful—he had barely aged a day in five years. He looked up and saw me, and a huge grin broke out. We hugged and laughed, the goodness radiating off him, the sweetness. He was sixty-four and had more than three hundred fights, and he still held pads for people. He still trained and even ran a little, a walking argument against the oft-touted long-term damage of muay Thai. "Oh Sam, you fat," he cried mournfully and rubbed my belly, and we laughed about it. Apidej was never one to mince words. He had been chosen to help direct a fund that provided for old boxers, because of his compassion and his legend.

Training was over for the day, and back in the Internet café I ran into big Bart again, and braved his "fuck-off" expression to ask him how he was going to dry Steve out.

"Basically, I'm going to dehydrate his skin," Bart said. "The body holds water in the muscles and skin, and I'm going to deplete his sodium levels and strip the water out of his skin without touching the water anywhere else."

Bart, it turned out, had earned a degree in nutrition in Australia—and he also had won Mr. Universe, the biggest amateur bodybuilding event in the world, for Thailand in 2004. Philip had read about him in a newspaper and hired him to help start a massive new facility in Pattaya, the beach town to the south. I had more than a passing interest in what he was doing because I had had such a bad time cutting weight.

Bart was happy to explain. "I can grab a lean body part, a shoulder or something, and test how much water a fighter's holding in his skin—you push the skin into the muscle, hold it, and then release and see how long it takes to spring back, and about every second is a liter of water. That's not an exact science, of course, but just a way to get an idea. I tested Steve, and I reckon he's carrying six kilos of water, so I'm confident that I can get him to shed that by weigh-in. When it comes time to fight, he'll have plenty of steady energy. In the first round he'll seem a little slow, but he won't diminish as time goes by. His energy will remain constant, just like a train, chugging away through the rounds."

Early the next morning, I was up drinking coffee, and Steve went and weighed himself and he was still way over, at seventy-six kilos—and people were panicking. Bart, however, remained calm. He was in the same suit and it was still immaculate, and he went off with Steve to the weigh-in a few hours later.

Fairtex was very bittersweet. They had my article that I'd written about my first fight there framed on the wall, and they were giving away copies of my National Geographic video, and I still saw people wearing the T-shirt I had designed for Anthony so long ago.

The biggest shock was the early morning runs. Now, instead of outside, the pro fighters ran in the gym, racing on treadmills under the TV, like it was Gold's Gym. It made sense, it kept them out of the traffic, but it was still disconcerting.

Philip was around all the time now, and the camp was in a sense more serious, but it also more obviously catered to the *farang*. There were still top-level fighters, Beya, my old friend, among them. Beya had been a promising prospect, destined for greatness, when I had been at Fairtex the first time. He was now a highly ranked star, in the top four or five in the country in his weight class, and he'd fought in Japan. Philip told me that the camp had never made money, it was all about his love for the fight game—but now, with the changes and ability to accommodate so many *farang* at once, the camp was turning profitable, and the gigantic gym and health spa he was building in Pattaya would be even more so. Still, Philip's primary business was textiles; in a sense, these were all hobbies.

The changes in the camp reflected a shift that had been under way even when I'd been in Thailand years earlier: the shift of muay Thai from being supported by Thais to being supported by *farang*. When we went to Lumpini years ago, there were maybe five thousand Thais in the audience, and thirty or fifty *farang,* and now I was told that on most big nights there were two thousand Thais and two hundred *farang.* Foreigners were training everywhere, out on the islands, all over Bangkok and in every city. The introduction of cable TV and the popularity of English Premier League football had supplanted boxing as the sport on which to gamble; in Thailand, certain parts of the country followed certain teams. The foreign interest was keeping muay Thai alive.

The elephant swamp was gone, developed, and now there was a huge concrete wall that blocked out the sun. They couldn't do anything about the ants, I was relieved to find. The ants were still in the rooms and on the walls, unimpressed with the changes.

Hamid and I and a few other *farang* went into town to catch the fights later that day, the deepening press of Bangkok folding in around us as we came out of the suburbs.

It was hot, humid, and overcast, with the low gray sky threatening to pour rain on us but never delivering. The golden temples and palace glistened dully in the far background on the flat marshy plain of the old city. The fair was huge, an open-air festival, and thousands and thousands of Thais pressed in all around the ring, milling and calling and slightly drunken, willing to be pleased by just about anything.

The tournament was called S-1, a knockoff of K-1. It was a round-robin, from eight competitors to four to two, so the winner would have to win three fights. Hamid told me that the pool was not exceptionally strong. There were two Thais, the rest foreign, and only one of them was any good, a *farang* named Arslan, who was also a model, with long black hair and an aristocrat's pointed face and blade nose. Hamid had fought him in K-1 and lost a decision.

To everyone's relief (and secret surprise), Steve had made the weigh-in at 72 kilos, just under 159 pounds, but he looked a little pale. Bart wore his habitual expression of doom and gloom. Hamid and I wandered around the backstage area under the tents, watching the other fighters get their massages and complete their prefight rituals.

The fights started and went *exactly* as Bart had predicted. Steve fought a young, heavily tattooed Russian who swarmed him and won the first round, but he weathered the storm and came back, and by the third round was clubbing the guy all over the ring, and won by decision. He rested briefly, got massaged, and then fought Arslan, who was the favorite to win the whole thing—and Steve beat him by coming in aggressively with his elbows chopping instead of jabbing his way in. Again, by the third round, Steve was the strongest.

The final championship fight was against a Thai, an older fighter, an ex-champion who used his face and emotions aggressively in every fight, widening his eyes and shaping his mouth in an *O* of surprise, trying to convince his opponent that he was already beaten, the fight was over. There was a deadly finality to his kicks, but Steve was unconvinced and fought him tough, pressuring him, and at the start of the third round bum-rushed him with a few elbows and caught him with a knee to the head and knocked his ass flat out. It was a good thing, too, because there was no way Steve was going to win a decision—not against a Thai ex-champion who was kicking well and stealing rounds on the queen's birthday.

I was sitting next to Bart and shook his hand afterward and said, "Well, that went pretty well." He nodded. "It almost didn't," he said. "He was here without me for a few hours, and he was feeling really badly so his [Thai] trainer took him to a store for some Gatorade—and when I heard that, I nearly walked away, because if he'd started in on that he would have felt better, and about fifteen minutes into the fight he would have crashed horribly." Steve had luckily waited for Bart and kept to the regimen.

I had Bart give me the whole rundown as we sat there and waited for the crowds to diminish. "Well, normally I'd take all the salt out of his diet about two days before the weigh-in, but in this case, we didn't have time, so I used a potassium-sparing diuretic. Sodium holds water in the skin, and potassium holds water in the muscles, and we don't want to touch that muscle—the heart, after all, is a muscle. You know that steroids aren't banned from bodybuilding shows—just diuretics. Too dangerous.

"Now, everyone is panicking in the morning, when Steve still weighs seventy-six kilos, but it was just the start of the process. Basically, Steve had to piss all the water out of his system, out of his skin, and if he stops pissing, you have to make him start again, by giving him water, which seems counterintuitive. Get him flowing, and his body starts flushing, and overflushes, without touching the water in his muscles. He made seventy-two kilos for the weigh-in. The trick is putting it back in; he's dehydrated and needs electrolytes, and he feels like crap.

"Every half hour I'd ask him how he was feeling, and slowly put the electrolytes and carbs back in him. Don't give him anything high in sugar—he'll spike his insulin and then he'll crash—and in the beginning nothing with salt, only an hour before the fight. It'll help him hydrate. I gave Steve potato chips: salts, fats, and carbohydrates. As we got closer to the fight, more sugary foods, chocolate bars, electrolyte drinks, an apple. He was feeling pretty bad until about an hour before the fight, and then he started coming back. But you saw how he maintained."

With his composure and his prophecy, Bart had secured Philip's trust. It was all the more impressive because Steve had not been highly touted going into the match. In the end, though, it was Steve who did it. He showed tremendous heart, and he obviously had been in excellent shape. Two weeks earlier, he had fought for free, just to get a fight, and now he was a name. Now he had a belt. Bart had gotten him there, had put him in the right position, but Steve had made it happen.

When I had first come to Thailand, Apidej, my teacher, used to meditate sometimes after training. He'd sit alone in the quiet ring cross-legged, with his eyes closed and his hands neatly in his lap, for ten or twenty minutes. The young Thai fighters would roll their eyes and shake their heads, but you couldn't really do that to a guy who'd won more muay Thai titles than anyone else in history. He'd been doing something right. When I asked him about it, he said meditation had been very helpful to him before fights, to see everything an opponent might try to do.

I was still waiting on word from Myanmar and hadn't heard anything—about either training or fighting. In the meantime, I thought I should examine meditation to some degree. In Thailand, nearly every male will spend a rainy season at a temple at some point. It's a part of Buddhism. Beya spoke wistfully of becoming a monk, once his fighting career was over. It was what he wanted more than anything. Many of the Japanese martial arts have a meditation component, the Zen. Apidej said it had helped his concentration, and maybe it could help mine. I knew from Virgil how important concentration could be.

I found a somewhat famous meditation center far in the north, called Wat Thaton, near Chiang Rai, close to the Myanmar border. The wat practiced *vipassana* meditation, although I couldn't have told you what that meant. I knew you were supposed to be silent the whole time. That sounded like a challenge. Which led me to Chiang Rai and being picked up by a monk, Panyavudo, from the temple, who spoke perfect English, and a driver, Sukhit. Panyavudo asked me if I wanted to take a tour of the Golden Triangle. If I would pay for gas, we could do one.

"Sure," I said.

It was good just to be out of the oppressive heat and grit of Bangkok, healing for the heart to be out in clean air and the countryside, with the jungle dark dull green on all sides and rounded hills and mountains rising around us. We drove through a series of towns and wandered the grounds of the ancient wats; it was interesting being the walking companion of a monk in orange robes. The Thais were respectful and the *farang* curious and staring.

Panyavudo was a young man, maybe thirty-five, small and slender with an acne-scarred face, a pleasant smile, and thick glasses. He began to fill me in on some of the basic tenets of Buddhism. He had been ordained about six years before, and briefly disrobed (become a layperson) for two months to sort out some family troubles. He had an eagerness to please that was touching, and a tremendous amount of nervous energy. We walked around on ancient wat that was slowly being reclaimed by the jungle, and he stepped carefully around ants on the ground, stopping to pay respects to the *chedi,* the big stone column or cone with the Buddhist relics inside. We looked over the rows of amulets and statues for sale; grassroots Buddhism in Thailand has a strong current of animism, and there is a thriving trade in amulets, charms, and lucky statues.

Back in the car, competing with the roar of the windows, I explained myself and the book I was writing to Panyavudo by saying briefly, "I don't want to hurt anybody. I just enjoy the action and striving." I wondered if that was true.

We drove up along the Mekong, a broad brown eel with its tiny ripples like scales in the humid sun. More temples and shrines, and then a brief stop at the Myanmar border. Panyavudo walked frenetically—he would have been right at home in New York—and I realized that this was a real treat for him. He got to leave the temple every two months, and he wanted to look around. His ankles were strangely black and blue, and I wondered why.

Back in the car and driving to the wat, I asked him about meditation and what I was going to learn. "You become aware of the processes of the body and mind," he said. "By becoming aware, you can understand that there is no ownership of body or mind, that thoughts are just illusions, and that suffering can be overcome." *Sounds good,* I thought, and leaned back and watched the green hills roll by and become more mountainous as we approached Wat Thaton. We turned in through some massive gates and wound up past lower temples and outbuildings (the wat exists on nine levels on the mountain) until we reached the Meditation Center. It was dark, and Panyavudo showed me to my little cabin and said he would see me in the morning. No computers, no cell phones, no reading. Nothing but meditation and reflection, eating and sleeping.

The cabins for the meditators were small white cottages set on stilts on the steep hills, surrounded by thick jungle, with one room and a little toilet with a bucket and bowl for bathing. The bed was a one-inch pad on the floor; there were two folding chairs and about ten feet by fifteen feet of hardwood floor. There was a sense of reduced scale, a little like Tokyo—the light switch next to the door was at mid-thigh.

I fell asleep and awoke sometime later in the dark to the ringing of bells and then a sonorous, amplified nasal chanting that went on for at least an hour, and then I fell back asleep, and in the morning walked down to the Meditation Center, through a shaded road with about ten cottages like mine and dogs lying idly about.

The view was breathtaking, out over the low, flat floodplain with a river snaking idly across it, to some rows of high and mysterious mountains in the far distance, like a vision of ancient Asia from an emperor's palace. And then I went inside and began meditating.

The kind of meditation practiced at Wat Thaton was dynamic (moving) *vipassana* ("to see things as they really are"), and the key concept is mindfulness. Through meditation, in which you focus entirely on the immediacy of the action, on the *feeling* of the action, you build up the strength of your mind and your awareness. As your awareness grows, you become better able to see your own thoughts for what they are: illusions. You become able to see things more clearly, to see the truth through feelings such as greed, jealousy, and even joy. This leads to an end of suffering and, eventually, maybe, enlightenment. I was down.

I started learning the various kinds of meditation; there are sitting, standing, lying down, and walking versions, although in practice all anyone does is walk and sit. For walking, there were patterns on the floor of seven steps in one direction (for the petals on the lotus and as part of mindfulness and so on) and then a nearly military pivot and seven steps back in the same line. The idea is to focus entirely on the feeling of the movement, to be entirely present in the moment. There is no past and no future, just the present, and every time a thought creeps into your mind, you are supposed to let it leave and resume focusing on the movement.

The sitting meditation was similar, sitting cross-legged (or half or full lotus, if you could) and moving your arms in prescribed patterns, over the belly button, up to the heart, and back down to the knees. Again, the intention is to focus on the movement, being totally aware and present in that precise instant; every time your mind wanders, bring it back to the movements.

It was excruciating. I have never been so bored as I was during the first five days of meditation. It should have gotten better after three days, but apparently I have a noisy mind. Because you focus on every movement and are so present all the time, the days pass with agonizing slowness, every second is present and accounted for. Even the walking meditation can go on forever. I was put on a schedule: meditate for a half hour in one form (walking) and then switch (to sitting). I would check the clock after what felt like twenty minutes and see that a whole three minutes had passed. I cannot describe the boredom in sufficient terms.

The worst was sitting. Because I have very tight hamstrings and lower back, sitting cross-legged became painful quickly. Most first-time meditators can sit for ten or fifteen minutes without pain; for me, the pain started in five. And I was sitting for half an hour. In meditation, Panyavudo told me with his huge smile, "Pain is a friend. It is a reminder to mindfulness, and it tells us in the end that it is only pain, another illusion, and this helps our understanding." He could sit for an hour and a half, and some monks can sit for four or more hours, but for them there is always pain, and dealing with it and working through it are part of the process. Sometimes the bones in your ankles would grind into the mats, and I realized why Panyavudo's ankles were black and blue. Enlightenment through agony.

So I would sit and sweat as the pain came in waves from the back and knees and tendons, moving my arms faster and faster in an attempt to speed up time, trying to remain mindful, trying to stay straight but with my back invariably bowing, and the clock moving with indescribable slowness. The days, because of the focus on the intense instant present, become absolutely epic. They would go on and on and on and on . . . and I'd still be only halfway through. I did come to realize that time is a human concept with no reality; there is only the present, impermanent. And there is a tremendous difference between knowing something by having read or been told it, and *knowing* something, by having it become clear to you through intuition.

As a meditator at an intensive meditation retreat, I was not supposed to speak; eventually, I was supposed to stay in my room and "study," just meditate, for the entire day.

The day began at three-thirty a.m. with bells, an ancient alarm clock, a call to chanting. The bells would ring, and then ring again, faster and faster until it was a continuous *ding-ding-ding,* and then a long pause, and then a repeat. Sometimes the dogs would join in, howling and yelping in the darkness. This invariably made me giggle.

After I heard the bells, I would put on my white clothes (laypeople wear white) and go to the chanting hall in the pitch-black darkness, leaving my flip-flops and umbrella (it was the rainy season) at the door. In Thailand, you never wear shoes inside anyone's house, it's disrespectful and dirty; and when you approach or enter a wat, you are expected to remove your shoes.

The chanting hall was a large building, like a small church, but with no pews or furniture, just a long, hardwood floor with thin mats laid down in strips. At the far end was a collection of large golden Buddhas in various postures, tapestries, pictures, and candles. On the floor in neat patterns were the monks' cushions, inch-thick pads on which they sat, some brocaded or colored. At any given moment, about half would be occupied by monks in their orange or brown robes, sitting cross-legged or kneeling.

The chanting was led by a heavily tattooed, rail-thin older monk, or by the meditation master up on the dais with his back to us, facing the Buddhas. The chanting was in Pali, an ancient dead language from India, the home of the Buddha. The Buddhist scriptures, written five hundred years after Buddha's death, are in Pali and Sanskrit. For many hundreds of years in Thailand, the monks had chanted without even knowing what they were saying, until sometime in the last century a monk decided that it was time to understand what he was saying every morning and evening. The Pali is a wailing, nasal, bubbling song, droning, rising and falling with a heavy cadence, and serves two purposes: to remember and pay homage to the Buddha, the Dhamma, or Dharma (his teachings), and the Sangha (his disciples, the body of monks around the world—themselves), and second, to train the breathing, as it is a difficult performance, with short, sharp inhalations and long, slow powerful chants. This was also the religious part of things, something I observed but didn't take part in other than sitting quietly until my legs screamed and my back ripped holes of fire into me. It was the medieval aspect, the kowtowing and pressing the forehead to the floor, the unthinking worship of the Buddha.

After the chanting ended, we would meditate as a group; most of the monks would continue to sit, while the laypeople would get up, slowly, joints stiff and bent up like cripples, and begin the walking meditation.

I would walk for a half hour and then leave, go back to my room and put on shoes to walk up the mountain, as we were allowed to do walking meditation on this path. I would stride briskly and with some attempt at mindfulness, umbrella firmly in hand through the darkness, past the silent dogs and through the gloomy jungle. The road wound up and down, past smaller temples and a huge *chedi* being built and past the abbot's and higher-ups' ornate houses. It was strange to be alone in Thailand; you're almost never alone. Eventually, after a mile or two and maybe a seven-hundred-foot climb, I would come out at the Standing Buddha, the best part of my day.

The Standing Buddha was a massive golden statue, thirty feet tall, on a high, raised, tiled platform, miles above the valley. The river ran below, thousands of feet down, through the thick Asian jungle, and wound mysteriously away into the mountains at my back. The view was incredible, distant mountains shrouded in low clouds, the storm-tossed sky ripped in blues and blacks as the dawn approached.

I would do my tai chi form out there on the high ledge, in front of the massive golden Standing Buddha. Almost immediately, my form had begun to feel better, the chi flowing from my palms. Ajahn Suthep, the meditation master, had shown me some *chi gung* exercises, and I tried those, too.

Afterward, on the walk back, I would often meet the only other *farang* at the retreat, a quiet German girl named Britta, and some of the hill tribesmen coming up from their valley behind the mountain. On my first morning, a young boy, maybe six years old, silently fell into step with me for most of the walk back, and I slowed to accommodate his churning short legs, and we didn't speak but walked together.

Sometimes I walked up in the rain clouds, with mist thick and low around me and water saturating my breath, and sometimes I walked in the torrential rainy-season deluge, the water sheeting in streams across the path, waves and ripples and eddies forming.

Back at my hut, the light cool and growing, I would "shower" with the bucket in the cold water and nap and wait for the food, which arrived at seven forty-five in a column of covered pots stacked together by a clever handle. This was my other favorite time of the day, I took a lot of photos of my food because it was so pretty. But you had to make sure that you ate only half and saved the rest for lunch, because that was all you got. Also, you had to keep the food safe from ants. There was a poisonous or repellent chalk that did the trick; you would draw a circle on the floor with that and put the food inside it.

So I would eat, mindfully, slowly chewing and savoring each bite, and the food was usually bland but good and of good quality, a little tiny bit of meat, rice, and a lot of vegetables.

Then I would lie down and rest until nine or so, and start meditation. And so went the days. One night, after chanting, when I was walking again in the hall, Ajahn fell into step with me, to help me increase my mindfulness. You would often see the monks do this, heads slightly bowed, walking together, helping each other increase in mindfulness.

It reminded me of the intense brotherhood relationship you see sometimes with Sufi mystics. Ajahn must have been about five foot three
inches, and he reminded me of nothing so much as the little boy I'd
walked with that first morning, so long ago.

Ajahn had a kindly round face. He spoke barely intelligible English and
looked fifty, but it was hard to tell with the shaved head. All the monks
shave their heads together on every full moon, and the Thai Buddhist
monks also shave their eyebrows; they are the only ones who do this.
The story goes that it shows loyalty to the king. Back in the ancient
days in Ayuthaya, the old capital of Siam, the monks found out that a
Burmese spy was coming disguised as a monk, and so they all shaved
their eyebrows so the spy, not knowing about it, would be revealed.
Another example of the tremendous popularity of the monarchy in
Thailand.

Ajahn was born in 1949 ("the year the Communists took over China")
to Laotian immigrants living in Thailand, a farming family. He showed
promise and his mother worked hard to get him an education, and he
lived with his uncle at a soldier's camp. His uncle would beat him every
day, and he saw that the life of a soldier "had no value." He won a scholarship to a famous school and lived there and in the temple for two
years but didn't become a monk. He didn't like monks. He thought the
meditators were locked up in their own minds, ignoring the world,
something I was feeling as well. He eventually went to a famous university for agriculture and animal husbandry, and he "lost awareness"
of the sin of taking any life. He was elected student council president
and led the students in a massive demonstration over some complicated
tuition changes, and even met with the then dictator of Thailand in
parliament. He was subsequently kicked out for embarrassing the university. The student body collected money to send him away to finish
his education overseas, but instead he joined the Communist Party—
because he was angry. He became an important figure in the underground, organizing in high schools and universities. There were power
struggles and a coup d'état in Thailand, and in 1976 he was forced into
hiding and spent years in the forests, as a deputy political commander
of the Thai Communist Party, fighting and hiding. "I had so many
names," he said, laughing, when I asked what his real name was. In
those days he was Somdet.

Later, the international movement for communism died down, and China changed its policy. The Thai government allowed the former illegals to return with amnesty, and so he came back, and even went to Australia. He gave me a secret smile and said, "I have a joke: I am a failed animal husband and farmer, and a failed in the business and a failed revolutionary, so now I am a Buddhist monk, where they cannot fire me!"

He had an equally tortuous path as a monk, but finally, after a seventeen-day intense retreat where the meditation went on for thirteen hours a day without stopping, he realized that the million different thoughts weren't real; the walking was real. He has worked with HIV patients and built temples and had visions of an interfaith meditation center, and he was reading a lot about Tibetan concepts of death and dying. He had even thought he might be a holy man once, but now he just wanted to teach meditation everywhere and help people find the truth. His bluntness and lack of mysticism were refreshing, and he delighted in poking fun at mystics.

We had a few dialogues at night, over tea, sometimes joined by Britta and then another foreigner, a young man from Singapore, who came later. The dialogues wandered, and at times it was hard to understand Ajahn's heavy accent, but his good nature was encouraging. When I first met him, he mentioned that he had read in the paper that a man had been in an accident and lost his legs, and his eyes teared up instantly, brimming with compassion.

It was rainy season, "the Wet," and although Bangkok was dry, the north wasn't. The rains came often, first with a breeze and then a wind rushing in the trees, swirling and threshing the foliage in ponderous whipping circles, and the sky cooled and darkened. Sometimes there was thunder, but sometimes not, just the spattering that might turn into a real barnstorming downpour, or it might stay at a steady patter for hours, dripping among the broad heavy leaves.

Alone in my room, with heightened senses, I could hear the lizards on the roof as they patrolled the tops of the windows for insects lured by the light. Sometimes I would catch very clear rock or Thai pop music wafting through my windows, and at first I thought it was from the town below. *Man, someone is pumping that crap up,* I thought. One day, when I was just finishing a thirty-minute seated stint, in started the techno, and I burst outside, looking for the source, and found it was coming from the basement of my cottage. I banged on the door but received no answer. Later, when I spoke to Ajahn about it, he was contrite, and said, "Oh, yes, that's a monk, he's my cousin."

"Can you ask him to use headphones or something?"

Ajahn gave me a long look. "We'll move you," he said finally. "He's a little crazy."

If I ever do a stand-up routine about living in a Buddhist meditation retreat in northern Thailand, it will certainly have a bit called "The Monk in My Basement." Another monk, a Thai who had been to college in Indiana, fell into step with me a day later and commiserated. "That's too bad, to disturb you like that," he said. "Here you are to be in isolation and he's blasting techno. What the fuck, huh?"

On the fourth day, after evening chanting, when everyone was standing slowly to start walking, Panyavudo came across the hall to me and asked directly, "Have you ever had black magic practiced on you?" in the manner of asking an obvious drunk, "Have you been drinking?"

"I don't think so," I said.

"I can see these red bands around your chest, right here over your ribs," and he motioned with his hands right over my damaged ribs. I was fairly shocked.

My ribs had been bugging me, and perhaps he had seen me massaging them, but I certainly hadn't mentioned them to anyone.

He led me to a quiet corner, where I sat down, and he sat behind me with his feet against my back and directed energy through me to loosen the bonds, and who knows? Maybe I felt better.

Afterward he said, "You have to be careful. Sometimes a fighter will be given something to eat or drink, or a curse may be put on him several days before a fight." Had I eaten something that made me feel funny? Common practice in Thailand.

It took some time, but I eventually got Panyavudo to talk to me about black magic. There are certain monks who do magic, who understand it and work to counteract the bad magic they find, the ones who make blessed amulets and who work with the more superstitious Thai people. Apparently, Panyavudo was one of them. Ajahn Suthep, emphatically, was not. He would laugh, then tell a story of a famous magic monk who made powerful charms, "but he still go to the hospital when he is sick. Why? He still gonna die. I don't believe." Ajahn would giggle like a fat happy kid.

Panyavudo had been told to ignore the magic, and he had tried to, for four years. Recently, he had decided that he had to embrace it, discover it, and then he could let it go and move on toward enlightenment. He felt that to understand it was now part of his duty, a very important concept for the monks.

"Magic is about intensity of concentration," he said to me, his eyes blinking behind thick glasses (but not as thick as Ajahn's). A practitioner can concentrate, find you mentally, and affect your mind with alien thoughts. The way to combat this is with awareness, with mindfulness, and you can keep your mind strong and able to defend itself, to recognize thoughts that are yours and thoughts that may have been planted.

"You must not give out your time of birth to *anyone,*" he said, as apparently that will help them locate you. To counteract, you must be aware and know yourself, and trust your feelings. If someone hands you something to eat, feel it for a few minutes, feel the vibe of it.

He said that my practicing tai chi would help, as would meditation and awareness. I could also try "compassion meditation," where you reflect good thoughts on people you love, people you like, people who are neutral to you, and people you dislike. Keep it to the same sex. "But not dead people, because that can bring spirits around." The pain may be residue of spirits that have been injured—the spirits of the ants I washed off my toilet, for instance, or the spirit of someone whom I have wronged. That last got me thinking.

"Negative forces can come back to us, and we have eighty years of life [he said that so carelessly], so be careful, because it can accumulate and hurt you. Give loving kindness."

Panyavudo was an intelligent, educated man, who lived in the Netherlands and Germany between the ages of two and twenty-four and who had had import-export and parliamentary jobs in Bangkok. He was not a silly superstitious native; he'd been a part of the modern world.

He looked at me for a long time and then said, "There is a band of metal around your head, around your forehead, a narrow gold band," and he gestured around his temples and around his head. "Does that mean anything to you?"

I shook my head.

"Well, you might want to look into that," he said, and as always, gave me a huge smile. "You need to see the spiritual side of fighting and self-defense, as well as the physical and mental. People train to build up the will to fight, and black magic can destroy that."

By day six I had turned a corner of some kind, and my bouts of deep boredom were fading, because what is boredom? It's just another feeling, just an emotion, just an illusion—it's not real. Boredom is like the pain, it comes to show you the character of boredom itself. The pain arises to teach you about pain. Once I sat for forty-five minutes, and stopped more out of shock than out of pain. Ajahn, when he went into deep meditation, would sit for six and a half hours. My mindfulness was increasing, and I found it easier, could fall into it with more familiarity. Things did start to become clearer. I could see more angles on my thoughts—I was starting to see 360 degrees around all of my problems.

I also had adjusted to the lack of food, and the six hours of sleep, and felt energized and strong all day without the coffee crutch. In part, too, the contentment came from the lack of all the technological intrusions that had been part of my life, the endless electric hum of microchips that surrounded me. It was like being a little kid again. I rediscovered the ability to stare at clouds and trees for long periods of time. There was a sense that this could go on forever, but there was also the world calling outside my window, through the jungle. The wind would come winding and twisting through the thick trees and dense bamboo, the drops on the leaves. There was constant noise, the thrum of far-off engines, a scooter on the road, the wind, cicadas, the boys next door chattering in liquid Thai, solitary monks clumping past my window.

In the darkness on my tenth morning, I climbed into the car, back in my civilian dark clothes and out of my pure, simple whites that had been such a comfort, such an ease of mind to wear. I had deodorant on, and it stunk through my Bruce Lee T-shirt. All the chains and accessories of society—technology, money and credit cards, tickets and passports, and a friend's borrowed cell phone: each heavier than the last. Ajahn invited me back to write a book about what he was doing, the meditation and the experiences of *farang* at different temples. I think he was inviting me in the sense that Buddhist monks sometimes *invite* laypeople to come and work with them, to build temples and so on, to build merit for themselves.

"Mindfulness can be brought to bear on everything, can be a part of everything, of your training, and of your fighting," Ajahn told me. The monks had no trouble at all with the fact that I was a sometime fighter. "If you are mindful in boxing, then you can be aware and not trapped in a same movement, you can be formless, and formless cannot be beat—as long as you are strong inside and have your feet rooted," Ajahn said. Virgil would have agreed with him.

As we wheeled through the misty countryside, past the tribal hill people in traditional garb walking alongside the highway, he turned from the front seat and said to me, "Mindfulness will help you see without illusion."

I nodded and said, "Hemingway was all about writing the 'true' sentence," almost to myself.

"*The Old Man and the Sea*," he said to me, and smiled. "Good story."

7

GAMENESS

A dog fight in the Philippines.

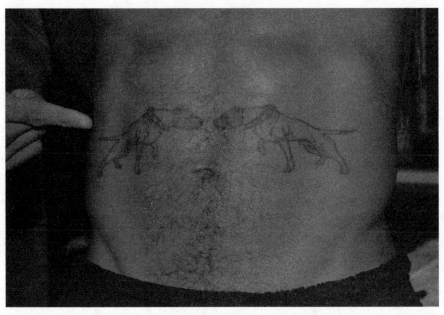

Paulo Filho, member of Brazilian Top Team,
Brazil, December 2004.

But in the corrida, *the matador is not exposed to physical and emotional damage by duty, or conscription—he is a volunteer, a true believer, a lover with his love. And there are no limits to love, it is quite merciless.*

—A. L. Kennedy, *On Bullfighting*

I was lying awake in the heat and dark when the alarm went off. It was three-fifty a.m. I dressed, Tim knocked on my door, and we went quietly down the tiled halls, broad stairs, and through the lobby.

It was pitch-black and hot outside, not the roiling heat of the day but a friendly, swampy mush, the cooling sea not far off. We were on the outskirts of Pattaya, in Thailand, down near the gulf; and it was still the rainy season. The house dogs, disturbed as we left the hotel, rioted without ferocity. We clambered into the car.

Tim drove through the night, the low grass and jungle, to his farm, which was around the corner and down a rutted dirt road. We loaded Herbie into the crate after checking his weight. Herbie was dense, lean to the point of starvation, and muscular, a tawny red pit bull with a big head, a "head like a brick," his co-owner, whom I'll call Monty, said. Herbie was ecstatic to be off the chain, a dense ball of energy thrusting against his leash, tail lashing the air. He was an American pit bull, of course—serious dogmen wouldn't dream of fighting anything else. Herbie was a decently bred dog, Tim knew his lineage back five or six generations, but today was his first fight, his first test. He was thought to be a good dog, if not a world beater.

Herbie was slightly above weight, a hundred grams or so, but a good shit and a piss would take care of that. "He drinks a lot of water," muttered Tim in his broad Australian accent. "I've never had a dog do that. Usually, by the end, when they're in condition, they don't drink much."

Tim CEK (Combat Elite Kennels, his personal group and the name he wanted me to use) was a bookish man in his early thirties, gray hair starting to belie his youthful face. He was half Thai and half Australian, and although he was perfectly fluent in both tongues, he was often mistaken for *farang* in Thailand. He was my guide to the dog world. He was the expert. He had about fifteen dogs, and he and Monty (a white British safety engineer) were co-owners of Herbie. "You'll see yards where they have hundreds of dogs, but those dogs are all shit, and they don't know what they've got. They're just hoping to get lucky. You need to keep your yard small, with high-quality dogs, so you can understand what you have," Tim said.

International dogfighting is a mixed bag of enthusiasts. Tim's friend Ike X was a relaxed Asian man in his late thirties or forties who had been to Harvard and spent ten years as a cowboy in Montana. He was now basically a professional dogman. We didn't talk about Harvard.

The weigh-in was for six o'clock. They wanted to fight the dogs early to avoid the heat of the day and also to limit the visibility to prying eyes: Dogfighting was illegal in Thailand, as it is in most places. The dogs were supposed to weigh 18 kilos, just under 40 pounds, and Tim's opponent, Art, weighed his dog first. The dog (also an American pit bull) was meek and yellow, his tail whipped down between scrawny legs, and he weighed in at 17.9 kilos. They weighed the dog on a hanging electronic scale slung from a low beam, with a strap made from an old seatbelt cinched around the dog's body, right underneath the forelegs. The dog hung there nearly upright, twisting idly, tail twitching slightly but otherwise still, eyes staring. He was a good-looking, friendly-faced dog with soft eyes.

The Captain, who fancied himself judge and referee (even though he was neither), was an older man of Afghan descent, a skipper in the Canadian merchant marine who had sixty years experience with dogs. He was a stickler for details, and his watch beeped urgently at six a.m. Herbie still hadn't shat or pissed, and despite some vigorous walking, came in at 18.1 kilos. The Captain, with some satisfaction, gave Art the forfeit money.

When you agree to fight dogs, you set a weight, and if your dog doesn't make the weight, you must pay forfeit money, maybe a quarter of the money you put up to fight, and then it is up to the opponent to decide if he still wants to fight.

The forfeit was twenty thousand baht (about five hundred dollars U.S.), and Tim was a little annoyed because he had given Art breaks before with weight; they had fought many times, and all he needed was ten minutes to get Herbie to void his bowels. Art was glad to give him more time, but Art's partner took the money, and Tim said, "I'll remember that."

In the world of dogfighting, I found, there is a fanatical adherence to the rules. Honorable dogmen, good dogmen, have a very strict code of behavior, predicated on camaraderie and desire for fair play and a fair test of their dog. They look down on dogmen who are just in it for the money, trying to build a name for themselves and hyping their dogs out of proportion in order to sell pups. They are also secretive and incredibly tight-lipped, and word of mouth and reputation are everything.

The pit had been set up, the dogs were washed, and the handlers, Tim and Art, came out carrying their dogs like toddlers who had grown too big to be carried easily, legs dangling and awkward. They clambered into the pit, and huddled over their respective dogs in the corners. The pit was a simple wooden square, just a few feet high, and the opposite corners—the scratch lines—were supposed to be fourteen feet apart.

Suddenly, the moment arrives (the referee calls, "Face your dogs—release!"), and the dogs dash into each other like brown streaks, spinning around and up and down with a continuous snapping, snarling frenzy. They writhe furiously like snakes, twisting and spitting and slavering, growling like bears. Fury epitomized. Their tails are wagging, this is what they are meant to do, and they're fulfilling their purpose, they're *becoming*. There is blood, but the dogs don't care, turning and pinning, fighting off their backs and then clawing their way to standing. They're biting, and letting go, and biting again, searching for new holds, for a vulnerable spot. They feel no pain—or any pain they feel is overwhelmed by the desire to get the other dog. I know that feeling. The fight stretches to fifteen minutes, to twenty.

Tim said to me the day before, "It's not the best dog that will win, it's the best man. You are fighting the man, not the dog; the dog's just a weight." In a sense, he's right, and the dogmen always talk about "when I fought him" as if they were doing the fighting themselves; but of course that comment was absolutely shimmering with irony. I was reminded of something Willie Pep, a great boxer, said: "I had the bravest manager in the world—he didn't care who I fought."

In this fight, the dogs were evenly matched, and neither one had a "hard mouth" (a big crushing bite that can break bones or rip off flesh), so the outcome would come down to conditioning. Which dogman had conditioned his animal better?

The dogs bite and bite, their mouths locking onto each other with a horrible clack and snap of fang on fang. The teeth sometimes grind together and sound as if they are breaking. Herbie is more active and a better wrestler; he often has the other dog pinned down. This isn't necessarily bad for the other dog, as long as he's getting good "holds," or bites, but it isn't really good, either (a little like jiu-jitsu). The dogs go silent, panting, and when they freeze "in holds," their bellies work like bellows, desperately breathing to try to shed heat. Blood covers Herbie's face and teeth, as the other dog has chewed up his jowls a little.

The sun climbs up and strokes the pit, the players, and the dogs, and their shadows leap into being on the wall. Soon heat will be a major factor. Tim and Art pace warily around the dogs, looking and whispering, "tch-ing" and sometimes asking the dog to shake once he has a good bite, to shake and break something. It is eerily quiet—the Thais murmur occasionally, and the dogs pant.

There is the first "turn" call. Art's dog has "turned," and they go to "scratch." This means that Art's dog, for a brief second, has turned from Herbie, has turned from the fight, has shown a little bit of cur. Art and Tim dive in and pluck up their dogs, "handling" them. Immediately, a voice from the crowd begins counting the seconds, and both handlers in their corners face their dogs away and work vigorously with a wet sponge, trying to cool them down. As the count nears thirty, the referee calls on them to face their dogs, and Art's dog, having turned, has to "make scratch." The scratch lines are fixed in the corners, and to make scratch means you let your dog go, and on his own accord he attacks the other dog (who is being held in his corner until your dog comes to get him). Art's dog comes off the scratch line like a bullet—he scratches hard, and the Thais murmur an appreciative sound. They like that. It means nothing, really—a dog that scratches hard and a dog that scratches slowly are the same until one won't scratch. The dog and Herbie come together in another whirling tussle.

Now that they have scratched once, every time the dogs are "out of holds" (when neither has a bite), they have to be separated, to scratch again, alternating. The handlers stay close, and each has to seize the right moment to pick up his dog so that the other dog doesn't get a chance to sink in a free bite. I could see why the dogs can't be people-aggressive, because if they were, in the fury of the fight they would bite the handlers. I could also see that what was important, what was critical to the fight, wasn't the battle itself—it was the scratch. Hair-splitting definitions and measurements of courage, that's the dog game.

At thirty minutes, the dogs are obviously tiring. Tim's yard man, a Cambodian who'd been in the Khmer Rouge and scared all the other Cambodians senseless, is circling the pit, calling, "*Goot* boy, Herbie," and the twenty or so people in the audience are trying to encourage their money.

Each time they scratch, Art's dog comes hard; but Herbie just trots out from the scratch line when it's his turn, not in a blazing dash, but with no sign of stopping, either. Monty mutters, "The tide has turned," and then Art's dog cries out. I watch Herbie learning as the fight goes on. He figures out where to bite, and to bite harder and longer, going after the throat more. And finally, after thirty-five minutes, he starts to dominate.

Art's dog scratches slower, and then finally he sits down, right at Art's feet, his tongue flapping, belly jerking. Art exhorts him, and even gives him a tiny jerk with his legs (which is illegal; you can't touch a dog trying to make scratch), but it's no good, and Art knows it; his efforts are half-hearted. His dog is through. Herbie is still twisting and turning in Tim's arms to get back into the fray. Tim is utterly expressionless; you can't tell whether he's won or lost. Monty is thrilled—although he knew that Herbie wasn't the greatest dog the world had ever seen, he's still happy with him. Like a racehorse owner whose horse comes in, it doesn't matter if it was a slow race, you have to be happy about it. Plus, he and Tim are a couple of grand richer.

I had first become aware of the dogs in Brazil. Pit bulls were everywhere, as symbols for jiu-jitsu schools and *academias,* and tattooed on people—and not always the cartoons, sometimes photographs were rendered, like someone having his son's picture tattooed on his arm. The first dogman I met, Escorrega, had his first dog tattooed on the inside of his arm, as did many of the other guys. As I talked to him at great length about the dogs, I started to realize *why* fighters prize these dogs so much.

The key to understanding dogfighting is the concept of *gameness.* Gameness could be described as courage, but that's simplistic. I've heard gameness described as "being willing to continue a fight in the face of death," and that's closer; it's the eagerness to get into the fight, the beserker rage, and then the absolute commitment to the fight in the face of pain, and disfigurement, until death. It's heart, as boxing writers sometimes describe it, with a dark edge, a self-destructive edge; because true gameness doesn't play it smart, it just keeps coming and coming. No matter what.

The important principle here is that dogfighting is not about dogs, or even dogs fighting, it's about *gameness*. That's why a dog turning is so critical, and that's the whole point of the endless scratching: We almost don't care how good the dog fights, the fight is just an elaborate test to check his gameness. John, a dogman in Oakland, told me, "Give me a game dog any day, a dog that bites as hard as tissue paper but keeps coming back, and I'll take him." Gameness was more important than fighting ability. He illustrated the idea with a story. "I was in Arkansas at a fight, and one dog was whipping the other for about fifty minutes, and at the hour mark, the dog who was winning jumped the pit wall." John laughed uproariously. "He was mopping this dog *up,* and then he jumped the wall. I wish I still had that tape, you'd die laughing."

I met three real dogmen—Escorrega in Brazil, John in Oakland, and Tim CEK in Thailand—and with their help I started to see how dogs and men were linked in fighting for sport. The quest for gameness in dogs is more pure, more basic, and less encumbered by illusion than the quest for gameness in men.

The capacity for violence has a direct correlation to entertainment value, which means money. Escorrega, my first dogman, had been involved with dogs for thirteen years, and he told me of prices and prizes that seemed absurd, fifty thousand dollars for certain dogs of truly spectacular proven bloodlines. A good prospect would run fifteen hundred to five thousand dollars, and good pups might fetch five to fifteen hundred. There was a dog in the United States that had generated total income of more than a million dollars, something my friends in Oakland didn't believe but that Tim CEK confirmed, although that dog had since died. There were fights in Korea for hundreds of thousands of dollars, and tales of fights in Hawaii for a quarter million.

"Now, if you say fighting dog, you mean from the U.S. or Mexico," Escorrega said. A pit bull (not an exact breed, but something quite specific) is a cross between the bulldog and the distinguished terrier. "The bulldog supplies the strength, the appearance, the low pain sensitivity, the loose skin; while the terrier supplies the intelligence, heart, and gameness. Terriers are fast, strong, and smart—they can get a skunk out of a tree—and they are very, very game animals."

They were all dog lovers and students of history. The members of the "fancy" knew their dog history—they could rattle off stats and names, breeds and bitches like a baseball fan could talk about ERAs and RBIs. Escorrega even had breeding cards with pictures and statistics, just like big baseball cards, and he could name famous dogs like you can name movie stars. Tim and John were also students of breeding and genetics. There are massive books of breeding, going back to the 1800s.

A champion is a dog that has won three fights, and a grand champion is a dog that has won five—these are the distinctions that owners of game-bred dogs want to breed to. John told me of Banjo, a famous biter that was a grand champion at three years old, which is young; so that means he probably wasn't getting challenged with tough fights. "Banjo would run in and destroy the whole front end, but maybe a good wrassler could have handled him, and popular belief is Banjo was secretly a cur—he's never reproduced." In the end, though, winning is still winning.

Fighters, whether dog or man, have to win to matter. You can say what you want about Mike Tyson or Muhammad Ali, but if they hadn't been winning, no one would have paid attention. Tim even said to me once, "I don't care about gameness—I just want to win."

My only previous experience with dogfights had been the film *Amores Perros,* and this got a big snort of derision from Escorrega. "It's very Hollywood. The owners are not shooting dogs and all crazy like that, and you would never fight a rottweiler against a pit bull, not at any kind of weight similarity."

The American pit is the standard for fighting dogs. Pound for pound, the pit, with its lower pain sensitivity, thicker skin, higher bone density and muscle thickness, and, above all, greater gameness, will destroy any other dog. Rottweilers are bred to be guard dogs—they are big, heavy, and slow, but intimidating, and they are people-aggressive, unlike pits. Pit bulls don't make good guard dogs, because if they are finally trained to become people-aggressive, they will go for the throat, not the arm or leg. Any dog will fight for a few minutes, but only a pit will go on and on.

Dogfighting is legal in Japan, and there they have a thousand-year-old tradition of fighting the big dogs, the tozas. Those dogs are all over a hundred pounds, big and slow-moving compared to the explosive pit. A really big pit, even one at seventy or eighty pounds, would tear a toza up.

Pits are wonderful pets, and are not inherently dangerous, but their gameness and toughness make them animals that need to be understood, or there can be tragic results. They have been bred specifically to fight other dogs for hundreds of years, like a greyhound has been bred to run. Pit bulls make great pets as long as you know what you've got, and you know what you are doing. They're almost more of a farm animal, an outside animal, and they are very sensitive and intelligent but need a lot of stimulation and attention—especially a "game-bred" pit, in which these characteristics are most defined. The problems happen when pits get left alone too much, or when they are tortured or mistreated. If a pit has been "turned on" to fighting, meaning it has been fought a little, it will want to fight and kill basically any dog it comes into contact with. Ike X said that dogs so aggressive are a fairly recent breeding phenomenon, only since the seventies, as before that puppies used to be allowed to wander the yard. John said, "I had a bitch once named Renegade who would kill a puppy, anything walking, she would jump it—basset hound, Chihuahua, anything." His dog was a fighting dog, game-bred; and that was how it interacted with the world. I thought of boxers and pro fighters who end up beating their wives. The fighting dog has learned that interaction with the world is through its teeth, and the fighter, sometimes, has learned it is through his fists.

Pit bulls are responsible for so many dog attacks against people mostly because so many dogs are pits; they are in some areas the most popular breed in the United States. The various pounds in the Los Angeles area were killing eight hundred stray pits a week in 1996. They have been bred to fight—and to forget that is foolish—but they are great dogs. I lived with two in Oakland and loved them. They don't have a "locking jaw," as some people think, but they do have a powerful bite and, of course, tremendous will to hang on. With an adult pit, you use a "breaking bar" or "stick" to get it to release its bite, by working the bar in and levering its jaw just a little, and then when it lets go to readjust its bite, you pull the dogs apart. John had a young pit bite another dog, and luckily the pit was young enough that when John took the hose and sprayed water right in its eyes, it let go. "He never would have done that if he was a year or two older—he never would have let go," John said. You have to know what you are doing if you own a pit.

Many game-bred dogs don't have the big bulkiness and intimidating silhouette of a show pit bull, and it isn't until they yawn, and you see the massive jaws and huge fangs (sometimes called tusks), like a small lion, that you realize that these aren't ordinary dogs.

Just like human fighters, dogs have to be conditioned properly before a fight. The program is called "the keep" and runs anywhere from six to thirteen weeks. The keep is strict isolation and a workout program with nutrition and mental conditioning thrown in. It strikes me that the isolation is the real torment for a pack animal; it is part of what makes the dogs so aggressive and must feel like a form of madness. Certainly, human fighters need the isolation and go into camps for weeks or months before a fight, separated from families and women and anything not to do with the fight. I think the isolation must change your brain chemistry, just like a dog's, and make you more focused, more aggressive. I had heard no sex for three weeks before a fight from a hundred different sources.

This is where the true barbarism of dogfighting lies, in the life on the chain—not in the fight. These dogs are never allowed to be with other dogs, and for so keen a pack animal it must be torture. Especially once they've been fought, the dogs can never be allowed in contact with one another, because they'd tear one another to shreds.

The owners put the dogs on an electric treadmill for stamina and a manual treadmill for bursts and strength, and then do all kinds of other exercise, such as bite work, dragging chains, pulling tires. Nutrition is monitored—precisely. As with humans, the goal is to get the biggest possible athlete into the fight at weight. John used to do long sessions, sometimes eight hours a day (just to "peak" a dog), and Tim shook his head when he heard that. "It's overtraining a dog, just like an athlete. Is the dog going to fight for eight hours? No. At most, he'll end up fighting three, so why would you train him more than that?" Tim favors shorter, more intense workouts.

In the distant past, cats were used as bait on the treadmill and then given to the dog to kill right before the fight, so the dog would learn that all that work finally paid off. But that isn't done anymore, and isn't considered necessary. There are guys who fight their dogs against stray mutts, but that's "just ignorant," said Escorrega. "It doesn't do anything for your dog but get him used to easy fights."

The fight takes place in a pit, under what's called "Cajun rules," which have become the standard all over the world, reflecting the dominance of American-bred dogs. The pit is supposed to be sixteen by sixteen feet square, with a two-and-a-half-foot wall running around it and scratch lines fourteen feet apart. Before the fight, the dogs are washed by either the opposing handler or his second, to make sure that no one has used poison or any chemicals to confuse the other, such as a "bitch in heat" smell, for example. They are even washed in milk, occasionally.

As in boxing or jiu-jitsu, when the dogs fight, anything can happen. Some dogs bite the legs, some switch from back to front, some dogs bite the nose, some the kidneys, others the chest. Chest biters can keep the opponent off, can keep him from walking, but that is considered boring—it's ugly to watch. Some dogs make a career biting ears. They will sweep each other, and take each other's back, just like grappling.

The main thing is that if the dog doesn't want to fight anymore, he can leap out of the ring, or just refuse to continue. The dogs should never die in the pit. The one thing they do die from, if the fight goes very long, is shock and stress, from either a burst heart or failed kidneys.

"Pride is the whole damn thing," Escorrega said. "Vanity can blind you—your dog is dying, but you won't let him quit, hoping that he can win." John said that "a dog should never die of kidney failure—those guys don't know what they're doing." It's a little like chess: Good players don't need to get to mate; once someone realizes that his position is untenable, he'll resign. In this way, if your dog is losing badly but still game, you should pick him up, because you can breed him on. If he hasn't quit, pick him up. Real dogmen don't need to see a dog die. "If you've got a decent dog, you would never let him die—it ain't about winning, it's about not quitting," John said. "If I got five generations of something that won't quit, I might get something." When dogs fight past an hour and a half, which isn't uncommon, you need experienced dogmen to keep them alive after the fight. They need IVs to rehydrate, and their systems are very fragile, on the edge of shock. It's in the "deep waters," where a lot of money is at stake, that dogs die.

"When I started, it was all about gameness, and the dogs, and I was the only black dude there. It was mostly hicks." John had been into dogs in the eighties, with his partner; they called themselves CMB, for "Cash-Money Brothers." He and his partner got ahold of some dogs from a famous stud dog, Jeep, and they started beating everybody, because they had good dogs. They would go way out into the countryside, and there would be a picnic, and then later the dogs would come out, sometimes a couple of fights, sometimes just one. The game has changed, and the dog scene has devolved in the United States and moved into Mexico. The great breeders are all old men now, and a lot of the legendary kennels have been broken up.

One of the reasons dogfighting is so demonized, especially in the United States, is that it has become linked to the drug world and to criminals. A lot of these guys don't know what they're doing, don't love their animals, and have weak dogs but fight them to kill one another. These aren't real dogmen and would never be admitted into the tight world of big money and international dogs. It's a secret world of reputation, of personal knowledge. Real dogmen love dogs. However, love is not always simple, and we can be cruel to what we love. The dogmen love dogs, but they, like fighters, are often damaged themselves and have little pity; their love of dogs is a cruel, desperate kind. Dogs that lose are culled; dogs that cur out are killed directly after the fight, or at best given away (although that is problematic). When John talked of the dog that had jumped out of the pit, he laughed and said, "You got to cull him right there in front of everyone, to show you're serious." These dogs are not pets, but more like farm animals, and sentimentality has no place on a farm.

Escorrega had gotten out of dogs. He still loved the fight, but he loved his dogs more; pit bulls feel no pain when they fight, but they are flesh and blood. "I devote my life to the church," he said. "I know gambling is a sin, but I love to watch the fight. I like to fight myself. I've been hit before, I had my ass kicked before: I know what it looks like, what it feels like." It was the days after the fight, nursing his dogs back to health, and their pain and slow recovery, that put him off dogfighting. In the end, he loved his dogs too much to see them suffer.

Even Tim CEK, as professional a dogman as I'd ever met, had a soft spot for his good dogs. He and Monty had a dog that was a four-time winner, and one more win would make him a grand champion, which was worth a lot more money in terms of breeding, but Tim wouldn't fight him; he was five and a half years old and "it wouldn't be fair to him."

"Filipinos are the black people of Asia," said Tim CEK. He had to yell it in my ear over the din at Bedrock Bar in the Malate district of Manila. Tim and I had come to the Philippines to see a big dogfight show, a "convention," on the following night. Tim was drunk on gin and tonics and had his arm around me in the easy Thai familiarity.

The band was about three feet away and covering R. Kelly with tremendous enthusiasm.

"They are the most musical, and every bar and fancy hotel in Asia—in Japan or Thailand or anywhere—has always got Filipino singers. They're the best," he said. "They love black culture. In the U.S. the Filipinos don't hang out with other Asians; they hang out with black people."

He was right about the singing; we'd been to a couple of different music bars and I had already heard at least five singers who would have been in the top ten on *American Idol*. Tremendous voices, rich and deep and incongruous coming from these sweet round Asian faces. Their taste was mainstream pop. At the Hobbit House, a *Lord of the Rings*–themed bar staffed entirely by midgets (brilliant!), I heard a tall Filipino girl with a sad face and a bitter air do the best Led Zeppelin cover I'd heard—she was better than Robert Plant.

Manila was big and dirty, and full of seedy fun. The streets were crowded, and everyone was out for a good time, though there were not many foreigners. Manila used to be a big tourist destination (especially when the U.S. military bases were there) but had been eclipsed by Thailand and the rest of Southeast Asia. My dad had been stationed in Manila for a time, which he remembered fondly.

Tim was something of a wunderkind in the dog world; he had only been matching dogs for five years, but through a combination of meticulous research, intelligent planning, luck, and having good dogs, he was nearly undefeated in that time. He had the science, and the discipline; he had earned respect, particularly in the Philippines, where he had matched five times and never lost. Tim had the quiet, watchful air of a careful judge who is reserving his opinion, impenetrable and inscrutable. Even with ten gin and tonics in him, it was hard to know what he was thinking.

Jo, his best friend in the Philippines, was a battered-looking chain-smoker with long hair and the features of an American Indian. He was a good dogman, and like all good dogmen he was honest, loyal, and friendly (which still didn't make him a Boy Scout). He worked as a designer, specializing in Web sites, but when Tim asked him a technical question about software, Jo shook his head. "I'm an artist, man," he said.

The bars reeked of cigarettes—everyone was smoking, and it became harder and harder to bear just drinking water and Coke.

Although I wasn't in training, I wasn't out of it, either. I didn't have a fight set but thought I might fight in Myanmar, or MMA again, back in the States.

Eventually, we headed back to the hotel. We watched a dogfight on Tim's laptop, and at twenty minutes one dog was overpowering and mauling the other, and the losing handler let his dog lie there inert. He was letting his dog get killed—it was the first distasteful thing I'd really seen in dogfighting, the first time the spectacle made me uneasy. "The guy's an idiot," Tim said. "He should have picked up long ago."

Tim confided to me that here in the Philippines, sometimes they kill the dogs in fights; they want to see the dog die. When dogs are dying, it means the people don't know what they are doing. The exception is when both dogs are very good and well matched and the fight runs long.

Tim told me about one of the great fights in history, between grand champion Buck, a six-time winner from STP (a kennel in New Jersey with some of the world's greatest dogs) and grand champion Sandman, a five-time winner from Rebel (another famous kennel). The dogs were both getting old, but their owners decided they had to fight to determine who had the greatest dog of the era, and they fought at forty-seven or forty-eight pounds. After three hours and seventeen minutes, Buck won; and amazingly, he lived. Sandman died, of course, but for either dog to have survived a battle like that was extraordinary.

The next day, Tim, Jo, and I climbed into a hired van with another friend of Tim's and headed up into the hills. The seventy-kilometer drive took almost three hours because of traffic, but we were in no rush. "They won't fight the dogs until five or six, when it starts to cool off," Tim explained.

Tim had also worked with and around Thai fighters for many years, but he preferred the dogs. The dogs wouldn't betray you and throw fights for money, or not train properly; human fighters were too much trouble. The dogs were simpler, purer, and you could put your heart into a dog and get its heart in return.

There was a hazy sunset reddening the sky as we climbed into the lush glowing hills, the night sweltering down with the gentle whispering kiss of a thousand mosquitoes. We arrived and met with the Southern Men, Jo's group of dogmen. The Philippines is now one of the centers of dogfighting in Asia (along with Korea), and there was a "convention" every weekend this month. Tim had been there one night when they had thirty-one fights in two pits that worked simultaneously.

"There's nothing like this in Thailand," Tim complained, where there are sometimes private matches of just one fight, but few conventions. He had beaten everyone in Thailand so badly that only Art would still fight him—and Tim usually beat him.

That night there would be eight fights. Someone handed me a program:

1. MTK vs CROSSROAD	31.5 Male
2. KKK vs CHILIBOZ	38 Male
3. CROSSROAD vs JOGON (1W)	33 Male
4. RPK vs BWK	36.2 Male
5. F1 vs SM KILO (2W)	39.5 Male
6. PQK vs 3X/BAK	33.5 Female
7. DQZ ABBY (1W) vs BFK RED (2W)	33.5 Female
8. MJK BRENDA (2W) vs EBK CH. TINA (3W)	32 Female

Tim wasn't too impressed by the card, but fight number five, with Southern Men's Kilo, should be good, he thought. He explained to me that the Ws in parentheses were wins (so Kilo had two wins) and the numbers were the weight. We checked out some of the dogs, their tails thumping desperately in their cages, and to the untrained eye they all looked starved, with the ribs and muscles standing from their skin; but they were really at peak condition, at weight.

The pit was a high raised platform under a massive roof, surrounded by seats and concrete. When it was full, there were nearly five hundred people around it. The pit itself, about five feet off the ground, was walled in by clear Plexiglas for viewing and had seats for the time-keeper, the seconds, and the cameraman (someone was always taping the fights). Over in the corner was a food stall with numerous braziers and meat on sticks. "Filipino fast food," Jo said.

Tim and I met Tim's good friend Ito, who was putting us up at his nearby resort. He was a barrel-chested man of about fifty, with a broad Filipino face and a quick smile. Ito and his friend Joedic were already pretty drunk by the time we sat down at their table, and they proceeded to get a lot drunker. Their hospitality and friendliness were profound, as was their deep respect for Tim. They had a kind of old-world hospitality, and they wouldn't let us pay for anything.

The first dog was brought in, carried high in the handler's arms like a baby, and gently deposited in the pit. This was his first fight, and he walked around nervously, trembling with energy, his nose glued to the floor. He must have smelled the blood, the old fear and emotion of dogs before him struggling and dying, and I wondered if he suddenly began to realize the gravity of the situation. He was paraded around to give the audience a look so as to inform their bets; betting was the fuel of dogfighting, as in cockfighting,.

The atmosphere was laid-back and festive, relaxed and chatty like at a bar, but attention invariably wandered back to the center, with a thrum of anticipation. There were plenty of women and even girls in the audience, and a few kids running around, and a drunken, picnic mood.

The first fight started without barking as the dogs darted together, leapt up, and came down in a spinning tangle. People were paying attention but not unduly. The fights would all run past twenty or thirty minutes—everyone knew that—and there were going to be eight fights, so we would be here for a while. Conversations sometimes lulled and got caught up in cheering, but there was a steady buzz of laughing and talking, and traffic to the food stall and beer counter never slowed. The dogs twisted wildly up in the pit, snatching and crunching, looking for advantages, two dense whirls of muscle and teeth. The handlers hovered, shouting encouragement, *"Good boy, good boy,"* and getting right in there, inches from the dogs, pointing to where their dog should bite next, admonishing and uplifting.

"That dog is finished," Tim murmured as he glanced around, uninterested in these early, poor-quality dogs.

"How can you tell?"

"Look at his tail," he said shortly. The losing dog, desperately biting ears and face to hold off the stronger dog, had his tail sunk and curled around between his legs. The stronger dog's tail was still straight and wagging as he powered into the weaker dog. Eventually, the dogs tired, and the dominant one stood over the other with his tongue lolling, and the timekeeper began his count; the dogs were out of holds and, after thirty seconds of inaction, were whisked by their handlers into the corners, and from there they started scratching. The losing dog was obviously in trouble, and when it was his turn to scratch, he just sat there between the handler's legs, as the handler yelled and screamed and pointed and jerked his body in an attempt to get his dog to scratch. But it came to naught. The dog was through, and he sat there, tongue lolling in overtime, gazing around. He had "curred out," and the fight was over. The winning handler sometimes will make a courtesy scratch, and sometimes has to scratch to win, and the winning dog came out like a shot toward his shirking opponent. The fight was over, the dogs were separated, and the winner was far richer than he was before the fight began.

I sat pitside for one fight, right up against the glass, and the sights and smells were powerful that close, the smell of blood and raw dog emotion, the crunching and cracking of jaws. The dogs twisted and leapt up, snapping together, and came down with one on top, and then the other. They looked like lionesses when their muscles leapt into stark relief through tawny skin. The crowd fed off the emotions of the dogs, and the handlers, a way to feel vicariously the sheer desperate thrill of the struggle: This was man's best friend and proxy—you can fight and die for me. Real dogmen love their dogs—but we are merciless to what we love, as A. L. Kennedy wrote. There is some horrible truth to that, evident in one common factor in boxing deaths: in the father as a cornerman, sending his son in again and again, unable to throw in the towel.

The crowd had grown, and grown loud. The women shrieked at a particularly rough move, and the men ululated when they wanted their dog to shake. Suppose your dog (the dog you've just bet ten thousand pesos on) gets ahold of the other dog's foreleg, you want him to shake in that powerful twisting move (the shake that every dog does, the instinct to break the neck of a small animal that they've caught), to try to break something, to tear it loose, to do damage. The crowd picked favorites, the odds shifted, and sometimes the crowd even heckled the dogs and the handlers, and made jokes and catcalls. The handlers shouted too, *get-get-get* and *shake-shake-shake,* willing their dogs to win, to find good holds.

The dogs left blood heavy and swirling in brilliant red trails on the Plexiglas walls of the pit. Tim had told me that there were no knockouts in dogfighting, at least not between two well-matched dogs, but rather a slow accumulation of damage, and it took time because the dogs were so durable. "There aren't many surprises," he said. "You can see it coming." Packs of girls shrieked like it was a rock concert. Violence is entertainment: both sickening and thrilling, reactions that are surprisingly harmonious.

At some unknown hour, not long before dawn, we stumbled out of there. Ito and Joedic were long gone. They had lost money on every fight and left after the fifth or sixth, but we found Ito's resort and clambered up into his tree house to sleep.

* * *

We woke up the next morning to blasting karaoke at about ten a.m. Ito and Joedic were drinking already; it was Sunday, after all. After breakfast, we went to look at Ito's cock farm, with hundreds of cocks all tethered to individual lean-tos, with perches to stand on and crow. Cockfighting is the national sport of the Philippines, and it's legal. In Manila, there are huge stadiums and hundreds of fights a day during big festivals. Ito ran his own small cockfighting pit out here in the country, next to his resort.

Here Tim was the novice, and Ito and Joedic were the experts. They "rolled" some cocks for us, had them fight without spurs on, just to let them clash a little bit, to get a sense of the birds. Ito had something like 150 birds, and the volume of use is very high in the Philippines. They fight the cocks with long blades strapped to one foot, and most of the fights don't last a minute; the birds flare up, and when they come down, one is dead on his feet, bleeding out into the dirt.

It was hard for me to watch chickens fight, because I had no real idea what I was looking for. Ito explained that they wanted aggressive, hard-hitting cocks that strike first and strike hard. Because of the blades, they wanted cocks that kicked in a certain way, straight on, long and horizontal. Ito rolled some good birds for us, and though I still had no idea what was good, Tim seemed satisfied.

We went over to the pit to begin the real matches, and they had obviously been waiting for us—Ito the owner and his special foreign guests. The small stadium was half full with a hundred or so people, and a picnic atmosphere, a "Sunday afternoon with your kids" feel, although there were almost no women.

Tim took me to the "gaffing" room, where the gaffers were putting on the blades. They were professionals, hired out to each chicken individually, and they had brought cases of forty or fifty different blades, as each chicken had a slightly different foot. It was surprisingly elaborate, more complicated than taping a boxer's hands: There were supports and underworks that molded to the foot, and aligning the blade along the bird's natural spur was critical. When the bird struck, the blade had to be correctly positioned to be effective, or else the cock wouldn't be lethal. The blades themselves were amazing, two or three inches long, tiny razor scimitars lashed securely to the strange foot and then carefully sheathed until the cocks were in the pit—otherwise, the handler might get sliced to ribbons.

The birds were brought into the pit, where they were first annoyed by two bait cocks that wouldn't be fighting. The handlers then grabbed their cocks' heads and pulled them back, exposing the necks, and they brought the cocks together and allowed them to take a little nip out of the bared neck, really pissing the cocks off.

The crowd din grew as the betting reached a crescendo, with yelling and gesticulating, hands fluttering like stockbrokers' on the floor of the exchange. Tim bet with tiny nods to a man in the pit, and then the pit cleared out and the two handlers tossed their chickens gently down, about five feet apart. The crowd went dead silent as the cocks oriented on each other, and then darted forward and leapt up kicking. Often, that was it; one bird would be mortally wounded in that first exchange, and would stumble and then sit down. The referee sometimes picked them both up and reset them, to see which was still game. The longest fight of the day was shorter than three minutes.

After the fights, the gaffers were at work again, this time sitting in the corner with butchers' smocks on, sewing up the winners in brutal instant surgery; the damaged winners were saved for breeding if they could be kept alive. The dead losers had their blades cut off and were hung in a shed, to be eaten later, the row of plucked dead birds growing as the day went on, with the tremendous wounds from the fight plain to see, like murder victims in a morgue.

The day meandered on, and the cocks died again and again. Just a few threshing bursts, splashing up together in their lizardlike fury, and one staggered, drooped, and failed to rise. I didn't really get it, although cockfighting is tremendously popular around the world and supposedly the oldest spectator sport, dating back three thousand years. I'd read that Abe Lincoln earned his nickname "Honest Abe" during his days as a cockfight referee.

The next day, Tim and I flew back to Thailand. Driving into Bangkok, I asked Tim a question that had been on my mind. I remembered Escorrega in Brazil telling me about love, and how important that was for dogs, and I wanted to know what Tim thought. How important was the bond between the dog and the handler—how important was love? Tim didn't spend all that much time with his dogs, his Cambodian yard man trained the dogs and had them kept according to Tim's specifications because Tim had a full-time job and a family.

"It's extremely important," he said, without taking his eyes from the road. "I wish I could spend more time with my dogs, especially right before a fight. You can do a lot with a real tight bond, you can raise them up. If your dog is on the bottom, getting chewed up, you can get in there and raise him up with encouragement. You can turn the whole fight around. There are dogmen that sleep with dogs [in a crate] for the week before a fight to increase that bond. If I could spend more time with them, my dogs would fight better. You should really invest from a puppy onward."

Tim dropped me off, and I jumped into a cab, winding through Bangkok traffic. Evening rush hour was just peaking and everything was jammed solid, a city-sized parking lot, and the taxi guy laughed with me as I got in, and said, "Thailand number one traffic!"

I was not disgusted by the dogfights, even though I love dogs. The knee-jerk reaction that I get whenever I mention the dogfights, "Oh, I couldn't watch that, it's so cruel," has always struck me as hypocrisy—unless you are a vegetarian, don't wear leather, and think that what chicken farmers and cattle ranchers do is unusually cruel. It's telling that cockfighting is still legal in parts of the United States, because animal cruelty laws could be applied to the poultry industry, as well. Ike X said that "the S.P.C.A. uses the 'scourge' of dogfighting as a fundraising tool, mostly . . . and then they save fighting dogs by taking them away and killing them." And what about breeders that raise puppies for the pet store window, and when the puppies don't sell, send them to "no-kill" pounds—which in turn pass them along to pounds that put them down?

The fight itself is not cruel. The dogs love to fight—it is what they do, and their tails are wagging. It is a joyful, mad rage that has been bred into them. What is cruel is the life on the chain, being kept from physically bonding with one another or a human owner, and especially the isolation of the keep for a pack animal: *That* is the cruelty of dogfighting, like solitary confinement for prisoners, like the endless training and denial for fighters.

The losing dog is either killed or given away. He won't fight again—once he has curred out, there is nothing to be done for him. Tim tried to give away the dogs he couldn't use, as opposed to killing them—"I don't like killing dogs," he said—but they are hard to find homes for and don't make great pets if they have been fought or rolled. So, usually, a losing dog is killed. Ike X said, "The exception is when a dog is sick or has had a poor keep, or maybe is a little too young—then you pick up before he is broken. There have been quite a few great dogs that lost and went on to win again."

But often the loser is culled.

Killing them when they lose is rough, but these animals are like chickens or beef cattle. They would not exist if not for man's intentions. That cows never get to walk but are just pumped full of food and hormones until they are slaughtered seems just as cruel to me. The demonization of dogfighting is tied to the anthropomorphizing of dogs, and that is not an illusion that I subscribe to.

I am not for or against dogfighting; it exists without my approval or disapproval. I was drawn to it because of the close relationship it has with men fighting for sport, and the parallels between the two; and I wanted to understand them both. I had a professor once tell me that man cannot view himself clearly; only less complicated organisms can be completely understood.

It hit me when I read the description of a "game test": When a dog has been fought to exhaustion, you bring in a fresh dog to face him; and if the exhausted dog is still game, then you keep him and breed him. That quality of gameness is so specific, so valuable. In *A History of Warfare,* John Keegan makes the point that the evolution to modern combat happened with the Greeks, who would stand and fight and die in the phalanx. Primitive warfare had no such discipline; the fighters would posture, and yell, and throw spears, but not stand in and fight. Giving his warriors a willingness to stand in and die was how Shaka Zulu conquered much of southern Africa, how modern warfare came to be. The British navy, the "hearts of oak," won many sea battles because of gameness: The British would always fight and loved to fight; they were eager for a scrap. That quality of gameness allowed them to conquer the world. "Never mind the maneuvers, go straight at 'em," said Lord Horatio Nelson, the British sea commander who won a series of battles that set the stage for England's domination of the world in the nineteenth century, knowing that aggressive gameness was a strategy in itself. Decisive, competent aggression, sheer willingness to fight, was a tremendous advantage in a sea battle. It is no coincidence that the sports of dogfighting and prizefighting grew together in popularity, with the same fans, as the bloodier sports of bull- and bearbaiting and the tradition of dueling faded.

The appreciation of gameness, then, is probably both cultural and biological. The love of aggression, a willingness to fight regardless of safety or consequences, is a biological key to success, to domination.

Basically, I have been game-testing myself.

* * *

I finished up my stay in Thailand at Fairtex, and I found out a lot of things, about old friends who had thrown fights, about the inner workings of the camp, and I finally began to comprehend my own naïveté and lack of understanding—the American in the Orient, who thinks he understands when really he sees only the tiniest bit, the scratches on the surface.

My skills had come a long way; after Hamid and Steve left, I was the best *farang* in the camp, the only one with decent form. I was way out of shape, but Philip told me my form was very good. If I wanted to stay around for a year or two and get some fights, I could fight in K-1. That seemed a little far-fetched, but I did feel good, and Apidej would regularly remind me that he liked how I thought, how my brain worked. I still felt like total shit—you need a month just to get to the point where you can train hard—and I sweated like a pig. But I noticed when we worked the bags that I was the only guy in there who left sweat in a ring around the bag; everyone else left it in just one place—they weren't moving laterally.

My ribs felt better; I could train hard but didn't want to start sparring yet. I went to Yangon in Myanmar for a little while, which was a step back in time, like visiting Bangkok sixty years ago. I couldn't find any real places to train; none of my three or four contacts pulled through for me. I trained in the one place I found Burmese boxing, at the YMCA in Yangon, but it was not for professionals. There was no equipment, just two homemade bags hanging from the rafters, one pair of bag gloves we would all alternate using. The teacher was interesting, and he showed me a different kind of head butt, one using the side of your head, back and *behind* your ear, not the spearing attacks I expected. He was good, but the training wasn't, so I returned to Thailand and ended up back at Fairtex.

Finally, a promoter I didn't know got me a fight in Myanmar, but it was only three weeks away, and I wasn't in great shape. I got really excited, but when I mentioned it to Philip, he was adamant, immediately shaking his head. "No way," he said, "you're not going to be ready. The reason you did well when you fought before was you were in shape, great shape. Those guys will try and kill you." I thought about it for a few days, but in the end I agreed with him, because I wasn't such a good fighter that I could take a fight on short notice. I didn't have the experience. I only had two fights, after all. I needed to be in much better shape than any opponent because my work ethic was the only advantage I had. Some guys with great skills, or a lot of fights, they can take fights when they're out of shape and fight smart and be economical, but I was emphatically not one of them. The promoter wrote me some e-mails, saying things like "Don't worry, nothing will happen to you," which had the opposite effect from reassuring me. It was a fight—why would you keep telling me that? I wanted six weeks or eight weeks to train with *lethwei* guys and then I would fight, and instead here he was telling me he could teach me all the tricks I needed to know in the two days before the fight. That was the final straw. He was going to teach me head butts, and how to defend against them, in two days? I declined the fight. I just didn't know him. He hadn't returned my e-mails for years, and then suddenly he was overly friendly, and it put me off. I'd been burned enough times by promoters, I guess. I wasn't going to allow myself to get rushed into something stupid. I wasn't out to prove anything; I'd fight when I was ready. I'd go back to the United States and get another MMA fight with promoters I could trust.

8

COOLER THAN REAL

Pat "Hollywood" Miletich on the set of *Death and Life of Bobby Z*,
September 2005.

Paul Walker rehearses with stuntman Tommy Rosales Jr.

The sight of a gladiator performing well and dying courageously was held by spectators to be an ennobling and uplifting experience, and well worth the price of a life.

　　　　　　　　　　　　　　　—Don Atyeo, *Blood and Guts*

I flew back from Thailand and arrived in Los Angeles. I was shocked by the hordes of gigantic white people. I thought about fighting; my friend Kirik in Massachusetts was setting something up for December, an amateur MMA fight.

I kept thinking about the ties between fighting and entertainment, the game test, and the big punch. Every single action movie I could think of had the climactic battle when the hero fights the villain, and without fail, the hero gets bashed around and it looks as if he will lose; and then he shows gameness, he makes scratch, and comes back from the edge of death to snatch victory. And action movies and fight movies always had big clean punches, huge shots that would kill a full-grown polar bear, just like in pro wrestling—to galvanize the crowd. Movie fighting is where most of us learn about fighting, especially at a young age, and I was starting to wonder if my exploration of fighting for the twenty-first-century American man should include some kind of investigation into the cinema, into the emotional drama of fictional violence and how it is made. How different is it, really, from the old gladiator arenas? Sure, the action is staged, but it *looks* real; making it feel real is a whole industry. Does your subconscious know it's just a movie, that none of it's real? Isn't that when a movie fight is great and exciting, when it fools you emotionally?

I was about to leave L.A. for the mania of the cross-country drive back to the East Coast when I got an e-mail from Pat Miletich. He was consulting on a film to be directed by John Herzfeld, who did *15 Minutes* and was a huge fight fan. (He'd given an older UFC hero, the Russian Oleg Taktarov, his start in that film.) Herzfeld had been in contact with Pat for months about a UFC *Rocky*-style movie that had stalled in development. In the meantime, Herzfeld had taken on a thriller, and he had brought Pat down to Mexico, where they were filming, to be the fight coordinator.

The movie, *The Death and Life of Bobby Z,* was an action-thriller based on a book by Don Winslow, about a convict in a prison who is recruited by a shady DEA agent to impersonate a famous drug dealer—Bobby Z—whom the convict resembles. Mayhem ensues. Paul Walker, the handsome, boyish actor who came to fame in the tremendously popular B-movie about illegal car racing, *The Fast and the Furious,* was going to play the convict, and the shady DEA agent would be played by Laurence Fishburne.

Herzfeld, in a combination of hubris, prescience, and philanthropy, was filling the supporting cast with MMA stars, former Ultimate Fighting champs. Not only Pat, but Oleg was back, as well as members of Pat's MFS stable: "The Maineiac" Tim Sylvia, Ben Rothwell, Rory Markham, and "Ruthless" Robbie Lawler were all playing various convicts and bad guys, and the UFC light-heavyweight champ, Chuck Liddell (notoriously hardheaded and heavy-handed), was playing the baddest guy in prison, Maddog. Pat told me to come along if I was interested, and I was. Maybe this chance to take a look behind the curtain would shed some light on the whole experience of fighting.

I drove from L.A. down past San Diego and across the border into the Mexican countryside. The concrete jungle of Tijuana gave way to desert and crystal blue sky. I drove around and around, got lost and found and lost again, until I stumbled onto the set, hours later, and met one of the producers, Keith Samples. He was friendly but a little surprised to see me. "You made it here, huh?" he said. "Well, score one for persistence." He looked at me for a long moment and then asked, "Do you have any tattoos?" I nodded, and he said, "Great, we'll use you in the Aryan Brotherhood."

The set was an abandoned, half-finished Mexican prison being used by *la policía* for training purposes, with empty guard towers standing sentinel over a rocky void. I drove hours back to where the crew was staying, and I was relieved to see Tim Sylvia's massive, forbidding head through a window, watching TV.

It was great to see him again, and Pat was there with a chew in, and instantly I was back in the MFS family, back in the fold, made welcome into that jock wrestling-fighting world where it's share and share alike and favors are asked and granted. Pat and I fell right into conversation, as though it had never stopped. It felt good to be on the inside. There was another heavyweight I vaguely remembered, a young monster named Ben Rothwell, down to play another bad guy. They got the beds, I got the couch cushions and my sleeping bag.

Pat was a little nervous about his role as fight coordinator and wasn't sure how things were going to go around the Hollywood people, and he missed his little girls already—but he was happy and curious, enjoying the novelty of the situation. He also had a healthy case of Mexico paranoia: He worried about the water, needles on the beach, getting robbed, and getting shaken down by the police. To be fair, we did get pulled over a few times, just for being gringos, and once we were about to be extorted when the policeman recognized Tim and started laughing and shaking his head. "Arlovski, eh?" he asked. (Andrei Arlovski was the guy who had beaten Tim and now had the UFC heavyweight title.) Several other people who were working on the film got shaken down for a hundred bucks here or there. What you really worried about were the *federales,* the state police.

The next day I was on set. John Herzfeld, the director, had been high school buddies with Sly Stallone and was of a similar vintage; he also had an assistant named Adrian he would yell after, adding a note of farce. He, Pat, and Oakley Lehman, the stunt coordinator, were talking their way through a pivotal scene early in the movie. Paul Walker's character is being pressed by Maddog to join the Aryan Brotherhood, an evil white supremacist gang that runs the prison, and Paul slashes Maddog's throat with a license plate.

John asked, "Who's in here as part of Maddog's gang to jump on Paul after the slash?" and Pat said, "Well, Tim and Ben will be here." John looked thoughtful and said, "We should have one more," and I piped up with, "I think I'm supposed to be in this scene as another gang member." John looked at me like he didn't remember who I was, and

Pat and Tim waited to see if my little gamble worked. I wanted to be a part of things—I can't stand sitting around. John nodded okay and started talking details with Oakley.

I got my prison costume: a cruddy pair of jeans, slip-on shoes, and a blue federal button-down shirt (like the stuff I'd gotten from the Washington Department of National Resources back in my firefighting days). I then proceeded to stand around with all the other extras and fighters. And stand around. Moviemaking seems to be a pretty miserable experience; there are only a couple of good jobs on the set. The actors have it okay, and the director and the DP (director of photography, same thing as a cinematographer) are pretty busy, but everyone else does a ton of waiting, waiting, waiting. I drank coffee and ate cookies off the snack table for hours and hours. The DP, John Bailey, muttered to me, "Sit down whenever you can—I learned that from Phil Lathrop."

Chuck Liddell was a nice guy, big and a little wild-eyed, but friendly and open and exactly "what you see is what you get." He was somewhat amused by his character's antics: "If some kid was punking me out like this guy is," he said, referring to the way Paul Walker's character was mocking Maddog, "I'd just crack him and lay him out—there wouldn't be any talking." Chuck had a prosthetic neck made for the license plate slash, and his abnormally thick real neck had deeply impressed the makeup people. His massive neck had a lot to do with his hardheadedness; a thick neck makes you harder to knock out. Virgil had always been thinking of new ways to exercise a fighter's neck. The Thais used to do it with a piece of cord tied to weights; you bite down on the cord and do neck curls. I'd never done it. Rory said he'd done it until it started to screw up his teeth.

Chuck was one of the first American MMA fighters to make real money—he'd just gotten a sponsorship from Xyience, a supplement company, and he wore designer jeans and texted restlessly on his Internet phone. He was old school gone new school; he had just kept beating people until they realized he wouldn't go away, and then the UFC embraced him.

Chuck's two heavies were Tim and Ben. Tim was an old friend, and although he'd lost a couple of fights since I'd seen him last, he'd won his most recent fight with a spectacular head kick that had KO'd his opponent, Tra Telligman. Pat had heard a funny story: After the fight, in the locker room, Tra didn't really know where he was. His corner told him that he'd just fought in the UFC.

Tra: I just fought in the UFC?
Corner: Yeah.
Tra: Who'd I fight?
Corner: Tim Sylvia.
Tra: I just fought Tim Sylvia in the UFC? . . . What happened?
Corner: He knocked you out with a head kick.
Tra: Tim Sylvia knocked me out with a head kick in the UFC?!

Pat had a good time telling this story.

Ben was much younger but still experienced. He'd started fighting MMA in high school, and he'd fought and lost to Tim at nineteen, a fact Tim never let him forget. Ben was huge and played the simpleton, but he was, like all these guys, a lot smarter than he seemed. He liked to hoot and holler and yell "Fuck" in his heavy midwestern accent, but it was an act: He was no fool.

The four of us, along with dozens of prison extras, waited for our scene. The prison was high and cold and empty, the bare unfinished concrete lit by the brilliant klieg lights of Hollywood and patrolled by a half dozen Mexican PAs (production assistants, the lowest of the low, gofers) with headsets, shushing people constantly and taking up the call of "Rolling!" whenever filming was going on. All offscreen chatter was supposed to cease; sometimes it did, but sometimes it would just subside to a low murmur until everyone started yelling, "Quiet please!"

We rehearsed our little scene, with Chuck getting slashed and falling at my feet, and big Tim Sylvia punching Paul Walker down, and the rest of us piling on, stomping and kicking. Oakley was Paul's stunt double as well as the stunt coordinator, and he went through the motions that Paul would go through, with a wig pinned to his head (Paul's hair was long for this scene).

Oakley Lehman was a former desert motorcycle racer and horse-packing guide who had been friends with Paul in Burbank as kids, and they had gotten into movies separately, Paul as an actor and Oakley as a stuntman. Oakley's specialty was first bikes, then cars and horses. When they ran into each other later, Oakley instantly noticed that they had similar builds and complexions, and he asked Paul if he could double him; they had been working together ever since. This was Oakley's first film as the stunt coordinator, but he was a talented, competent guy, young and friendly in a very L.A. surfer way: "That sunset is bitchin'." I liked him immediately, and he knew enough to respect

Pat and they got along famously. Pat said he'd teach Oakley to fight if Oakley would teach him to surf.

John Herzfeld came in and took a look at the latest rehearsal. "I want something faster, more violent—just a quick smash of Paul," he said. "Why don't we try it with just the knee?" So instead of Tim throwing a right elbow and then a big knee, he would throw just a leaping knee—a small thing, perhaps, but it showed me something. The director, a fight fan, was going to put his stamp on the action and modify what the real fighters would have done, fighters who were all consummate street brawlers and had been in these fights a hundred times in and out of the ring. John wanted something that looked a little different—that looked cool instead of being real.

Finally, after what seemed like several days, with the cold desert night settled in like a blanket over the prison, prying at the corners, we were shooting. The cameras went in, and then the extras: about thirty tough-looking guys in prison blues, who all looked a lot rougher than me, older Mexican guys, young white tattooed dudes, and black Muslims. I found myself in the near background with the camera in front of me, and suddenly I had to *act*. It felt very strange, and unfamiliar. I had acted in high school, but since then hadn't done anything but the stuff that almost all guys do with their friends—funny voices, stupid girls, movie quotes—the typical screwing off. But there I was, at the forefront, watching Paul fall again and again, and then leaping into Oakley and pounding on him, over and over. You know the camera can see you, so you have to act. You don't have lines, but you still have to act.

It took hours, but we got through the scene—from various angles, with dozens of prison extras in the background, kicking and stomping Oakley, and then we stomped some cardboard boxes that stood in for Paul, then Paul himself, careful not to kick him too hard. I tumbled to the ground on every take, dragged down or shoved down by a guard. As long as we were doing something, it was fairly entertaining—not something I'd want to do every day, but fun in small doses. It was funny to hear the various assistant directors coaching the extras—"Remember, you're in prison, you hate it here." "I want to see that prison walk." "This is a living hell for you guys"—like the assistant directors had ever been any closer to prison than watching *The Shawshank Redemption*. That's one of the problems with movies: You have guys making films about mobsters who have learned about mobsters from watching *The Godfather,* which is fantasy itself. Movies get further and further away from the truth if their only reference to reality is other films. Later, however, I noticed that John was consulting with one of the extras— who had been in prison—about the way the guards held their guns, so that was good to see. I had a friend in L.A. who was working on a script about a death row inmate, a legal thriller, and he had never been in- side a prison or visited death row.

Moviemaking has elements of an endurance test: Can you stay interested and do good work at three a.m.? Finally came the gleeful call of "It's a wrap!" and we all scuttled for our gear and the vans, like at the end of a rave, desperate to get home.

The days turned to weeks. Pat and I would run on the beach in the morning, and then go to the set for the rest of the day. He'd do some consulting, helping with this or that, how to hold a gun (he'd learned this from all the Controlled FORCE work he'd done), but often just watching and drinking coffee.

Oakley was young, just thirty, and his stunt specialties were cars, horses, and motorcycles, not fighting. Pat was the fight coordinator, and of course he had tremendous fight experience, but he had never worked on movies before. To set the producer's mind at ease, Oakley had asked for some help from one of the best guys in the stunt-fight business, Mike Gunther.

Mike had been in the business for a dozen years and had a résumé that was five pages long. He'd worked on the *Matrix* series and *Under- world, Elektra,* and *Catwoman,* as well as a hundred other films. He was broad-shouldered and athletic, with short black hair and tired eyes; at six foot one and 180 pounds, he was the perfect leading man size. "I was lucky and the right size to double a lot of guys," he said. He was not just a fighting guy, though; he had done everything. "I was fight- ing on the national karate circuit when I got into stunts, but I cross- trained to death because I didn't want to get pigeonholed as a fight guy. I would do anything on the set, rig this or that, be water safety, ride a motorcycle—and it made me more marketable. I wanted to be involved, to be a filmmaker. I got my DGA [Directors Guild of America] card, so I can direct, and my SAG [Screen Actors Guild] card and I've sold a script, so I'm a writer in the WGA [Writers Guild of America]." This was a small-time movie for Mike, but he had been traveling for years and been on various sets all over the world and was trying to stay closer to home, to see his fiancée in L.A. and to develop his own projects.

Mike was excited for a chance to work with Pat, and he recognized more than anyone what an opportunity this was for a fighter: You've got the best trainer in the world in MMA at your beck and call, just hanging around. We all hit pads on the set, in the darkness, and I held for Pat and put the Thai belt on, so he could throw body shots—his specialty. He threw shots that stunned and staggered me, almost knocking the wind out of me every time, digging in and turning and, *boom,* blasting me on the pad. Shadowy pain rippled across my chest, and I would back off and put my hands on my knees. "Stop being such a pussy," Pat said, laughing, and I wheezed, "I'm not tough like you guys," and he hit me again and said, "Shut up, you're such a liar." Who knows what Mike thought, but he could hit pads pretty well.

Pat was truly a wonder to watch. He was friendly and honest and open, and after Paul Walker, he became the most popular guy on the set. His face was rough, in contrast to the smooth actors and sallow crew; he looked more battered than I remembered, his nose and brows polished by an accumulation of blows—something like a seal, or a shark, sandblasted, and his ears were nubs. An assistant director confided in me that they all had had reservations about Pat coming in, bringing the fighters, that Pat would be out of control or throw his weight around; but all those fears had evaporated. "He's awesome," said the AD. "He's relaxed, he's smart, he's intuitive—he should do this for a living." Oakley said something similar. He had been concerned that Pat wouldn't listen to him, wouldn't respect him because he wasn't a fighter, but that had never been a problem. "I realized that fighters are performers, too," Oakley said. "If they are boring, then they won't get fights." Very few people in the world knew more about fighting than Pat; he'd been in hundreds of street fights and was a five-time UFC champion, and he'd trained fighters for years. But he was well aware of his limitations in the movie world, and to his credit, he learned more from Gunther and Oakley than they did from him.

Pat and I trained and ran, and we worked hand fighting on the beach, Pat pressing relentlessly forward and his breath sweltering through his battered nose. We were out under a scuddy, remote sky, with a handful of cargo ships low on the distant horizon, anchored and patiently pointing into the wind. We sparred, going light, and of course I tweaked my ribs again, this time courtesy of Pat. He didn't even hit me that hard, just a clean shot that didn't bother me until later that night. I was so sick of it that I wanted to shoot myself.

Pat reassured me that it wasn't just me, and he lifted his shirt to show his own ribs, which were notched and nobbed all up and down the bones. He had me feel the lumps and deformities, where Alvino Peña and other pro boxers had shred him up. "My ribs were destroyed all the time—we all went through it," he said. "You got to tense up." What he meant was that you had to be constantly tense, and then flex your body when you knew a punch was landing. I'd heard this before but had never been able to do it.

The set was the most social place I'd ever been. You'd end up talking for hours to everyone, getting their life stories, anecdotes about this film and that film; the fighters had their own brand of gossip. It was a kind of forced, convective bonding. The fighters' interaction with the movie people was a little awkward at first: There was friendliness, a slight sense of mutual disdain coupled with genuine interest and curiosity, but inside, both sides were secure in their own form of arrogance. There was flirtation, on-set romances kindled, flared, died in front of your eyes. And there was celebrity.

Celebrity is an interesting phenomenon in the United States, directly tied to power. A famous judge is more powerful than a non-famous judge; celebrity is its own currency and is worth something very specific, set dollar amounts for so much notoriety. I think the roots of movie celebrity lie in basic biology, and in our subconscious. The human being is programmed to read other humans' faces, and to read them intensely and closely—indeed, manipulating those ten thousand facial muscles is what movie acting is all about. I don't *know* Harrison Ford—I've never met him—yet I have *seen* him up close, in a wider range of emotional states than I've seen in any of my friends. I've seen him laugh and cry, undergo tremendous suffering and joy. The fact that it's all fictional is secondary. I know him, in a sense, better than I know my friends and family. I've spent hours staring at his face and identifying with him—and not just him, but the most heroic and pure version of him that the writers could come up with. This is just an example—I'm not a Harrison Ford fanatic—but it is the kind of thing that happens to some extent with all movie and television people. When fans approach with the "mad joy" in their eyes, the camaraderie of an old friend, that shouldn't surprise anyone. In a way, they *are* old friends.

It's the same with fighters. You've seen a man fight five or six times, you've been with him through his struggles, and you know him now;

in a sense, he's your friend, an intimate. You've seen him show his courage, come back from adversity, fight through pain—you've seen him game-tested.

In Hollywood, they call that initial reaction being starstruck, which happens when you first meet a bona fide celebrity and you react to all the one-sided time you've spent together, before you begin to recognize the real person underneath that famous flesh. It's interesting to watch celebrities deal with it, because they can sense it, and it sometimes makes them uncomfortable, as it would anyone. It's why meeting new people is exhausting for them.

There was some of that when I met Paul Walker, a familiar face, even though I didn't know all his movies and certainly wasn't his biggest fan. I stood around nervously for a while, trying not to appear impressed, trying to get a sense of the reality of the guy.

He was a good-looking, slender guy with intense blue eyes, some of the bluest eyes I'd ever seen. The first thing I got off Paul was that he just wanted to surf. He was laid-back and very polite and friendly in a Southern California way, and he would hang out and bullshit with the PAs or makeup people as readily as with the other actors or the director. He wasn't buying into the whole diva routine—he came from a pretty humble background and seemed like he knew he was lucky to be where he was. He was going to work hard and deserve what he got. And then go surfing.

My first reaction was similar to what I felt with Andre Ward; I just didn't want to bug him. I hung around and got to know him a little better, and helped Pat train him and Oakley one Sunday on the grass in front of the ocean at his hacienda. Oakley joked that he'd learned to fight on a movie set: "Reach way back and grab a bottle from the bar" was how he had been taught to punch, with a huge western windup, old John Wayne stuff. Paul was serious, he took what he did seriously and wanted to be good, he wanted to make good movies.

Paul had a darkness to him, an edge that I was a little surprised to see. When he hit pads with Pat, he was intent, and he was a good athlete and picked it up faster than Oakley did. He understood what "bad intentions" were, and he knew about MMA. He had even started jiu-jitsu with a famous Brazilian, Ricardo "Franjinha" Miller, rolling in the *gi,* part of the surfer/jiu-jitsu interface, before the movie started. He was psyched to have Pat around, and he confided in me that he wanted to train, and maybe fight someday—even though he knew he would probably never have the time to learn enough.

After we trained, Paul and Oakley took Pat and me surfing on the break right beneath Paul's place. We shrugged into borrowed wet suits and listened dutifully, the roles of teacher and student reversed. Pat had fins and a boogie board, but his body was so dense he sank it, and he swam like a lead weight. His buoyancy was about the same as concrete. I got the biggest longboard they had, and I lay sideways on it to protect my jacked-up ribs and paddled in the freezing cold, battling to catch a few waves. My favorite part of surfing is sitting out on the board, just watching the swells roll in, looking for the right wave. I shadowed Paul and Oakley, spending eight times the energy to get to the spots they easily paddled to, while Pat worked even harder, chopping away with the flippers, working against wind, waves, and his own nature. We sat there bobbing on the swells, in the cold wind and warm sun, and Pat and I watched Oakley and Paul catch a big wave. Their surfing styles were similar, with their arms cocked behind them. It looks so easy when someone else is doing it. Pat muttered, "This is pretty cool, dude—we're surfing with Paul Walker."

The most important thing a movie actor does is look good on camera; and it's a weird phenomenon, how certain people just look better than others on film. On camera, Paul's face picked up a definition and roughness, an edge that it didn't have in plain sight. One of the stuntmen told me that Sharon Stone was crazy like that—you would look right at her and think, *She's pretty,* and then look at the monitor and think, *Who the hell is this girl? She's amazing.*

We wrapped the prison scene, and Tim and Ben returned to Iowa. Pat was working on two major fight scenes with Mike and Oakley and had sequenced them out in steps.

The first was between a bad guy, played by Stefanos Miltsakakis, and Paul, in a trailer down by the beach. It was going to be brutal, smashing the trailer to pieces, breaking windows, and generally tearing shit up. The second fight was to be filmed later, at a set the construction guys were building out in the desert, colloquially called Split-Rock in the script. That one would be Paul versus Pat, Rory Markham, and Robbie Lawler. They joined us on set, Robbie utterly laconic, while Rory was more excited; he shamefacedly admitted he'd taken acting classes in Chicago.

Stefanos was a fascinating character, a massive, craggy man who had played bad guys in several Van Damme movies but was also a real fighter; he was 5–0 in MMA. John Herzfeld had seen him fight in Los

Angeles and hired him to be in his movie. He was Greek and had been on the Greek Olympic wrestling team in 1984. He'd trained with Rickson Gracie and had won *vale tudo* fights in Brazil. He was educated, European; he told me I had to read Emile Zola's *Nana*, and I promised him I'd get right on it. He also looked great, an unbelievably rough, handsome, leonine face, massive hands, the steely blue eyes of a German U-boat commander. He was great for movies. He was forty-five and looking for a shot at the UFC. He had a deep respect for Pat, as well as lot of his own ideas about how the fights should go—some were good, and some weren't. He wanted to maybe kick the gun out of Paul's hand, but Mike shook his head: "That's a little *Charlie's Angels* for me." There was a move that eventually got cut of Paul banging a pot on Stefanos's head; Mike felt it was slapstick and said, "I didn't know we were making a comedy," and Stefanos replied immediately, "We're not making Shakespeare."

Fighters watch movie fights and are experts of a kind; they know what they like, and they know what a real fight is like. When Pat started working with Paul and Oakley, he wasn't teaching them movie fighting, he was teaching them real fighting—the basics: footwork, balance, keep your hands up. Pat knew you had to teach feet first. "The arms are the chisel and the body's the hammer," he'd say, and you have to move your feet to swing that hammer. What Pat and I had to learn was movie fighting.

"The difference between movie fighting and real fighting—the big difference—is that in a movie fight, the guy *getting* hit is more important. It's a dance, you have to have a good partner or the fight won't work. The person getting hit—he's got to sell it. Or it looks fake," Mike told us.

Oleg Taktarov had a funny story about that: He was doing a Russian film, and one of the extras told him that he really admired him and was thrilled to be working with him; in a scene where Oleg was getting beaten by five or six guys, that same extra kicked him in the face, hard, trying to make the scene look real. Oleg laughed and said, "That was the only kick that looked fake, because it surprised me so I didn't react properly."

Communication is critical between the parties in a movie fight, and you have to maintain eye contact. In a real fight, you don't do that; or maybe you use your eyes to mislead, look high and kick low, but in a movie fight, you *need* to telegraph your punches, not only for your partner but also for the audience. When Chuck was beating up an extra in the prison kitchen, he momentarily forgot and did what he normally did, which was use his eyes to mislead. He threw a light slap that the extra didn't expect, and that one, although it landed, looked fake, because the extra wasn't ready to sell it. Oakley had done sword fighting on *Timeline* and said, "For swords, eye contact is really key, because now you've got actors with weapons."

The other big part of shooting a fight scene is where the cameras are; profile on the actors is the worst, the hardest to sell. You want to be either in front or behind, or at some kind of three-quarters view, so that the camera flattens out the distances and the punches appear to connect. Matt, one of the main cameramen, said, "You always want the action coming at you, move the camera into it. It's a game of angles." They do a lot of messing with the speed, the frames per second, too, depending on the type of action, and whether it will be slow motion or ever so slightly speeded up. Normal speed is twenty-four frames a second, and action might be shot at something around twenty, while slow motion is ninety-six. But there are all kinds of in betweens and exceptions, and Mike said, "Certain action looks better at different speeds."

The shoot continued, unabated, and the whole crew moved from Rosarito to Ensenada, a few hours down the road south, to be nearer to the hacienda. The shoot moved to a fancy vineyard where American owners were making serious attempts at turning this part of Mexico into a wine name. We drove in, down washboarded dirt roads before sunrise, the warm blue of the sun still down below the horizon, the light suffusing and lifting details one by one from the rugged countryside. I remember passing a Mexican man on his bicycle—he paused as we dusted him out (our Mexican drivers would never slow down)—an older man in his mid-forties with a mustache and a hooded sweatshirt against the morning chill. He watched us roll past with utter indifference, and I wondered where he was going at five in the morning, deep in the desert mountains before the sun was even up over *las montañas*. He probably had a family out here in the scrubland, in one of the dirt shacks.

That night, Pat and I were back in Ensenada, working on the trailer fight scene with Oakley, Mike, and Stefanos. Paul and John were going to show up later, for a serious rehearsal.

Between us we had worked it out over the past week, sometimes with Stefanos, sometimes with Oakley, and I had necessarily stood in for whoever wasn't around. Paul, the leading man who was in nearly every scene, was constantly busy, and when he wasn't, he was exhausted. Being a movie star isn't breaking rocks in the hot sun, but it isn't a cakewalk, either. The shoots are long, nonstop, thirty or forty days of shooting, all of them twelve or fifteen hours long; you have to be present, focused, and powerfully active. The money, of course, is ridiculous; so it's worth it—but it's not *easy*.

The fight scene started with Stefanos disarming Paul, and then went back and forth with kicks and punches, head butts and fishhooks, body slams, triangles; the kitchen sink was in there. It ended with a spectacular neck break from Paul, dispatching the monstrous Stefanos. It was something like sixty separate steps, broken down into beats of four or five exchanges, where we would cut, reset, and rehearse the next beat.

Paul and John showed up and we had a real rehearsal. John was raring to go. "If I can't make the violence rough and raw with you guys, I can't do it," he said. We started to go through the scene. Pat would walk Paul through the beats, and then Paul and Stefanos would run them. Stefanos was tough—he was a real fighter—and he moved forward like a machine, massive and forbidding. It quickly became apparent that there were some kicks in there that Paul was supposed to do that he couldn't quite get right. Pat had put in a little piece of footwork that someone who had trained in muay Thai would be able to do, but it was hard for someone who hadn't. Oakley couldn't do it, either. "What about Sam?" he asked. "Sam, you do it," said John, and suddenly I was in there, doubling Paul Walker. I went through it once with Pat, and then with Stefanos, and it was a lot different to be in there with him—he was big and quick and hard, and I was just trying to remember the moves and get it all to flow. Stefanos liked it. "This guy can do it good, kick me good," he said in his broad Greek accent.

John, the director and the final word on everything, was far from convinced, and he frowned at me. "We'll see if we need him."

Pat was musing to Mike, "It's funny how Paul is actually pretty serious about this," referring to training, and Mike replied, "Paul has anger in him." It made me think about fuel again, in these different contexts, what drives people, especially to fight, to hurt. It is more obvious to me now that fighters were almost all street fighters first, and then they found an outlet in the cage or ring. Rory said he used to go out and get in a fight every Friday *and* Saturday night, without fail, for years. His hands were covered in scars. Nearly all fighters are from broken homes.

Pat's father abused Pat and his mother. "My father was a jerk," he said, "and my mom was my buddy growing up and I still talk to her every day. She's a saint. I really want to make enough money to get her out of that crappy house I grew up in and move her to Montana, where she's always wanted to go. I've got to get it done while she's still young enough to enjoy it."

Rory nodded. "I'm working to get my mom off her feet, too." Rory, at twenty-four, was still fighting in small shows, for five hundred bucks a fight; he was eyeing the acting gig with a lean and hungry look. He was tired of being broke, and there is so little money in MMA.

The next morning, we were out in the vineyard again, to rehearse the fights some more and for the free food. Oakley had a scene in which he had to take a horse and jump a fence with a kid on the back of the horse. A very small man named Banzai Vitale was in to double the kid. Banzai was friendly, and I started picking his brain about selling punches.

"The head snapping around is the most important thing to sell," he said. He looked like a jockey: small, tight, athletic. "Let the body part that gets hit first lead the reaction," and he showed me in slow motion. "Let the jaw lead the head, which turns the body. Twist your shoulders to sell it, and then instantly come back to center and reset." He demonstrated several times quickly, his head snapping around with imaginary punches, his shoulders twisting afterward, jaw slack and snapping.

"If you twist diagonally, you'll jack your neck, so just twist side to side." In rehearsing a fight scene, you had to keep in mind that you might be doing twenty takes, so you had to be able to do the moves again and again without getting hurt.

"The most important thing is physics," Banzai continued. "Every action has to have an equal reaction. The reaction needs to match the punch—if you throw a huge looping punch and I just twitch my head, it won't sell."

Banzai helped me rehearse, out in the cold, early desert morning, with horses eyeing us curiously over the high barbed-wire fence. The vineyard owner's wife bred Andalusians with some Mexican breeds and these were her gentle gray babies; we had a scene with gunshots coming, and I knew they wouldn't like that. The sun was slowly warming the chilly, foggy air.

"With body shots, shoot your ass straight back with your head up, just a little bump; don't let your feet get too high off the ground." Banzai showed me some body shots with Pat pretending to crack him, and Pat enjoyed it so much that he chased Banzai around for a while, giving him body shots, and giggling.

Mike walked up and said, "Now, the advanced stuff is to be throwing a punch when you get caught, so you're always in the motion of *about* to throw a punch when you get hit—you're not standing around waiting for the punch, you sell the in-between moments—that's big-time stunt stuff right there."

Later in the day, the director walked by, and he looked over and then walked up to me and pushed a lazy punch past my face, and I "sold it" according to how I'd been rehearsing all morning. I really went with it, snapped my head over.

"Well, okay," said John, but he still wasn't convinced.

For the rest of the day, we bounced ideas around for the Split-Rock fight, Pat, Rory, Mike, and I (while Rob slept sitting straight up in a metal deck chair). Mike leaned toward chop-socky and flash, while Pat always went with the basics of real fighting, combinations and the Controlled FORCE stuff. Mike would throw in some kung fu–style hand interplay and kicks, and Pat would counter with big heavy locks and the jab-cross-hook. Rory argued that the "real" stuff, the MMA stuff, was why we were here; Mike nodded and simply offered that movie fighting is different from real fighting, and if the action didn't kick ass, Pat wouldn't work again. "For this movie, I need cool more than I need real," he said. "Give me something real *and* cool."

By the end, we got somewhere, a basic idea of the sequences for all three fights inside Split-Rock—Paul beating Robbie, then Rory, then Pat. Then we went to watch the pool scene, which had a whole bunch of cute little extras in bikinis in the freezing-cold overcast day. Mike muttered to me, "That collaboration wouldn't have happened on other sets; you'd get the fight coordinator telling you this is how it is, and all you could ask is 'What do I do here?'"

Late in the cloudy, strange afternoon, with a low marine band of clouds hanging in over the mountains, Rory and I went for a run. Wide-open desert stretched out around us. We pushed on down the dirt roads and headed toward the foothills, past fancy modern ranch houses with massive sculptures out in dry desert fields, and past a Mexican grave-yard strewn with plastic flowers and the ornate gilt trappings of impoverished Catholicism.

We turned around and headed back, and the setting sun began to catch the underside of the clouds and gild them silver. Rory started talking a little bit about his hopes and dreams, and he said in his Chicago twang, "I have a passion for fighting and a passion for acting," his *passion* a long nasal sound. "It's just that once you start fighting, you reach that stage of intense concentration and excitement; I'm so *pure* when I'm in the final stages before a fight. I can't give that up."

Rory asked me a favor. He was broke and didn't have a return airline ticket—could I drop him off in Iowa when I drove back east? My first thought was, *What an imposition.* Pat had assumed I would do it—I was part of the team, wasn't I? And I realized he was right. I couldn't just continue being the selfish solo traveler. I was a part of things, so I said, "Of course. It'll be fun."

On the way home, in the van, as everyone nodded off, Banzai sat next to me and said quietly, "If you're doing it for the director, make sure you try and sell it big-time—because he doesn't think you can do it. That's just between you and me. I heard him talking, and he wants to bring in somebody else, so sell everything hard."

There is a very cowboy "nut-up-and-do-it" attitude about stunts: Don't say you can't do it, or your ribs are fucked, or anything—just do it. Can you do it or not? Here's my chance, I get to double the lead, get my SAG card, make money—just don't blow it.

The next morning we went to the beach set for the trailer scene, down the rugged, cliffed-out coast. I was nervous as I got my wardrobe and put on Paul's clothes, just like Oakley. Suddenly I was a part of things. I didn't say a word, but I felt like everyone could see straight through me as a hack. I sat in makeup and had my hair colored by the crew, a pale blond that didn't look too far off.

Pat shook his head a little bit when he saw me. "You're a lot bigger than he is," he said. Nothing I could do about that, but at least I knew the whole routine better than either Paul or Oakley, because I had rehearsed it with Pat, Mike, and Stefanos more than either of them had, by the pool in Ensenada. I had become acutely conscious of the sell, snapping my head with the punches, lurching with the knees, and snarling when I hit back.

I was called to set and felt extremely self-conscious as I entered the rarefied air of the actors and director and DP—the real movie.

As it turned out, Paul was doing 99 percent of the fight, because (a) he could do it, and (b) the trailer was tight and close and you could tell who was actually in almost every shot. In addition, because of time constraints, they'd cut a huge chunk of the fight scene, from sixty moves down to about twenty or thirty. As Mike had said, "When a movie starts to fall behind schedule, action is always the first thing to go, because it's not all plot essential." Action takes a long time to shoot because of all the setting up and taking down for each shot, and multiple angles. You need days and days to get a fight scene right, and there is always going to be compromise. One of the things Mike wanted to do was address this by designing the action beforehand, instead of loosely sketching it and then figuring it out as you went, which is how a lot gets done these days. By designing and having an exact shot list and careful plan, you can save time and money *and* get everything you need. Plus a lot of the time, the directors don't even know what's *possible* in stunts.

The kicks were still in the fight, and the little muay Thai footwork for a lead-leg kick that I was supposed to do hadn't been cut, so I went in and did it, kicking at Stefanos and trying to make it look good. I ended up not having to sell a punch at all. They even did a close-up shot of my feet, there was a little skip kick, but I doubted that would make it into the film. It was somewhat stressful, with the camera crew looming all around, but Stefanos was a pro, and I blocked everything out and just focused on the kick.

That was it, just a few minutes of work, then Paul was back in there. As I walked off the set, the AD shook my hand and whispered, "Congratulations, you just got your SAG card." And made $719, the day rate. I asked Robbie if it looked okay, because he was a guy you could count on for the truth—Robbie didn't care about your feelings. He nodded, and I sat and watched the monitors as Paul and Stefanos battled through the trailer, growling and roaring. I had a new appreciation for the way Paul took the hits, and Stefanos did a great job of acting; he really seemed enraged and frightening. He also had had a rough day, I'd leg-kicked him a little too hard (even though he'd asked me to) and he'd had to walk it off, and then he got smashed by Oakley several times into some cupboards made of balsa wood that didn't break as they were supposed to, and then he got burned on the stove. He laughed and said he felt like he'd been in a fight, but he was glowing with happiness and from exertion by the time the shoot ended, late at night. Because we went so long, I got overtime pay, too, which put me up to around $1,500, basically for sitting around drinking coffee all day and doing fifteen minutes of kicks. It's why everyone wants to be in the business.

* * *

We wrapped the trailer scene and went back out into another part of the desert to shoot Split-Rock, the huge fight scene between Paul and all the boys. I had been standing in for Paul for most of the rehearsals for this, too. Mike talked about the differences in the planning stages of action; he had just done *Elektra,* and the female lead, Jennifer Garner, had rehearsed the fight scenes for three months before the movie started, eight hours a day—one scene had a hundred moves and five attackers with bo staffs. On *Bobby Z,* there just wasn't the time. Pat and Mike had originally hashed out a big fight scene that went up and down the rock, with a ten-foot fall for Paul and Pat, and the director wisely wiped that out with a few words, because he had two days to shoot the entire sequence.

The Split-Rock set was a huge man-made rock triangle, placed out in the middle of a plain, in what felt like high desert but was only a couple of miles from the sea. Mexico was heading into winter like the rest of the hemisphere, but it had been a dry fall and a fire had started, and from the set the entire southern horizon was covered in roiling smoke, blowing out to the ocean. It was low scrub ground with very spotty fuels, and so I reassured anyone who was worried, as the smoke billowed up in black gouts across the sun, that we were in no danger—the entire plain was a safety zone, and the fire was miles downwind. But it was close enough to be spectacular, and as the sun sank, to turn the day a dreaming red.

It was Pat and his boys' chance to shine, and they did. Robbie, who had been sleeping all day, suddenly came alive. "He's a game-day player," said Pat. He looked great moving and coming around the rock with murder in his eyes. Paul dispatched him with ease.

Rory was next, and he came hard with his knife, but Paul was up to the challenge and disarmed him, beat him to picking up the knife, and slashed his throat. That was the first day.

The morning of the second day, I dressed as Paul again, and doubled him for the close-up of Rory getting his throat slashed. I watched what he had done on the monitors and then tried to match it, while keeping my face angled away from the camera. It was hard to remember everything in order, and to also use the gag knife, which had a blood bulb in it—I was supposed to squeeze it as it went across Rory's throat. (The effects guy laughed and said this technology was straight out of 1930.) It took a few tries, but finally we got the shot. There is a fair amount of stress in doing action live for the camera, because you want to nail it, get it right on one take, and sometimes you just go on and on getting it wrong. Rory did a terrific job selling the knife slash, his eyes darting from his head.

Then it was Pat's turn, and they battled back and forth until Paul caught Pat in a leaping triangle and elbowed his face about a dozen times. The director had the makeup guys put a thin trickle of blood down Pat's nose, and I thought, *Man, his face would be busted to pieces— it would look like an exploded tomato.* Paul's elbow should have been red with blood, too. That scene was the most impressive for Paul's commitment: He and Pat tumbled all over the place, they went up and down and up and down in the dirt, banging and smashing. "Movie stars don't *do* that," the AD said. Paul had wanted to make it good, and he wanted to hang with Pat, and Pat felt the same way. They pushed each other and got down and dirty, and by the end of the second day they were both exhausted and beat up.

The fires continued to fill up the southern part of the world, and the smoke drifted far out to sea in a hazy, dirty layer. The sunsets as we drove back to Rosarito were incandescent.

The film had bought both Robbie and Rory return airfare, so in the end, I wasn't going to have to take either one of them with me. I thought I had concealed my desire to be alone well, but Rory laughed and said, "This is good. I know Sam was going to leave me at a truck stop in Texas."

We watched the UFC that night. Pat had three guys fighting and they all won, and Paul sat next to me for a while. I liked Paul, although we weren't close; I think he is an honest guy, the real deal. Whenever he got a film, a circle of friends from his youth who worked in movies (stunts, effects, producing) would drop what they were doing and go with him; they kept him grounded—they would tell him when he was doing something stupid. He knew that some of the movies he'd made were cheesy, and he wanted to make good films, cool films. He was capable of it.

Paul had read the article I'd written about Thailand and said he might want to go and train there. He asked me, "Do you think you'll ever get this out of your system? You won't, will you? . . . It will always be there." He had the bug, a little bit: He wanted to train more, he wanted to fight.

I thought about his question. Maybe it *was* out of my system, I realized. I still wanted to train, to get better, to roll and spar—but I didn't need to fight, I didn't want to hurt anybody. Did I?

There is a question, an endless debate, over whether fighting makes you more aggressive and prone to violence, or less. In my case, it was definitely more. For the first time, I kind of, secretly, *wanted* to hurt someone. Before, I had been forcing myself to do it because I could, because I enjoyed the training, because I wanted never to be afraid.

I had looked deep into my heart for any sign of fear; what I found instead was boredom. I like getting hit in the head—I'm not afraid of it. It gets me psyched. I hate getting hit in the body, but that's because I get hurt and then can't do things for five weeks or whatever. Climbing into the ring or cage didn't seem like such a big deal. Staying in shape was boring; training all the time was boring. I was never going to be a great fighter, so maybe it was time to move on to other fears. I could walk away from it, I thought. I can walk away from anything or anybody, I've proved that, not that it's something to be proud of.

Suddenly, it was all over—at least the Mexico part was. Pat's role was finished, and the fight scenes were all done. The crew was packing up and getting ready to return to L.A., take a week for Thanksgiving and then two weeks to finish the shoot in the United States. I got up one morning at three-thirty and set off on the three-day marathon, driving diagonally across the country back to Massachusetts. I wanted to hit the border early, to get across before the commuter traffic began, but it didn't work. My eighth time driving across the country and the sixth time by myself. The magic was long gone.

I was surprised to see a few columns in Arizona, big fires pushing up smoke. It was late in the season, November, way late for Arizona to be burning.

9

A FIGHTER'S HEART

In consequence again of those accursed laws of consciousness,
anger in me is subject to chemical disintegration. You look into it,
the object flies off into the air, your reasons evaporate, the
criminal is not to be found, the wrong becomes not a wrong but a
phantom, something like the toothache, for which there is no one
to blame, and consequently there is only the same outlet left
again—that is, to beat the wall as hard as you can.
—Dostoyevsky, *Notes from Underground*

There comes a moment when we stop creating ourselves.
—John Updike

I was back in western Massachusetts, at Amherst Athletic, training for another MMA fight and on a deadline to finish this book. MMA still hooked me on a personal level, because of the added complexity of the ground game. Not that I had mastered stand-up, by any means—that is another endless quest. But with the ground element, MMA allows the thinking fighter more options, which takes away from some of the sheer athleticism and reflexes that win boxing fights. I don't have the reflexes, so I'm working on the thinking. Also, getting hit in the head is bad for you, and that's the main work of boxing.

I was working with my old friend Kirik Jenness, who had been involved with this project from the start, more or less. Kirik had taken me under his wing and refused all payment. "I don't take money from fighters," he said, even though he was privately training me every day for an hour or more. Kirik coached, refereed, and cornered for fighters

291

at all levels, from the UFC on down to the lowliest shows. He had a genuine love for the sport, and he ran the largest MMA Web site (www.mma.tv), but he wasn't trying to get rich. I was back in the amateur atmosphere, a small college town; for kids and men who fight in these amateur MMA shows, it wasn't about money, either. So what was it about?

Kirik and I did light MMA, we put on the little gloves and worked for position, and I came hard with knees and the clinch. "You've got a lot of aggression, which is good," he said. "You're relentless, and you're almost in shape." I had learned what fighting has to be—I understood the urgency of it. Aggression plays a big role.

The brain science, the "neuropyschology," of aggression (as my friend Michelle Ward, who has a PhD in clinical neuroscience, attempted to explain to me), places aggression in two regions of the brain: in the limbic system, which is in the core, and in the prefrontal cortex, which is behind the forehead. The basic thinking in the scientific community says that the impulses for aggression come from the core, and control of the impulses happens in the prefrontal cortex. So any damage to the prefrontal cortex can change things, Michelle said—"even slight brain trauma, often so light it is unnoticed, from head injuries can lead to more aggressive and impulsive behavior." Then what comes first for fighters, the chicken or the egg? They get hit in the head, which makes them more aggressive and more prone to get hit in the head.

It does mess you up—there's no question. All fighters joke about forgetting things, and all of us have gone home with a headache from sparring and not slept well and not been right for a few days. More than once. That's the long, slow road to punchiness—don't fool yourself, those are mild concussions.

There's a psychiatric tool called the Sensation Seeking Scale. You answer a bunch of questions, and the scale determines whether you are a "sensation seeker" or not, the idea being that the serotonin levels of certain people are lower than average, so in order for those people to *feel* anything—excitement or anxiety—they need greater than normal stimulus. This is a common thought—the idea of "adrenaline junkies" has been around for a while. I scored pretty high on the SSS, but I'm not an adrenaline junkie—I can stop anytime I want. Sure.

Michael Kimmel, in his book *Manhood in America,* talks about the "homosociality" of the manly arenas (sports, business); for a man, the most important thing is "his reputation as a *man among men.*" Men need to prove their masculinity to one another. I thought of the lack of women in all the gyms I'd been in; fighting is essentially a man's world. Of course, there are exceptions, but a woman fighter isn't important in a man's world.

Konrad Lorenz, the author of *On Aggression,* understands where this "homosociality" comes from. Lorenz studied tropical reef fish and geese, and used the observed behaviors to draw inferences about all vertebrates and thus ourselves. He first noticed that, on the reef, "fish are far more aggressive towards their own species than any other" (outside of eating and being eaten, of course). The male fish viciously attack other male fish of the same species, the females the females, while allowing the myriad others to coexist peacefully.

Lorenz papaphrases Charles Darwin when he says that "the strength of the father directly affects the welfare of the children" and goes on to say that in herds (and any family unit), the rival male fights lead to stronger males and greater evolutionary success. There is a "survival value" in herd or family defense that strong males contribute directly to.

So the strong homosocial element of masculinity makes perfect sense, in evolutionary terms. Those that fight each other harder do better. Lorenz takes interspecies aggression several steps further. He talks about geese and says that two furiously aggressive animals must bond and live together in a small space, all without weakening intraspecies aggression. They have evolved inhibitors, behavior-changing devices, that turns the aggression they normally feel toward others of their species into something else when they mate. The same thing, albeit in a more complex way, takes place among men and women of the same tribe or family unit, bound together for increased success against the outside world. Lorenz writes that friendship is found only in animals with "highly developed intra-specific aggression," and goes on to say that the more aggressive the animal, the deeper the friendship. The ability to love and form bonds has evolved as a way to temper aggression, to turn it into something more powerful when defending hearth and home. Friendship and love are essentially evolutionary by-products of aggression. Men and women who form these deep bonds—who evolved ways to mitigate interspecies aggression—have greater sucess in passing along their genes.

That's the secret: It's all about love.

Kirik and I sat around and talked about fighting, why Greco-Roman wrestlers are better at MMA than freestyle wrestlers. (Kirik thinks it's the higher base, which is more like a boxing or kickboxing stance, and the proclivity for hand fighting.) Kirik has refereed hundreds of these matches at the amateur level, and has seen it all. He talked about how the range for punching in MMA is different from that in boxing. You can't stand in and trade with four-ounce gloves on—you'll get sliced to bits—so you stand back and come in hard. The jab is more of a straight hard left than a light jab. I was reminded of the old bare-fisted fighters, who would throw two or three punches a minute, probably because bare-fisted would slice you up even worse. Zé Mario had said that about the old *vale tudo* fights without gloves, that they were bloodbaths.

We gossiped a lot about fighters we knew, as Kirik knew everybody, and one day I said, "Tim Sylvia has badder intentions than most big men—it gives him an edge." That train of thought led me right back to myself—I don't really have the bad intentions. I haven't been damaged. My father didn't beat me or leave—my childhood was great.

I could feel that changing a little, though: All the fighting had made me a little more receptive to the idea of hurting someone. I could do it easily now. But still, I didn't have the basic rage that you need to fight, and I said as much to Kirik. And then I thought, *Doth the lady protest too much?* I had endless dreams of fighting, and "knee-on-belly" was my new favorite thing, a position from which you could hit a guy but he couldn't hit you, and I would *love* to get there in a fight. Which meant I wanted to hurt somebody.

I went to the only shrink I knew, a nice guy named Stuart Bicknell; I'd gone to high school with his daughter. I asked for his help, and we had two sessions (which he said wasn't really enough). I wanted to know what *he* thought of me, what was the psychiatric evaluation of this whole quest?

Stuart told me that "when one hears about kick-boxing and 'cage-fighting,' the response is often revulsion and contempt tinged with curiosity. 'Who would do such a thing? You'd have to have a death wish—or at least be a little unhinged—to put yourself in that arena.'" He looked at me for psychopathology and, in his own words, "found none." Stuart gave me a big-picture look at the diffent theories on aggression:

> Instinctual, catharsis theory argues that aggression is the self-destructive (death) instinct turned outward, away from the self and toward others. In so doing, in discharging this instinctual aggression, a basic human need is satisfied. The frustration-aggression hypothesis proposes that aggression is simply a generic response to frustration, a response to provocation. Social learning theory argues that aggression is learned behav-

ior, which is reinforced. Reinforcement comes from praise (for being aggressive) or from the discovery that it reduces tension. And, of course, the nature/nurture debate becomes part of the discussion. It's nature; the interaction between high whole blood serotonin, testosterone, and chemical activity in the frontal lobe—not to mention the concept of an "aggression gene"—plays a key role in determining one's degree of aggressive behavior. Those in the nurture camp argue for the influence of family, neighborhood, and peers. Environment is the determining factor. . . . Any explanation of aggression relies as much on interpretation and soft speculation as it does on hard science.

Confused yet?

Stuart's thought was that while my environment didn't have any red flags or smoking guns, the fact that my father was a Navy SEAL was probably significant, if only from a genetic viewpoint. The Freudian thought would be that I was still in competition with my father—although I have a great relationship with him, and we haven't competed for years and years, and we never did except in friendly play. But when I graduated from college, my dad did say, "The one thing I regret is not being able to make you into a world-class sailor," and what was the first thing I did? Sail around the world. So there.

I think Stuart was closer when we talked about my discovering boxing in college. "Love at first punch" was how he described it, and then, "For you, whose modus operandi has been to take it to the limit, the journey from boxing at Harvard to fighting in a cage was, with a few detours, a predictable one."

I thought of what Dan Goossen had said to Gabriel Ruelas: "You can't make fighting come out of you. It has to be in you."

We rolled a lot, and I was finally starting to pick up on the ground game—although I was a long way from having one. Kirik maintained that the ground game needed a two-pronged attack, as one attack would be easily countered by a halfway skilled guy. You had to distract him, keep him from thinking, and have two separate but related attacks going on at once and be able to flow from one to the other. I could grasp that conceptually, if not in practice. I started to learn to control the hips, using direct pressure as well as pressure on the head, shoulders, arms, or legs, all to limit his hips. If you shut down a guy's hips, he's halfway beat.

Kirik's other main focus was on the transition, "the scramble," the time between things in a fight. These were the times, going from standing to the ground, or in reverse, that a fighter might be vulnerable, and in MMA you needed a relentless attack, so that in the scramble you were always coming, because it might be the only chance you got at a clean shot for the whole fight.

Kirik was an interesting guy, tall and rangy. His dad was working in Ghana, and Kirik had been named after the noise that a bird in Alaska made, a gray jay, when his father was doing his anthropology study (with his young family along) in a small Inuit town. I considered him as we rolled.

Kirik had been in martial arts and fighting for a long time, around thirty years; he still trained all the time and was toying with the idea of fighting again. Yet he was one of the sunniest guys I'd ever met, smiling, relaxed, and happy. He claimed to be a happy drunk, not a mean one; and I bet most of the girls he knew thought he was just the sweetest, nicest guy in the world. They would be horrified, perhaps, by his knowledge of and attitude about fighting. I have a friend who said that older guys who were still really into fighting had "missed something," that their development wasn't quite there. I didn't think that was the case with Kirik, or some of the other guys I knew, who'd let the tough-guy stuff fall by the wayside but had become involved in the craft of fighting, in the expertise of it.

I wondered if it all was just a smokescreen for a manhood rite. Kimmel writes that for men, one of the deepest fears is that "others will see us as less than manly, as weak, timid, frightened." In American manhood, there is an incessant fear of failure—you aren't a man without constant, endless success. The point he keeps harping on is that in America, manhood is never something that is over and done with—it needs to be constantly proved, a "relentless test." Was this all MMA was, Brandon Adamson's idea of "clout," a new manhood initiation rite? People will always point to *Fight Club* by Chuck Palahniuk, which is a terrific book and was made into an even better film, but it was essentially a middle-class nihilist fantasy, which is revealed when the narrator claims that "fight club isn't about winning," because it would be, especially when the blue-collar kids got involved. The issue is more complicated. The real fight clubs aren't proving grounds where guys look for beatings just to feel alive, although that may be a part of it. Kirik and I had laughed about how fighters, almost without fail, sit backstage before a fight—in the moments before the bell, when the absurdity of the situation becomes clear—and wonder why the hell they do this. But I think I know: They train hard to win fights, so that no one will be able to dominate them, to damage them where they have been damaged—but in the end, they train hard to make themselves better. The test is necessary. It completes the training, and it changes you.

Fighting is not just a manhood test; that is the surface. The depths are about knowledge and self-knowledge, a method of examining one's own life and motives. For most people who take it seriously, fighting is much more about the self than the other.

Leah Hager Cohen, who wrote *Without Apology: Girls, Women, and the Desire to Fight,* noticed that boxers always embrace after fighting, and she wondered at it. She eventually realized that it was genuine, that afterward the fighters saw each other in a grateful light—"the happy eventuality that permitted them to take their own measure." She saw what the fighters were providing for each other.

The person agreeing to fight you is doing you a great service, allowing you to test yourself against him or her; they agree to abide by the same rules, to meet you on an exact date in a specified location. The opponent allows you to strive fully, without reservation, and you do the same for him (or her). When you think about it, fighting in a ring is incredibly civilized. We'll try to kill each other, but we agree to stop the instant the other wants to, or is hurt, we'll shut down all the killer instincts inside us the moment we feel a tap on the leg. The embrace after a fight is not false, or forced, it's respect and gratitude. Usually, the issue of dominance and mutual respect has been decided one way or the other. It's why I had to train with these guys to get to know them, because men before they fight are filled with contradictory impulses of hierarchy, while afterward things are decided: I am the student, you are the teacher. But not just that; someone who has agreed to fight you has agreed to serve as part of your test, your struggle for knowledge, your quest to make yourself better.

Fighting reveals the truism that Kimmel is bent on and which I agree with, that manhood, that endless test, is a sham, an illusion of sorts; because when you start fighting, you realize there's never an end to it, there's always somebody better—stronger, faster, bigger, younger, whatever, something. Brandon told me how he used to destroy people when street fighting, and that when he walked into Pat's, he thought, *There's nobody who can fight me at 155 pounds* (his weight class), and then he ran into Jens Pulver. A lot of these guys were street-fighting terrors, but when they get in the cage or boxing ring against strong, trained guys, they are the bottom of the barrel, because there are monsters out there. The quest to be the toughest in the world is an empty quest, and fighters realize that pretty quickly, I think. Muhammad Ali might have been one of the greatest strikers in history, but when he and Frazier got into a prefight scuffle, they ended up on the ground, rolling around ineffectually. You might be the world champ in your weight class, but a decent guy twenty pounds heavier will give you fits. There's always someone out there who can beat you. It's about being the best you can be, bringing yourself closer to the perfect version.

Of course, there's a manhood aspect to it—we want to know ourselves under stress, in pain and in adversity—we want to know if we are game. If you don't think gameness is a critical concept in our culture, think about the game test, in which they fight a dog, and when he's exhausted send a fresh dog at him to see what he'll do. Now think about every single climactic fight scene in every action movie: The hero fights, starts getting beat, looks like he's about to lose; and then he demonstrates pure gameness and comes back hard and wins the fight. Every damn time. It's for dramatic tension, but also more: It's satisfying because he's shown that he's game, he's proved himself worthy of our love. He's a worthy member of our pack.

Manhood, or the pursuit of masculinity, is really about the "hunter" virtues that had survival value for prehistoric man: strength and speed, courage and loyalty, skill—all things that have obvious survival value in the extreme conditions in which *Homo sapiens* first eked out existence. It wasn't that long ago. Society and technology have changed, but biology hasn't, at least not as much. You still want to see gameness in your friends, your family, your leaders, the men you hunt with and who protect you from wild animals—the old savage gods. As man mastered animals, those hunter virtues became the virtues of the warrior, as interspecies aggression in the form of warfare came to dominate human activity.

As far as watching fighting goes, the same rules apply: We are drawn to the spectacle of violence for hereditary, genetic reasons, but here, too, I think there is something more, and it's not easily accessible— you have to watch a thousand bad or mediocre or even good fights before you see one that is truly great, truly transcendent. In *Reading the Fights,* a collection of essays, Ronald Levao writes:

These are forces played out on the physical stage—the raised white canvas is a blank and basic *platea*—which make it possible to see great fighters as great artists, however terrible their symbolic systems. It may be, and perhaps should be, difficult to accept the notion that a prizefighter's work merits the same kind of attention we lavish on an artist's, but once we begin attending to and describing what he does in the ring, it becomes increasingly difficult to refuse the expenditure. The fighter creates a style in a world of risk and opportunity. His disciplined body assumes the essential postures of the mind: aggressive and defensive, elusively graceful with its shifts of direction, or struggling with all its stylistic resources against a resistant but, until the very end, alterable reality. A great fighter redefines the possible.

Fight fans keep watching, hoping for the great one, that fight that transcends and becomes art.

Down in Mexico, on the movie set, I met muay Thai legend Rob Kaman. He was the real thing—lived in Thailand for years and years, fought all over the world. He's the guy who should have written this book. He was a great champion and among the very best in the world in his day. A friend of Stefanos's, he was a hard-faced Dutchman in his mid-forties, but he had that glorious human warmth that the great Thai fighters had, a real friendliness, lack of ego, and compassion. We talked a few times, and he said to me, "When I stopped fighting, I thought I could start living—drinking and partying—but I found that wasn't the case." I felt the same way: The minute I pulled out of the fight, even though I had the time to write, I felt bereft of purpose. Why work out? Now what do I do? Rory said he felt pure when he got close to a fight, and I know what he meant—there's a refreshing purity of purpose.

I spoke with an old professor of mine, Gregory Nagy—a leading classical scholar—and he told me that the athlete in antiquity underwent a spiritual transformation during competition. It can happen only if the athlete is connected to something bigger than him- or herself. I was reminded of Zé Mario in Brazil, who said that after training for five months, he could feel the presence of God in a fight. Greg said that for the ancient Greeks, when the athlete is in the highest moment of competition, when he is in his "deep waters," he comes face to face with divinity—and is reborn on the other side. But in order to achieve that, the fighter has to be connected to the sacred somehow; otherwise, it's just games.

I examine my heart for fear and don't find any. If I found any fear, I would force myself to go straight at it; but without fear I have to wonder what the point is, because I'm not going pro. If I were ten years younger and where I am right now, maybe I would take two years and find a gym and live there and see what happens, but I am thirty-one. Is it time to move on? I wonder if getting out of fighting will be as easy as I think. Is there something wrong with really enjoying getting hit?

But there is something *else*. There is a quality around these men, the good fighters I've met—they are among the best people I know. Kirik, Virgil, Andre, Zé, Rodrigo, Master Chen, Pat, and Apidej are some of the best examples of humanity I can think of. They've been face to face with divinity—they've swum deep waters—and been reborn in the fight.

These men who have fought, and who really *understand* what it's about, have left their egos behind, in the tough-guy sense. The pressure of proving masculinity has been removed. You're more interested in seeing if your skills are better (like Jens said in Japan) than your opponent's than whether you are a man or not. It's a form of enlightenment; lack of fear leads to nobility of character. Not all fighters develop like this, but a surprising number do; the really good ones seem to. They stop street fighting, because untrained men don't interest them. Pat said he used to walk through the mall and feel like a shark among seals. And that power, in the great fighters, breeds restraint, understanding, wisdom—even gentleness, except when in the ring. I've seen it in different corners of the world, in totally different cultures. That's the other part of the fighter's heart.

Having a fighter's heart, having gameness, is about knowing yourself and not being afraid of losing. You become a better version of yourself. Nobility is a by-product of that attitude, just like love is a by-product of aggression.

Kimmel gets a little personal when he writes about "a new subgenre of travel literature" where "the journeyman/writer/hero" is "testing manhood in a Land Rover." He talks about that kind of literature as a way to prove masculinity and to escape the dangerously feminine city, and his voice is dripping with sarcasm. I'd never talk that way to him.

Luckily, I can easily refute that statement. I do things out of a genuine interest, a desire for knowledge, a deep and abiding curiosity that I think is the birthright, the God-given duty, of a citizen of the world.

You could argue that I have just been dabbling—fighting got me a book deal. I don't want to be pigeonholed as a fight writer for the rest of my life. But I'm not done with fighting, I know that. I doubt I ever will be, completely. It's been six years and seven continents since I first fought in Thailand, and although I'm desperate for a break, I know I'll be back in a gym somewhere, getting pounded on, before too long.

Cormac McCarthy wrote a book called *Blood Meridian* in which the character of the judge makes an argument that war is the most essential of human activities. He starts by saying that men are born for games, and that everybody, even children, know that "play is nobler than work." If that is true, says the judge, then what changes the quality of the game but the stakes? And what could be a more valuable stake than your life? So war, the game you play with your life, is the greatest of human endeavors.

In that same argument the judge says that "war is God" because it is the test of wills between two parties. Moral law is subjective, and man must submit before the "higher court," which will provide a conclusive decision. In a fight, the truth will out.

When I read this, it really bothered me, and I spent a few minutes reading and rereading the argument. And then I saw the fatal flaw in the judge's logic, and read on with an easy mind.

I do not believe that men were meant for games, that that is their highest purpose. Work is nobler than play. I believe that men were meant for work, that their highest calling is to build, not destroy or even protect. Learning to fight, trying to embody the virtues of the hunter and warrior—these things are useful and important, even essential. But don't be content with being a warrior, be a builder as well. Make something. The true calling of man, real manhood, is about creation, not destruction, and everyone secretly knows it.

ACKNOWLEDGMENTS

Thanks . . .

Harvard: Tommy Rawson, Gregory Nagy

Thailand: Apidej Sit-Hirun, John Deroy, Anthony Lin, Waring Partridge, Philip Wong, Bart Van Der Molen, Tim CEK, Ike X, Yarpie, Judy Blair, Merit, Daniel Boone, Ajahn Suthep, Phraratha Panyavudo (Vayagool), Blue, Neungsiam, Beya, Yak, Kum, Coke

Myanmar: Truth, Nobility, the YMCA in Yangon

Iowa: Pat Miletich, Rory Markham, Rob Lawler, Sam Hogar, Tim Sylvia, Brandon Adamson, Marshall Blevins, Spencer Fisher, Justin Brown, Ben Lowy, Josh Howit, Tony Fryklund, Ryan McGivern, Ben Rothwell

Brazil: Mario Sperry, Murilo Bustamante, Rodrigo Nogueira, Gustavo "Bomba" Toledo, Scott Nelson, Tony Desouza, Gabrielle Bermudez, Mariana de Faria Benchimol, Olavo Abreu, Carlos Lemos Jr., Paulo Filho, João da Silva, my tutor João Casaes, Matt Mochary, Darryl Gholar, Denis Martins, Farés el Dahdah

Japan: Hikari Ohta, Luis Alves, Luis Dórea, Amaury Bitetti, Marco Bruschelli, Danillo Villefort, Roland Kelts, Bebeo, Turi Altavilla

ACKNOWLEDGMENTS

New York: William C. C. Chen, Max Chen, Tiffany Chen, Claudia Vick, Connie Vick, Molly R., Mathilda, Suki, Imetai M. Henderson, the University Club, Matt Ross

Wenner Media: James Lochart, Mike Slenske, Mark Horowitz, Will Dana, Bob Wallace, Corey Seymour, Erica Kestenbaum, Nina Pearlman, special thanks to Kate Rockland and Jann Wenner

Oakland: Virgil Hunter, Andre Ward, Antonio Johnson, Robert, Nate the Great, John, Sheila Glenn, Kevin Thomason, Heather Hartman, Goossen Tutor, Gabriel Ruelas, Don Clark, Rachel Charles, Jacob "Stitch" Duran, Amos and Stitch, James Prince

Philippines: Ito, Joedic, Jo, the Southern Men

Amherst: Charles "Pain Train" Bishop, Kirik Jenness, Kip Kollar, David Roy, Kathy Robertson, Leon Aldrich, Caleb Bach, Stuart Bicknell

Los Angeles: Danny Passman, Shana and Don Passman, Jessica Chaffin (D-), Jeremy Kleiner (D-), Patty Jenkins (A-), Michelle Ward, Francis Porter and the Porter family, a special "thanks for nothing" to David Olson

Mexico: John Herzfeld, Adrian Vina, Keith Samples, Brandon Hill, Brandon Birtell, Paul Walker, Oakley Lehman, Mike Gunther, Troy Brenna, Banzai Vitale, Tommy Rosales, Matt Wiener, Tony Adler, Roland Fullajtar, Matt Moriarty

Grove/Atlantic: Morgan Entrekin

Special thanks for the vision and support to David Kuhn

An extremely heartfelt thanks to my editors, Panio Gianopoulos and Jamison Stoltz, for a miracle of readability.

For all those I've forgotten (I'm sure there are plenty): I apologize—I get hit in the head sometimes